LEARNING IN TWO LANGUAGES

LEARNING IN TWO LANGUAGES

From Conflict to Consensus
in the Reorganization of Schools

Edited by
Gary Imhoff

Transaction Publishers
New Brunswick (U.S.A.) and London (U.K.)

LC
3731
.L43
1990

Library of Congress Catalog Number: 90-31710
ISBN: 0-88738-319-X
Printed in the United States of America

Library of Congress Cataloging-in-Publication Data

Learning in two languages : from conflict to consensus / edited by
    Gary Imhoff.
        p.   cm.
    Revised papers originally presented at a conference with the topic
public policy issues in bilingual education, held in Washington,
D.C. in April of 1989.
    ISBN 0-88738-319-X
    1. Education, Bilingual — United States — Congresses.
2. Intercultural education — United States — Congresses. 3. Language
policy — United States — Congresses. 4. Minorities — Education — United
States — Congresses. I. Imhoff, Gary.
LC3731.L43   1990
371.97′00973 — dc20   90-31710
                                                                                    CIP

Contents

Figures

Tables

Introduction

Gary Imhoff

To get some idea of what reading meant in the two centuries following Gutenberg's invention, consider the case of two men—one by the name of William, the other by the name of Paul. In the year 1605, they attempted to burglarize the house of the Earl of Sussex. They were caught and convicted. Here are the exact words of their sentence as given by the presiding magistrate: "The said William does not read, to be hanged. The said Paul reads, to be scarred." Paul's punishment was not exactly merciful; it meant he would have to endure the scarring of his thumbs. But unlike William, he survived because he had pleaded what was called "benefit of clergy," which meant he could meet the challenge of reading at least one sentence from an English version of the Bible. And *that* ability alone, according to English law in the seventeenth century, was sufficient grounds to exempt him from the gallows. I suspect the reader will agree with me when I say that of all the suggestions about how to motivate people to learn to read, none can match the method of seventeenth-century England. (Postman 1988, 151–52)

The argument over bilingual education may not be the most divisive, most acrimonious, or most virulent debate within American public education today. There is also a ferociously angry controversy over sex education, as Rudolph Troike reminds us in his article in this volume. But the dispute over sex education is largely between professional educators and some segments of the general public, while bilingual education has divided professional educators themselves.

From an international perspective, *bilingual education* denotes many different educational approaches to many different groups for many different purposes. In the United States, however, *bilingual education* refers to a specific set of programs. The approaches taken by bilingual programs can be distinguished from those taken by structured immersion programs or English as a Second Language programs by an increased emphasis on the student's home language and culture, by the teaching of academic subject matter classes in the student's home languages, and by the deliberate pace of the introduction of English into the curriculum.

The groups for whom these programs have been designed in the United States are primarily minority-language students with limited proficiency in English. These students are predominantly members of immigrant groups and of racial or ethnic minorities (more specifically, they are predominantly Spanish-speaking and Hispanic), and they come primarily from economically lower-class backgrounds.

In April 1989, a conference was held in Washington, D.C., that attempted, if not to resolve this debate over bilingual education, at least to define some of its terms. Called "Public Policy Issues in Bilingual Education," it was the first national conference to bring prominent advocates and critics of bilingual education together at the same time and the same place to speak with each other. As I told the experts whom I invited to participate, the conference was held in order to lower the temperature and raise the tone of the debate. We did not hope to be able to resolve any of the questions surrounding bilingual education, since the process of resolving these issues will take many years. But we had two reasonable expectations about what we could accomplish by meeting each other and speaking together.

The first purpose was simply to get to know each other on neutral, or even on relatively friendly, grounds. As participants in this debate, we need to be able to credit each other with honorable motives, and to do that we must become acquainted. We must believe that those of us who are concerned with the education of non-English-speaking children, whether we are proponents or opponents of bilingual education, really care mainly about the welfare of these children. The participants in this debate currently share no such trust about each other's motives. On the contrary, we have engaged in heated rhetoric that calls each other's motives into question.

Let me exaggerate the terms of this division, for the time being ignoring its subtleties and shadings. Advocates of bilingual education fear that its opponents are racists who would deliberately give non-English-speaking children an inadequate education that is inappropriate for their cultural backgrounds, in order to maintain them as an oppressed class in the United States. Critics of bilingual education suspect that its proponents are racialists who would intentionally give non-English-speaking children an inadequate education that is inappropriate for their future in American society, in order to preserve and foster ethnic separatism. These sincerely held fears and suspicions do not lead to a great deal of understanding between the two sides.

I believe that this conference did lead to some personal understanding among its participants and its attendees. It certainly exploded a number of stereotypes that advocates and critics held of each other. Advocates of bilingual education expressed some doubts, reservations, and qualifications that, in a more partisan atmosphere, would have branded them as blood-sworn enemies of bilingual education. Similarly, critics of bilingual education expressed varying degrees of support for the aims of bilingual education and for bilingual programs. We found that, removed from the political and partisan atmosphere of the public debate, all of us were more realistic and reasonable than we had given each other credit for being.

Unfortunately, this measure of personal rapprochement did not and does not yet extend far beyond the bounds of our conference room. The funding for this conference was given by U.S. English, a nonprofit public-interest organization in Washington, D.C.; U.S. English has been viewed as an opponent of bilingual education, though its position is much more nuanced than that (see Imhoff 1990). Linda Chavez, who was the president of U.S. English while this conference was being planned, believed that the time was right to have a meeting between advocates and critics of bilingual education. She believed it would be possible to move beyond debate and into dialogue. However, because U.S. English participates in the political debate, we agreed that the organization would fund the conference without controlling it. U.S. English neither asked for nor received the right to invite or to veto participants, nor the right to review or edit their contributions in any way. As the conference coordinator, the choice of whom to invite to participate in or attend the conference was mine alone, and I simply invited the best people I could identify who represented a wide range of viewpoints. Linda Chavez was right. The response from both advocates and critics was enthusiastic, and nearly everyone who was invited to participate agreed to do so.

However, that does not mean that the political atmosphere surrounding bilingual education has become more civil. Some advocates of bilingual education attempted to dissuade their friends from participating. One prominent advocate, whose initial response to the conference call was extremely positive, withdrew after being convinced that it was "politically incorrect" to associate with critics. More seriously, Raul Yzaguirre, the executive director of the National Council of La Raza, attempted to scuttle the conference by demanding that Meridian House International, the conference site and hosting institution, withdraw its support. In a conversation with me, Mr. Yzaguirre said that "U.S. English is to Hispanics as the Ku Klux Klan is to blacks." He could not be convinced that the conference would be fair and balanced, partially because neither he nor two of his expert staffers recognized the names of any of the participants who advocated bilingual education—all of them among the most distinguished and prominent academics in the field. Fearful of criticism from Hispanic political organizations, Ambassador John Jova, at that time the executive director of Meridian House, tried to withdraw Meridian House's support for the conference. Fortunately, his staff convinced him to honor Meridian House's contractual agreement; the conference was held as scheduled and was successful; and there was no protest from political advocacy groups.

The second purpose of the conference was to try to reach some agreement on the terms of the debate. Before it is possible to determine whether bilingual education works, there has to be some agreement about what exactly it is expected to do. However, there is as much disagreement over bilingual education's purposes as over its success. One of the tasks of this conference, therefore, was to reach an understanding of the different criteria by which success could be judged.

A wide range of purposes has been advanced for bilingual education programs. In the 1960s and early 1970s, many bilingual educators suggested that their programs should be evaluated by students' linguistic proficiency and academic progress as measured on standardized tests. More recently, many advocates of bilingual education have suggested more subjective measures, such as students' sense of well-being and self-esteem. And yet other proponents of bilingual education suggest that measures of social change, students' empowerment, and economic progress are the most relevant tests of program success.

Any individual bilingual education program will have several purposes. Some purposes will be explicitly stated, and others will be implicit; some will be congruent with the aims of the wider society, and others will be at variance with them. Evaluating the relative success or failure of bilingual programs has been made very complex by the variety of aims and by widespread disagreement over and misunderstanding of these aims.

The first topic addressed by this conference was how to evaluate the relative success or failure of bilingual education programs or alternative approaches. Many studies have attempted to evaluate the success or failure of bilingual education programs, and meta-analyses of these studies have tried to determine whether, in general, they show that bilingual education is more or less successful than alternative educational approaches. But these studies will be much more useful if there is a common set of socially agreed-upon purposes for bilingual programs.

Obviously, the conferees did not reach any agreement on what measures of success should be used by schools and by our society, nor on the relative priorities and weights that should be given to these various measures. But we did arrive at some understanding of our differences on these matters. Some aims for bilingual education programs that have been advanced include, but are not limited to, the following:

1. Minority-language students' "metalinguistic awareness" (their understanding of language as symbolic representation)
2. Minority-language students' ability to speak, understand, read, and write their native languages
3. Minority-language students' ability to speak, understand, read, and write English

4. Minority-language students' progress in academic subjects other than languages
5. Minority-language students' knowledge of the histories of and their retention of the cultures of their home countries
6. Minority-language students' knowledge of American history and successful adaptation to American culture
7. Minority-language students' positive self-images and emotional well-being
8. Minority-language students' drop-out or stay-in school rates or rates of delinquency
9. Minority-language students' post-school economic advancement
10. Majority-language students' acquisition of the language of minorities in the community
11. Majority-language students' acquisition of knowledge of the histories and cultures of the home countries of minorities in their community
12. Promotion of an English/Spanish bilingual/bicultural society in America, or of multilingual/multicultural societies in some areas of America
13. Promotion of English as the common language of America
14. Promotion of students' sense of their cosmopolitan, global citizenship
15. Promotion of students' sense of their common American citizenship
16. Hiring and advancement of linguistic-, ethnic-, and racial-minority teachers and teachers' aides
17. Alteration of the balance of power among classes and ethnic groups in American society

As the following chapters show, we are still divided over which of these goals are legitimate and over what priority and weight to give to each of them. We disagree over the aims and priorities of American schools and over what should be done in them, as well as over the effectiveness of what is being done in them and over how to measure that effectiveness. But perhaps we can agree that, no matter how misinformed or blind or even stupid the people on the other side of the debate are, they are at least good people, well-intentioned people, groping towards the truth and the better society, just as we are.

In some ways, little has changed since 1605. We are all still looking for something that will bring society a bit closer to civilization, students a bit closer to enlightenment. However, today we hope to achieve those goals with motivations a bit less severe than the threat of hanging.

The Papers

The first three papers confront the question of the purpose of bilingual education.

James A. Banks brings a multicultural perspective to the subject of bilingual education. He argues that the rapid demographic change now taking place in the population of the United States mandates widespread multicultural and bilingual education. Over the next several decades, children from diverse ethnic and cultural groups must be prepared to be effective citizens. To accomplish that task, public schools must develop their students' "cross-cultural competency and cross-cultural literacy." The primary task within this mandate is to "clarify" students' identifications with their own ethnicity. Banks argues that students whose primary ethnic, cultural, and linguistic identifications are clarified contribute more effectively to our society and nation-state than do citizens whose cultural identifications are ambivalent and whose attachments are divided between their ethnic group and the wider society. In addition, Banks argues that schools must culturally empower minority students and students of color. Schools can accomplish this task by incorporating ethnic and racial cultures and minority languages into the curriculum.

In her paper, Rosalie Porter questions what she calls the "three basic assumptions that underly . . . transitional bilingual education." First, she questions the assumption that children benefit educationally from being taught in their native languages. Porter says that that assumption is based on flawed, politically based research. Second, she confronts the theory of language-skills transference. The transference theory predicts that students will achieve superior academic results if they gain skills and achieve literacy in their native languages before they are introduced to English—the language skills learned in the first language will be transferred to the second, allowing for easier learning. Porter argues that this theory has not been supported by actual educational experience. Third, she argues that research findings do not support Jim Cummins's linguistic-interdependence hypothesis. This hypothesis holds that children must be taught new concepts in their native language until they reach the age of abstract reasoning, about eight years old. Otherwise, the theory holds, children will not be able to grasp and understand these concepts.

Porter concludes that "there are a number of reasons for teaching children in their home language instead of the language of the majority community, such as promoting language loyalty, community closeness, and political hegemony and control by ethnic leaders. They are not necessarily reasons of equal education or effective second-language learning or integration."

John Edwards has frequently been characterized as an opponent of bilingual education. However, his paper shows that to be a complete misinterpretation of his position. Indeed, he writes that "bilingual education can be pedagogically useful and, in its transitional format, has a common-sense appeal." He emphasizes that a critical stance toward bilingual education is not necessarily a hostile one. In the United States, he believes, even maintenance bilingual education would not be able to preserve minority languages and cultures in the absence of segregation. Edwards also introduces a topic that is related to the political debate over bilingual education: U.S. English's support for naming English as the official language of the United States, a position that he opposes.

The next three chapters are based in educational research methodology. Public policy in education is informed and shaped by educational research. These presenters discuss the latest research evidence on the effectiveness and uses of bilingual education and of other, alternative methods of teaching limited-English-proficient students.

Christine H. Rossell's paper is based on her trial presentation in *Teresa P. et al. v. Berkeley Unified School District et al*. In it, she reviews the research studies that compare transitional bilingual education with alternative educational methods (structured immersion and English as a Second Language [ESL]) for limited-English-proficient (LEP) students. She argues that studies have not shown that bilingual education achieves results superior to those of the alternative methods. In fact, Rossell shows that educational research studies have not proven that bilingual education achieves superior results to submersion, that is, to having no special program for LEP students. In the case of the Berkeley Unified School District specifically, she argues again that the evidence shows that Berkeley LEP students in the transitional bilingual education (TBE) program do not demonstrate higher achievement levels than students in the Independent Learning Program (ILP).

Henry T. Trueba writes that many immigrant and refugee children live in poverty and cultural and linguistic isolation, leading to "cognitive underdevelopment, educational neglect, late exposure to literacy, and low school achievement, often leading to stereotypic classification into learning-disability groups." Trueba argues that there are English-only political movements that are attempting to curtail the use of non-English languages in schools, but that students' native languages must be used to ensure effective instruction, personality integration, and positive self-concepts for minority children.

Herbert J. Walberg writes that schools cannot control many of the factors that lead to effective learning by students, including the inherent skills of students, their preschool preparation, and their socioeconomic backgrounds. There are two factors involved in learning a second language that schools can control, however: time and content, the time spent on learning the language and the amount of practice devoted to learning the language. Research studies of bilingual education methods, Walberg says, have not proven these methods to be more effective than alternate methods. Students with limited proficiency in English, especially those from deprived socioeconomic backgrounds, can best be helped to learn English by being given exposure to English and time to practice it, and both of these factors are limited in bilingual programs.

The next three chapters address international and philosophical issues surrounding bilingual education.

Brian Weinstein contributes an international comparative perspective on national language policies. Language choices can be made "to maintain the state or societal status quo, to reform either one or the other, or to transform the state and/or the society." Weinstein views bilingual programs in the United States as reformist, rather than radical. Much more ambitious goals for bilingual education were advanced in the 1960s and 1970s. Advocates believed that bilingual education was part of a movement that would result in radical social transformation and shifting the power relationships among social groups in the United States. However, Weinstein believes that bilingual education as it has actually been implemented in this country has more modest goals and results.

Glendon F. Drake discusses the "sociology of knowledge." He writes about both the political and social roles of sociolinguists and also about the involvement of ideology in sociolinguists' work. Drake suggests that much sociolinguistic research has been motivated and shaped by the ideological motivations of the researchers, and that in the bilingual education movement much "definitional confusion, ideological conflict, technical difficulties, failure to inform public opinion, and an ahistorical stance" can be traced to this problem.

Joshua Fishman addresses two questions that are often raised in the debate over bilingual education: does the linguistic heterogeneity of a country exacerbate its internal civil strife, and does it lower the economic productivity of the country? Fishman has devised a project to test these questions empirically by performing an international comparison of nations' linguistic heterogeneity, degrees of civil strife, and per capita gross national product. The paper explains the project's measures of linguistic heterogeneity, civil strife, and productivity, and describes how the impact of linguistic heterogeneity can be disaggregated from other factors. It concludes that the linguistic heterogeneity of a society is not a redundant factor that contributes either to civil strife or to lower economic productivity. Instead, Fishman speculates, linguistic heterogeneity may have positive social effects.

The next two papers address bilingual education from two widely different perspectives, that of the former director of the federal government's bilingual education program and that of a classroom teacher.

Carol Whitten provides a summary of the history of how the federal role in bilingual education developed through legislation and litigation, and discusses the current role of the Office of Bilingual Education and Minority Languages Affairs in setting a national agenda for the education of children who have limited proficiency in English. Whitten expresses a strong preference for local control over school programs and for diversity in educational methods.

Sally Peterson is a third-grade teacher from the suburbs of Los Angeles who organized an organization, LEAD, to oppose the bilingual education policies of the Los Angeles Unified School Board. She describes how her initial hopes for bilingual education were frustrated by her and her colleagues' personal experiences with the method, and then describes her frustrations in dealing with the school board, the state bureaucracy, and the teachers' unions' bureaucracies. Her conclusion is that bilingual education is failing the non-English-speaking students of Los Angeles and California.

The final two chapters are summaries of the comments that were made during the conference by our two commentators, Rudolph Troike and Glynn Custred. Professor Troike rewrote, expanded, and edited his comments himself. Professor Custred's comments were transcribed and lightly edited by me, and I have retained the casual, conversational format of symposium comments.

Professor Troike argues that intensive education in non-English-speaking students' native languages, rather than in English, will improve their academic achievement. He supports bilingual education programs of at least six years in length, and says that the problem with too many bilingual education programs is that they spend too little time and effort in reinforcing the students' first languages. Professor Troike calls apprehensions about separatism resulting from bilingual education irrational paranoia.

Professor Custred's comments were originally presented throughout the conference day in response to various papers. Here, stitched together with minimal editing, they serve admirably to summarize many of the points on which conference attendees were able and unable to agree.

While Professor Troike's and Professor Custred's comments, because of the accident of position, may seem to be the last words in this dialogue, they are not. The dialogue will continue, and both points and counter-points will continue to be refined. If American history is any guide, the pendulums of intellectual favor and social practice will continue to swing between assimilation and pluralism in the future.

References

Imhoff, Gary. 1990. "The Position of U.S. English on Bilingual Education." *The Annals of the American Academy of Political and Social Science* 508:48–61.

Postman, Neil. 1988. *Conscientious Objections: Stirring Up Trouble about Language, Technology, and Education*. N.Y.: Alfred A. Knopf, Inc.

1

Fostering Language and Cultural Literacy in the Schools

James A. Banks

The Changing U.S. Population

The population of the United States and its schools is changing substantially. While most of the nation's immigrants during the 1950s and 1960s were Europeans, most people who come to the United States today from foreign lands are from nations in Latin America and Asia. About 82 percent of the legal immigrants to the United States between 1971 and 1980 were from Latin America and Asia; fewer than 18 percent were from European nations. The United States is experiencing its largest wave of immigrants since the turn of the century, when thousands of immigrants came to the United States from Southern, Eastern, and Central Europe. About 600,000 legal immigrants settle in the United States each year. In 1986, 643,025 legal immigrants made the United States their home (Immigration and Naturalization Service, 1989).

Other demographic developments are increasing racial, ethnic, and cultural diversity in the United States and changing the nation's ethnic texture. The percentage of whites in the nation is decreasing while the percentage of people of color is increasing. This trend has been occurring since 1900. The relative proportion of the nation's white population declined from 87.7 percent in 1900 to 83.1 percent in 1980, with a corresponding increase in the proportion of the population of people of color. The proportion of people of color increased from 12.3 percent in 1900 to 16.9 percent in 1980, a 4.6 percentage-point increase (Momeni 1984). The increasing proportion of the population of people of color has accelerated in recent years, due largely to the large influx of immigrants from Asia and Latin America, the relatively low birthrate among whites, and the aging of the white population. The median age of the white population in 1986 was 32.7, compared to 21 for Puerto Rican Americans. The growth in the population of people of color will continue to outpace that of whites in the foreseeable future. By the turn of the century, one out of every three Americans will be a person of color (Commission on Minority Participation 1988).

The tremendous increase in the population of people of color in the United States is having and will continue to have a major influence on the nation's social structures and institutions, including the work force, the economic system, the courts, and the schools. The effects on the work force will be dramatic (Berlin and Sum 1988). People of color will make up one-third of the net additions to the U.S. labor force between 1985 and 2000. By the year 2000, 21.8 million of the 140.4 million people in the U.S. labor force will be people of color (Johnston and Packer, 1987); 80 percent of the new entrants to the labor force will be women, immigrants, or people of color (Fly 1989).

As U.S. workers retire after the turn of the century, they will be heavily dependent on workers of color for their social security and other retirement benefits. During the boom years of the 1950s, 17 workers supported every retiree. By 1992, each retired worker will be dependent on 3 workers for retirement benefits. One of these three workers will be a person of color. By 2030, the ratio will have narrowed to 2.2 workers to one retiree (Here They Come 1986).

If the educational profile of people of color does not improve substantially, many of the individuals expected to be productive workers by 2010 will themselves be dependent on welfare and other social services. In other words, rather than contributing to the benefits of retired workers, these individuals may be needy and economically dependent on other workers and the government for support. This is a depressing but possible scenario if we do not act quickly and decisively to improve the educational achievements and status of people of color. While these groups made significant educational gains during the 1960s and 1970s, they experienced several drastic achievement reversals during the 1980s (Gay 1989). The enrollment of African Americans in higher education declined substantially between 1980–81 and 1984–85 (Commission on Minority Participation 1988).

The impact of an increasingly ethnically diverse population on the nation's schools is and will continue to be enormous. In twenty-five of the nation's largest cities and metropolitan areas, half or more of the public school students are people of color. By the turn of the century, about 42 percent of the public school students in the nation's largest cities will be either students of color or students who are from families living below the poverty level (Commission on Minority Participation 1988). In California, the population of students of color in the public schools exceeded the percentage of white students during the 1988–89 school year.

The percentage of people of color in large city school districts will continue to increase as we approach the next century, due to both a steady decline in the birthrate among whites and to the continuing exodus of whites to suburban areas and school districts. A salient characteristic of large-city school districts is that they are not only racially and culturally diverse; they are also attended disproportionately by students who are poor. Of the school-age children who lived in the central cities in 1983, 30 percent were poor (Challenges to Urban Education 1987). Urban schools are not only being deserted by the white middle-class, but by middle-class African Americans and Hispanics as well (Carter, Jones-Wilson, and Arnez 1989). Language diversity is one of the main characteristics of schools in central cities. In some districts, the students speak at least forty different first languages.

Education for Citizenship

The rich cultural, language, and social-class diversity of the U.S. population today poses a serious challenge to the nation and its schools. Our goal should be to prepare all of the children of all ethnic and cultural groups to be effective and reflective citizens of the nation-state. This goal should be attained in a way that is consistent with the idealized goals of U.S. society—that is, cultural democracy, human dignity, and respect for human rights. This means that we should help students from diverse cultural groups to become effective citizens of U.S. society without alienating them from their first cultures or violating their cultural and language identities. We should encourage students to maintain those aspects of their first cultures that help them to function effectively in a modernized society and that helps them to answer fundamental questions, such as metaphysical questions, that modern science cannot answer and that provide them with a sense of kinship and belonging. Rather than being harmful to a nation-state, citizens who have clarified cultural identifications and attachments are able to contribute more effectively to the nation-state than are citizens who have confused and ambivalent cultural identifications and attachments.

Our topic at this conference is language diversity and competency in two languages. Language is an essential part of an individual's culture. I am suggesting that competency in one's first culture, including one's first language, can help an individual become a more effective citizen of the nation-state. Cultural competency helps to empower individuals to participate effectively in the universal culture of the commonwealth.

Cultural, National, and Global Identifications

A major goal of schooling in a democratic, pluralistic society should be to help students develop the knowledge, attitudes, and skills needed to function effectively in their cultural communities, within their nation-state, and in the global community. Students who can function effectively in these cultural environments have what I call *cross-cultural competency* and *cross-cultural literacy*. The school should help students to develop clarified, reflective, and positive identifications with their cultural group, nation-state, and the global community (Banks 1983a). Individuals who have clarified and reflective cultural, national, and global identifications understand how these identifications developed; are able to thoughtfully and objectively examine their cultural group, nation, and world; and understand both the personal and public implications of these identifications.

Traditionally, schools in modernized Western nations have tried to make ethnic students effective citizens of the nation-state by alienating them from their first cultures and communities. The school often taught students contempt for their family cultures (Greenbaum 1974). It is difficult for students to develop positive attitudes toward other groups and a strong identification with the nation-state unless they have a clarified identification with their first cultures. Understanding and relating positively to self is a requisite to understanding and relating positively to other groups and people.

As important as it is for the school to reflect cultural democracy and to respect and understand students' cultures, it is also vitally important for all citizens within a nation-state — from each cultural group — to develop a reflective and clarified national identification and a strong commitment to the national political ideals. In the United States, these ideals include equality, justice, and human dignity. It is important, for national cohesion and unity, for all racial and ethnic groups to share a set of overarching values and goals. However, it is essential that all ethnic and racial groups participate in the formulation and interpretation of these overarching national goals and values. Otherwise, some groups will be alienated and will not have an allegiance to them.

It is essential that we help students to develop clarified, reflective, and positive cultural and national identifications. However, because we live in a global world society in which the solutions to humankind's problems require the cooperation of all nations of the world, it is also important for students to develop global identifications and the knowledge, attitudes, and skills needed to become effective and influential citizens in the world community. Second-language competency will greatly facilitate the attainment of the knowledge, attitudes, and skills needed to acquire a clarified global identification and to function effectively in the world community.

I believe that cultural, national, and global identifications are developmental in nature, that an individual can attain a healthy and reflective national identification only when he or she has acquired a positive and reflective cultural identification, and that individuals can develop a reflective and positive global identification only after they have a realistic, reflective, and positive national identification.

Individuals can develop a clarified commitment and identification with a nation-state and the national culture only when they believe that they are a meaningful part of the nation-state, and when it acknowledges, reflects, and values their cultures, languages, and them as individuals. A nation-state that structurally excludes an ethnic group from full participation in the national society and culture and that fails to legitimize the group's culture and language runs the risk of creating alienation within that group and giving rise to ethnic revival movements. Legitimizing a group's culture, incorporating aspects of it into the mainstream culture, and structurally including the group into the nation-state is the most effective way to reduce ethnic conflict and polarization and to help students attain the skills, knowledge, and attitudes needed to become effective citizens of their cultural communities, nation-state, and the world.

Cultural Literacy and Educational Goals

The school should help all students, including students of color, to attain several major goals:

1. Citizenship skills and competencies
2. Literacy in the basic skills
3. Economic empowerment
4. Cultural empowerment
5. The ability to interact and relate positively with people from diverse racial, ethnic, religious, and social-class groups

The knowledge, attitudes, and skills needed to attain these major goals are interrelated. To be able to vote and to participate effectively in the political process, students need to be competent in the basic skills. However, while literacy in the basic skills is necessary for economic empowerment and participation, it is not necessarily sufficient. Students of color who are literate in the basic skills may be and sometimes are denied job and other opportunities because of racial discrimination and/or because they are not knowledgeable about ways to function cross-culturally. Consequently, cultural empowerment is essential because it helps students to develop a clarified identity with their cultural group, a commitment to reform society in order to create equality for all groups, and the skills to function effectively within their own cultural group, within and across other cultural groups, and within the national society.

Cultural empowerment is related to literacy and economic empowerment in still another way. Research by Ogbu (1978) and Fordham and Ogbu (1986) indicates that students of color often do not achieve well academically because of a perceived lack of opportunity and/or because of a fear that high academic achievement is "acting white." African-American students who have internalized the belief that the quest for academic achievement is "acting white" are ignorant of black history and the strong push for literacy among African Americans both during and after slavery. In a recent and important book, Anderson (1988) richly describes the educational initiatives and institutions structured by African Americans in the post-slavery period.

The quest for academic achievement is an important part of the African-American historical experience (Bullock 1967; Anderson 1988). The degree to which young African Americans are unaware of this aspect of their history indicates the extent to which they are both ignorant of and, more important, disconnected and alienated from a significant part of their historical and cultural experience. This disconnectedness from their historical and cultural experience probably results from several factors. Black teachers and black history were major vehicles that kept African-American youths in touch with their past in bygone days. Prior to the civil rights movement and the reduction of housing discrimination that took place in the 1960s and 1970s, most African Americans, including members of both the lower and middle classes, lived in the same communities and went to the same churches and schools. Lower-class African-American youths had several important points of contact and interaction with middle-class African Americans who served as important models and sources of historical and cultural continuity for them.

Many lower-class African-American youths today — and the same may be true for lower-class Hispanic youths — have almost completely lost contact with middle-class members of their ethnic group, as Wilson (1987) points out in his significant book. He states that, in the past, middle-class African Americans lived in the same neighborhoods as poor African Americans and helped to empower them with knowledge of jobs and other opportunities.

All students, including those of color, still need cultural knowledge and continuity with their historical and cultural experience (Woodson 1933). As Glazer (1988) has pointed out, such cultural knowledge might be an important factor in the academic achievement of African Americans and Hispanics.

Schools alone cannot culturally empower students of color. Institutions in the ethnic community, such as the family, the church, the fraternity, and the sorority must play a significant role in cultural empowerment and continuity. *However, the school can and should play an important role in the cultural empowerment of students of color.* The school can help to culturally empower students of color by incorporating their voices, histories, languages, and other aspects of their cultures into the curriculum, by having high academic expectations for them, and by helping them to excel academically (Banks 1988; Banks and Banks 1989). High academic achievement is essential for students of color to experience success and cultural empowerment.

The school should also play an important role in the cultural empowerment of students of color because many of these students have parents who are poor, in need, or alienated from society (Banks 1989). In some cases, the school is the only institution in the lives of these students that has the capacity to empower them culturally, academically, and economically. Helping students to retain and refine their native languages is an important form of cultural empowerment.

As important as it is for students to develop cultural empowerment and connectedness with their own racial and ethnic group, it is essential in a pluralistic democratic society that students also develop the knowledge, attitudes, and skills needed to relate and interact positively with people from other groups. These two goals are interrelated in an important way because students must have clarified, positive, and reflective cultural identities before they can relate positively to outside racial and ethnic groups. Individuals who hold negative and confused attitudes and beliefs about their own cultural and ethnic groups will find it difficult, if not impossible, to relate positively to people from other groups. Helping students to develop cultural empowerment and clarified cultural identifications will facilitate their positive interaction with people who belong to other racial and ethnic groups.

Cultural and Language Literacy for All Students

The broad issues related to language literacy and competency for all students have often been confused and mixed with issues related to the cultural empowerment of specific language and cultural groups. In the United States, the term *bilingual education* is rarely used to mean that African Americans or white students will learn a second language. The term is often used to describe a program designed to teach a language-minority group, such as Mexican Americans or Vietnamese Americans, certain subjects in both their native language and in English until they have become literate and able to function exclusively in English. The student's native language is then dropped by the school. This was certainly the intent of Congress when it enacted the Bilingual Education Act in 1968. Most bilingual education programs in the United States are transitional programs rather than maintenance programs.

There are several problems with conceptualizing the major issue at this conference as bilingual education. First, the term is loaded with political baggage and has partisans who strongly advocate it and adversaries who strongly oppose it. Second, the term, at least in the United States, connotes compensatory entitlement programs designed to help specific ethnic and cultural groups, rather than the development of second-language competencies by all students. It tends to evoke "us-them" feelings and reactions.

While changing a concept does not eradicate old practices and conceptions or create a new reality, different and novel concepts can facilitate fresh thinking and the formulation of new assumptions and goals. Consequently, I think we are better off conceptualizing the issue at this conference as language literacy rather than as bilingual education.

A major goal of schooling in a pluralistic democratic society should be to help all students to develop literacy and competency in at least two languages. English is the shared, common language of the nation-state. Students from all ethnic, cultural, and language groups must be able to speak and write it fluently in order to be effective and empowered citizens (Banks 1983b). Several factors should be considered when determining the second language that students should learn, including:

1. Their first language
2. The extent to which the language is spoken by citizens in the United States
3. The extent to which the language will help the United States to enhance its economic and political goals
4. The extent to which it is feasible to teach the second language to students, beginning in the primary grades
5. The extent to which the second language will contribute to the academic achievement and cultural empowerment of language-minority students in the United States
6. The extent to which it is possible to offer students opportunities to practice and therefore to become functionally literate in the second language

The languages other than English spoken in the United States vary considerably by region. In the southwestern states and in California, New York, New Jersey, and Florida, Spanish is a frequently spoken second language because Hispanics are highly concentrated in these states. Eighty-nine percent of Hispanics in the United States live in nine states; over half of them live in California and Texas (Valdivieso and Davis 1988). Using the criteria above, a compelling case can be made that Spanish should be a frequently taught second language in the schools in the Southwest and in California, New York, New Jersey, and Florida. However, other second-language options should be available in the schools, especially Chinese and Japanese. Asian nations are becoming increasingly important in the global economy. Teaching Asian languages to U.S. students will help U.S. citizens to function more effectively in a competitive world economy, as well as to interact with Asian cultures with more understanding and empathy.

The selection of a second language for students to study should be done at the local level. The language resources of the community and the school, as well as the wishes of the community, are important factors that should be considered when a second language is chosen for study. A primary goal of second language teaching should be to preserve some of the rich language spoken by language minority groups in the United States, as well as to help all of the nation's students to become literate in English and at least one other language. The need for the United States to help its students to become literate in other languages was stated cogently by the President's Commission on Foreign Language and International Studies appointed by President Carter (President's Commission 1979, 1-2):

> Nothing less is at issue than the nation's security. At a time when the resurgent forces of nationalism and of ethnic and linguistic consciousness so directly affect global realities, the United States requires far more reliable capacities to communicate with its allies, analyze the behavior of potential adversaries, and earn the trust and the sympathies of the uncommitted. Yet there is a widening gap between these needs and the American competence to understand and deal successfully with other peoples in a world of flux.

The acquisition of competency in at least two languages should be a goal for all students in the nation's schools and not just for students who are members of language-minority groups. It is in the best interest of a nation-state to preserve some of its language diversity because we live in a highly interdependent world society, in which each nation must trade with and otherwise relate to other nations with different national languages. Only languages within a nation that have international utility, such as Spanish and Chinese, can be preserved for this purpose. Language diversity within a society reduces ethnocentrism and also helps a nation to deal more successfully with others. National policies that foster language diversity may promote national attachments and identifications among language-minority groups if these groups believe that the policies help to legitimize their languages and cultures.

To successfully set and implement a national policy of language diversity, however, a nation must also set, as a high national priority, the changing of social and economic conditions that will enable language-minority groups to become full participants in its social, economic, and political institutions. A nation that wishes to successfully implement a policy of language diversity must also take vigorous steps to help all of its citizens, especially members of language-majority groups, to develop positive attitudes toward minority-group languages, to view them as legitimate communication systems, and to learn to speak them. As long as language-minority groups remain structurally excluded from mainstream institutions within a society, and most members of the dominant-language groups remain suspicious and largely ignorant of minority-group languages, fostering language diversity as a national policy might exacerbate rather than reduce ethnic conflict and polarization. If only people of color become bilingual, then the future of minority languages is bleak. In this case, bilingual education is likely to facilitate the erosion, rather than the maintenance of, the minority languages.

A national goal to make all of the nation's citizens literate in at least two languages will facilitate the attainment of several important outcomes that are needed in the United States:

1. It will help U.S. students to become more culturally literate and sensitive to other cultures if the second or third languages are taught within their cultural contexts.
2. It will help to break down barriers between U.S. mainstream whites and language-minority citizens.
3. It will enable U.S. citizens to function more competently in a global world society in which cooperation among groups from different races, cultures, and religions is essential for human survival.
4. It will help language minority students become more successful in a range of careers in which a second language is vital, and it will thereby strengthen the nation.

Language Literacy and Global Competency

The most pressing and intractable problems that humankind faces, such as the eroding of the ozone layer of the atmosphere, the AIDS epidemic, nuclear proliferation, and international terrorism, are global in nature and cannot be solved unless peoples from diverse cultures, ethnic groups, religions, and nations work cooperatively. While human beings share a common destiny, various groups throughout the world are divided sharply by ethnicity, religion, and nationality. These groups, which tend to see their problems from unique and particularistic perspectives, do not frequently work jointly to solve difficult human problems. This is due largely to the fact that the world's peoples, both within and across nations, are sharply divided between the rich and the poor. These groups consume highly disproportionate shares of the world's resources and exercise sharply different amounts of power in world politics.

Two out of three people in the world live in poor and developing nations in Africa, Asia, and Latin America (U.S. Bureau of the Census 1987). Yet, the one-out-of-three people in the world who live in the developed nations consume most of the earth's resources and exercise most of the political and economic power in the world. The world is sharply divided between the few who are rich and well fed in the Western nations—who are predominantly white—and the many who are poor and hungry in the developing nations—who are predominantly nonwhite. These sharp divisions also exist within nations.

Allport's (1979) seminal theory teaches us that people from diverse groups can work cooperatively to solve problems only when they function in equal-status situations and when they perceive their fates as shared. We will not be able to substantially reduce international tensions and conflicts until most citizens in the world have a decent standard of living and a modicum of political power. Groups from different ethnic groups, cultures, and nations that have highly unequal amounts of power, cultural recognition and legitimacy, influence, and wealth are rarely able to work cooperatively to solve difficult human problems. A major goal of education for survival in a multicultural global society is to help students to acquire the knowledge, attitudes, and skills (including language competencies) needed to participate in the reformation of the world's social, political, and economic systems so that peoples from diverse ethnic, cultural, and religious groups will be politically empowered, will be structurally integrated into their societies, and will have cultural legitimacy and empowerment in their nation-states.

Helping students to acquire the competencies and commitments to participate in effective civic action to create equitable national societies is an important goal for multicultural, global education in the twenty-first century. A requisite to creating an equitable and just society is to legitimize and validate the cultures and languages of language-minority groups by making them a valued part of the U.S. mainstream culture. By requiring all of our students to learn a language such as Spanish or Chinese, we will not only legitimize and validate the language and cultures of Hispanic and Chinese-American students, but will help all students to develop the knowledge, skills, and attitudes needed to function effectively in a global world society.

Language Instruction and Multicultural Education

The infusion of language skills, insights, and competencies into the curriculum should be part of a comprehensive curriculum reform movement designed to restructure the curriculum so that the cultures of diverse racial and cultural groups will be integrated throughout it (Banks 1987). Language skills and insights should be taught within the context of a multicultural curriculum. To teach a language without helping students to understand its cultural context will not enable students to attain the kind of cultural knowledge, attitudes, and skills described above. Studying a language without examining its cultural context will also give students an incomplete understanding and appreciation of it.

Culture in the Curriculum

It is necessary for educators to have an in-depth and accurate knowledge of *culture* in order for them to help students to understand the relationship between language and culture and to incorporate important elements of ethnic cultures into the curriculum. There are many definitions of culture, and few on which all social scientists can agree. Kroeber and Kluckhohn (1952), in a comprehensive study of the definitions of culture, found more than 160. Most anthropologists emphasize the intangible, symbolic, and ideational aspects of group life as the most important aspects of culture. Some social scientists go so far as to exclude material objects (artifacts) from their definition of culture. Even social scientists who view tangible or material objects as a part of culture believe that the interpretation of these objects and the rules governing their use, and not the artifacts themselves, constitute the essence of culture (Banks 1988, 72).

It is the values, symbols, interpretations, and perspectives that distinguish one people from another in modernized societies, and not artifacts, material objects, and other tangible aspects of hu-

man societies. The essence of African-American culture is not soul food or other tangible aspects of black culture. Rather, the essence of African-American culture today is its unique values, beliefs, symbols, and perspectives (Gay and Baber 1987). A southern African American who has a strong identity with his culture may drive the same car as an elite Anglo-American Boston Brahmin. However, the values that the two individuals have about kinship and family may differ dramatically.

While social scientists emphasize the symbolic, ideational, and interpretative aspects of culture, often in the schools the cultures of ethnic groups are trivialized by focusing on artifacts such as tepees and sombreros and by depicting cultures as static rather than as dynamic and changing. Cultural artifacts, heroes, and ethnic holidays are often taught and celebrated in the schools, while the struggles and survival techniques that people of color have formulated to enable them to survive in a racially and class-stratified society are ignored. These approaches to multicultural teaching focus on the life-styles rather than the life-chances of ethnic groups. Bullivant (1989) describes culture as a strategy for survival. Students need to understand how a group's language and linguistic styles, whether Spanish or Black English, are part of its survival strategy and how eradicating a group's language might not only be perceived by it as an attempt at cultural destruction, but how destroying a group's language may actually threaten its survival.

Understanding Language Diversity in the United States

When discussing bilingual education in the United States, the discussion often focuses on Spanish and English, at least in the West. The rich language and dialect diversity in the United States is usually obscured in discussions about bilingual education. Students need to understand the rich language and dialect diversity in the United States. This diversity survives despite a strong assimilationist policy that has existed at least since the turn of the century when nativism, directed largely at the Southern, Central, and Eastern-European and Asian immigrants, was widespread (Higham 1972). In a 1976 survey, one out of every eight Americans indicated that they came from a minority-language background (Crawford 1989, 13).

Both students and teachers need to understand why language and dialect diversity is rich in the United States, and why it is likely to continue to exist for the foreseeable future, despite the passage of referenda in a number of states making English the official state language.

To understand why language and dialect diversity continues to exist in the United States despite powerful assimilationist forces, policies, and practices, students need to examine historical, political, and sociological issues related to race, class, and power in the United States. While U.S. mainstream leaders have espoused a strong assimilationist policy at least since the turn of the century, racism, class stratification, and exclusion have prevented groups such as African Americans and Mexican Americans from full structural participation in the national common culture where they would have had sufficient opportunities to master standard English and other mainstream values and behaviors. Thus, while U.S. political and educational leaders articulated an assimilationist ideology of inclusion, the nation's institutions practiced exclusion and rejection of groups that were nonwhite and non-European. The particularistic cultures, dialects, and languages of people of color in the United States are the consequences of efforts to structure survival cultures rather than to resist the mainstream culture of the nation-state.

Educators and students, as well as policy makers, need to keep the historical, political, and sociological origins and perpetuation of the languages and dialects of people of color in mind when they discuss, debate, and formulate public policies related to the languages of the nation's diverse ethnic and cultural groups. Human decency and fairness require that this be done.

References

Allport, G. W. 1979. *The Nature of Prejudice*. 25th anniversary ed. Reading, Mass.: Addison-Wesley.

Anderson, J. D. 1988. *The Education of Blacks in the South, 1860–1935*. Chapel Hill: The University of North Carolina Press.

Banks, C. A. M. 1989. "Parents and Teachers: Partners in Multicultural Education." In Banks and Banks 1989, 305–22.

Banks, J. A. 1983a. "Cultural Democracy, Citizenship Education, and the American Dream." *Social Education* 47:178–79, 222–32ff.

_____. 1983b. "Language, Ethnicity, Ideology and Education." In *Multicultural Education: A Challenge for Teachers*, edited by L. V. D. Berg-Eldering, F. J. M. DeRijcke, and L. V. Zuck. Dordrecht, Holland: Foris Publications.

_____. 1987. *Teaching Strategies for Ethnic Studies*. 4th ed. Boston: Allyn and Bacon.

_____. 1988. *Multiethnic Education: Theory and Practice*. 2nd ed. Boston: Allyn and Bacon.

Banks, J. A., and C. A. M. Banks, eds. 1989. *Multicultural Education: Issues and Perspectives*. Boston: Allyn and Bacon.

Berlin, G., and A. Sum 1988. *Toward a More Perfect Union: Basic Skills, Poor Families and Our Economic Future*. New York: Ford Foundation.

Bullivant, B. M. 1989. "Culture: Its Nature and Meaning for Educators." In Banks and Banks 1989.

Bullock, H. A. 1967. *A History of Negro Education in the South: From 1619 to the Present*. Cambridge, Mass.: Harvard University Press.

Carter, R. T., F. Jones-Wilson, and N. L. Arnez 1989. "Demographic Characteristics of Greater Washington, D.C. Area Black Parents Who Chose Nonpublic Schooling for Their Young." *The Journal of Negro Education* 58:39–49.

Challenges to Urban Education: Results in the Making. 1987. Washington, D.C.: The Council on the Great City Schools.

Commission on Minority Participation in Education and American Life. 1988. *One-Third of a Nation*. Washington, D.C.: American Council on Education.

Crawford, J. 1989. *Bilingual Education: History, Politics, Theory and Issues*. Trenton, N.J.: Crane Publishing Company.

Fly, Richard. 1989. "Introducing Dan Quayle, Competitiveness Czar." *Business Week*, Feb., 37.

Fordham, S., and J. U. Ogbu. 1986. "Black Students' School Success: Coping with the Burden of 'Acting White.'" *The Urban Review* 18(3):176–206.

Gay, G. 1989. "Ethnic Minorities and Educational Equality." In Banks and Banks 1989, 167–88.

Gay, G., and W. L. Baber. 1987. *Expressively Black: The Cultural Basis of Ethnic Identity*. New York: Praeger.

Glazer, N. 1988. "Education for Citizenship in the 21st Century." *Education and Society* 1:5–10.

Greenbaum, W. 1974. "America in Search of a New Ideal: An Essay on the Rise of Pluralism." *Harvard Educational Review* 44:411–40.

"Here They Come Ready or Not." 1986. *Education Week*, special report, 14 May.

Higham, J. 1972. *Strangers in the Land: Patterns of American Nativism 1860–1925*. New York: Atheneum.

Immigration and Naturalization Service. 1989. *Statistical Yearbook of the Immigration and Naturalization Service. 1988*. Washington, D.C.: U.S. Government Printing Office.

Johnston, W. B., and A. E. Packer. 1987. *Workforce 2000: Work and Workers for the 21st Century*. Indianapolis: Hudson Institute.

Kroeber, A. L., and C. Kluckhohn. 1952. *Culture: A Critical Review of Concepts and Definitions*. New York: Vintage Books.

Momeni, J. A. 1984. *Demography of Racial and Ethnic Minorities in the United States: An Annotated Bibliography with a Review Essay*. Westport, Conn.: Greenwood Press.

Ogbu, J. U. 1978. *Minority Education and Caste: The American System in Cross-Cultural Perspective*. New York: Academic Press.

President's Commission on Foreign Language and International Studies. 1979. *Strength through Wisdom: A Critique of U.S. Capability*. Washington, D.C.: U.S. Government Printing Office. Nov.

U.S. Bureau of the Census. 1987. *World Population Profile: 1987*. Washington, D.C.: U.S. Government Printing Office.

Valdivieso, R., and D. Davis. 1988. *U.S. Hispanics: Challenging Issues for the 1990s*. No. 17, *Population Trends and Public Policy*. Occasional papers. Washington, D.C.: Population Reference Bureau.

Wilson, W. J. 1987. *The Truly Disadvantaged: The Inner City, the Underclass, and Public Policy*. Chicago: The University of Chicago Press.

Woodson, C. G. 1933. *The Mis-Education of the Negro*. Washington, D.C.: The Associated Publishers.

2

The Disabling Power
of Ideology: Challenging
the Basic Assumptions
of Bilingual Education

Rosalie Pedalino Porter

Bilingual education throughout its brief history has easily been the most politically charged arena in U.S. public education. Two legislative acts of the 1960s initiated the federal government's commitment to improving the education of language-minority children. The Civil Rights Act of 1964 included a provision in its Title VI that children of limited English are not to be denied access to an equal education because of national origin or home language. The first Bilingual Education Act was passed in 1968, specifically mandating special programs to help these children learn English and participate fully in regular classrooms with their English-speaking classmates. The Supreme Court, in the *Lau v. Nichols* decision in 1974, upheld the rights of all limited-English students to special language programs, beyond what is available to the average English-speaking student, to overcome the language barrier to equal educational opportunity. Although the Supreme Court decision did not urge a specific remedy and the expressed will of the U.S. Congress did not dictate any particular program to achieve the stated goals, the idea was quickly promoted that educational equality could only be achieved by teaching the children in their home language while they were learning English. The legitimate demand for new educational initiatives to redress the neglect of language-minority children gained substantial support in many states. But the early establishment of the transitional bilingual education model as the only allowable option closed off the possibility of trying various approaches to second-language teaching to determine what works best in different settings with different speech communities and with children of different ages.

Instead of a search for a variety of educational solutions, the early advocates for the experimental bilingual education program proclaimed this model to be the only legitimate approach. Because of the earlier discrimination suffered by language-minority children, many well-intentioned educators were easily convinced that any program using only the English language must be bad, and that any special program that taught children in their native language must be not only equitable, but superior.

The original impulse for bilingual education and its major beneficiaries are Spanish speakers. It began as a Spanish-language issue since the large majority of children initially enrolled in bilingual programs (80 percent) were Spanish speakers. The negative side of this strong push for native-language instruction is that it created the impression that Spanish speakers are the first immigrant group that is incapable of acquiring a second language and that needs to be educated in its home language. This is, of course, a gross distortion of the true situation, but it has reinforced some negative attitudes among the uninformed towards the Latino community.

Bilingual education is part of the political movement for Latino equality, power, and influence in American society—a natural impulse of immigrant or migrant groups on the lowest rung of the economic ladder. However, it is represented as an educational program that will produce superior achievement for *all* language-minority children. Much has improved for limited-English students in the past twenty years as the investment of major resources has produced at least these visible benefits:

- The training and hiring of bilingual teachers, counselors, administrators, psychologists, and social workers
- The development of curriculum and teaching strategies
- The publication of native-language texts in Spanish
- The publication of English-language texts appropriate for elementary and secondary level students
- A heightened consciousness among educators in general that this

population has greater needs than the average children in a U.S. classroom.

The research projects carried on during this period, though, have not demonstrated the value of native-language instruction for extended periods as the key ingredient in achievement by limited-English students.

To ask the questions, "Is bilingual education effective? Is it more effective than alternative programs?" is to betray a lack of understanding of the reported research and of the application of education policy. The major conclusion of Keith Baker's and Adriana de Kanter's comprehensive study (1981) was that bilingual education achieved better results for students in the learning of the English language and mathematics in very few cases of the several hundred studies reviewed. It produced no better results than English as a Second Language (ESL) programs in several studies, and it was found to be less helpful than doing nothing in some of the studies.

More important than even the much-maligned research on bilingual programs is the fact that education policy, at the federal and state level, has been implemented with a very strong bias toward only one type of program for the past twenty years. Until spring 1988, when federal legislation changed the funding formula, 96 percent of all federal funds under Title VII were allocated to demonstration projects, teacher training grants, and research on transitional bilingual education programs! Only 4 percent was directed toward alternative programs. It is obvious why almost no research exists on the success or failure of ESL, immersion, two-way, or any other type of program for limited-English students. When we also consider that a number of states (eleven at the latest count) passed laws mandating transitional bilingual education and providing funding for only this type of program, it is easy to understand why there has been so little innovation in this field. The new legislation now allows up to 25 percent of the Title VII funds to be allocated to alternative programs.

During these past twenty years, not only the total number of limited-English students but also the variety of language groups needing special programs have increased dramatically. Spanish speakers now make up approximately 65 percent of the limited-

English students in our schools, with 145 other language groups making up the remainder (National Advisory and Coordinating Council 1987, 75–76). The language-minority population is growing at a faster rate than the rest of the population and is no longer found only in urban schools, but also in suburban and rural districts. By the turn of the century, it is possible that language-minority children will make up 20 percent of the school population, with speakers of Asian languages accounting for the largest increase. These demographic changes require a reexamination of a policy developed primarily in response to the purported needs of the Latino community.

It is timely, then, to review with a closer scrutiny the assumptions on which bilingual education initiatives are based. I look at these notions, which have come to be seen almost as natural law by an uncritical laity, from my perspective of fifteen years' involvement in the field. I am not a linguist or a sociologist, but a practitioner. I have worked as a Spanish bilingual teacher in the Puerto Rican community in Springfield, Massachusetts; I have directed the Bilingual/English as a Second Language Programs for the Newton Public Schools in Newton, Massachusetts; I have engaged in a variety of research projects as a member of the National Advisory Council on Bilingual Education; I have been a consultant and a lecturer on U.S. education policy in the United States and in England, Finland, Turkey, Italy, Japan, China, and Bulgaria. I have also had the personal experience of arriving in the United States at the age of six and sitting in a classroom in Newark, New Jersey, not understanding a word said by my teacher or my classmates.

I believe there are three basic assumptions that underlly the transitional bilingual education model, and they have been fairly widely accepted without much critical questioning until recently. Twenty years of practical experience with real children in real-life classrooms have led me to the serious questioning of these hypotheses.

Vernacular Advantage Theory

The case is made that there are good reasons for children who do not know the language of the school to be instructed in their home or native language for an extended period of time while they are learning a second language. This is the overarching idea from which the whole bilingual education enterprise developed. It is believed that using the familiar language in the classroom will not only ease the child into an unfamiliar situation but will have the following educational benefits.

- For young children, developing their first language well can help them learn a second language more successfully.
- Students who are taught all their school subjects in the home language, while they are learning a second language, will learn content better.
- Delaying the start of second-language learning until age eight or nine will avoid the confusion of "semi-lingualism" or the imperfect learning of two languages.

Early support for these notions came from the research studies of Finnish sociologists Toukamaa and Skutnabb-Kangas. Their works focused on the population of Finnish immigrant children in Swedish schools. These studies were often cited in support of the transitional bilingual education model when it was first implemented in the United States. This particular research has been discredited for the unreliability of the data and the apparent chauvinistic bias in the reporting. When I lectured at Finnish universities in Helsinki, Tampere, and Jyvaskela in 1981, I discussed the Toukamaa and Skutnabb-Kangas findings with several linguists who pronounced the work of these two to be ideologically motivated and very often not supported by reliable data. My Finnish friends expressed surprise that the unsubstantiated theory about the advantage of teaching children in their native language was still accepted in the United States and that it seemed to be the basis for national education policy.

Christina Bratt Paultson has studied bilingual education in Sweden and has written a critical review of the situation. Her conclusions make clear why we in the United States should not have become overreliant on the Swedish research. She claims that Swedish works on bilingual education are often very opinionated, and that many of the studies (Skutnabb-Kangas and Toukamaa 1978, for example) are written with the express purpose of making policy recommendations and so are biased and selective in their choice of primary data (Paulston 1982, 11). She totally refutes the notion of anything called *semi-lingualism*, denouncing it as a lay term with no empirical evidence to support it. She suggests that the term continues to be used because it serves as a rationale for Finnish groups in their demands for Finnish schooling in Sweden (Paulston 1982, 41).

In direct contradiction of the Toukamaa results, Paulston found solid evidence that children's proficiency in the Swedish language was not a direct result of their proficiency in Finnish, that school achievement in subject matter was independent of home language, and that there was no difference in motivation and school adjustment between students in Finnish- or Swedish-language classes (Paulston 1982, 50).

It appears that the whole rationale for bilingual education is based on flawed research reported for political and nationalistic reasons. And in the United States, as in Sweden, it has been aggressively promoted for similar purposes. Paulston agrees with an official whom she interviewed who said: "In the beginning the officials were duped into a mother tongue policy—then the bureaucracy took over." And, she adds, "the press helped in this duping with the best of liberal intentions" (Paulston 1982, 55).

There are a number of reasons for teaching children in their home language instead of the language of the majority community, such as promoting language loyalty, community closeness, and political hegemony and control by ethnic leaders. They are not necessarily reasons of equal education or effective second-language learning or integration. The promotion of linguistic and cultural separatism by community leaders fearing a diffusion of economic and political power provoked this caution from education writer Alfredo Mathews, Jr.:

> While bilingualism, from a political point of view, is meant to foster the Puerto Rican/Hispanic identity and consequently encourages concentrations of Hispanics to stay together and not be integrated, one also has to be wary that it not become so insular and ingrown that it fosters a type of apartheid that will generate animosities with other groups. (Mathews 1977)

Nothing in my fifteen years of involvement with this field has begun to convince me that delaying instruction in English for several years will lead to better learning of English or to a greater ability to study subject matter taught in English. This is still a hypothesis in search of legitimacy.

The Necessity of Mother-Tongue Literacy First

According to bilingual education advocates, children learn to read best in a language they know well, and later they will transfer these reading skills easily to reading in a second language. This may be a subset of the notion of vernacular advantage, but it is an assumption that has had far-reaching effects on the education of language-minority children in this country. Once again, the demand for schools to teach reading first in the native language to limited-English children was pressed on behalf of Spanish speakers. It was argued that learning to read in Spanish is easy because the language is so phonetic (only five vowel sounds, and the spelling is quite regular) compared to English with its more complex pattern of pronunciation (twelve vowel sounds) and its irregular spelling. There is no reliable evidence for this assumption, not for Spanish speakers or for anyone else. Even Kenji Hakuta, a staunch supporter of bilingual education who has been involved in bilingual classroom and community research for several years, has stated that "what is remarkable about the issue of transfer of skills is that despite its fundamental importance, almost no empirical studies have been conducted to understand the characteristics or even to demonstrate the existence of the transfer of skills" (Hakuta 1986, 218).

Nevertheless, bilingual education programs require that children be taught to read first in their home language, and, in fact, devote most of the school day in the first two or three years of school to instruction in the home language with only brief lessons in spoken English. I was ordered by my department head, when I was a bilingual teacher, not to begin reading instruction in English with my students until they could read at grade level in Spanish. As I was teaching fifth- and sixth-grade children from disadvantaged backgrounds, most of them were actually reading a few years below grade level in Spanish. It seemed irrational to me to keep delaying the reading in English since that is the target language, which the students would need increasingly for academic work. It seemed to me that there was not much time left for the magical "transfer of skills" to take place for these eleven-to-fourteen-year-old students who, for the most part, had been in the bilingual program since kindergarten.

Since 1972, we have had the evidence of the St. Lambert, Ontario, studies on the French immersion programs in Canada, through which over one hundred thousand English-speaking students have been educated in two languages. In these programs, all instruction is in French from the first day of kindergarten, and reading is taught in French also. The results of these studies show that the students learn to read and to do all academic work in their second language (French), and when the use of English, their home language, is introduced in the third grade the students began to read in English even though this has never been taught as a school subject (Hakuta 1986, 93).

U.S. advocates of bilingual education have consistently denied the validity of this type of program for our language-minority students, and have until recently successfully blocked these programs from being attempted. Educators have, in many cases, been more concerned with maintaining the correct ideological positions (that bilingual education must be preserved and that the various native languages and cultures in the United States must be maintained) and less concerned with the practical goal of giving our students the best academic skills for access to opportunities in our society here and now. There have not been many strong advocates for trying innovative programs that have already demonstrated a high degree of success elsewhere.

Some new initiatives are being attempted, nevertheless, and two reports from Texas make telling points. The Southwest Educational Development Laboratory conducted a six-year study, completed in 1984, comparing the achievement of students who read first in Spanish to the achievement of those who read first in English (Mace-Matluck 1984). These limited-English children, all Mexican American and from the same socioeconomic background, were traced from kindergarten through third grade. The most pertinent points reported are these:

1. Children with well-developed oral language in either Spanish or English have an advantage in learning to read.

2. Enrollment in the Spanish reading program generally had a negative association with learning to read in English.
3. Students who learned to read first in English transferred their reading skills to Spanish more easily than those who started reading first in Spanish and took up English reading later.
4. Knowledge of the English alphabet on entering kindergarten was strongly related to successful reading performance in grades 1–3.

The results of this study do not indicate much support for the assumption that teaching reading in the home language first is superior. It does argue the need for better early-language development for language-minority children, and if it is not happening in the home then more should be done through early-childhood programs such as Head Start.

The other study worth noting is the El Paso, Texas, Bilingual Immersion Pilot Project, which has just produced an interim report at the end of three years of a five-year project. Twenty-five hundred limited-English students in first through third grades are involved, all from Spanish-speaking homes and comparable backgrounds. Students in eighteen schools (the control group) are following the traditional bilingual education program, learning to read in Spanish first and being taught all subjects in that language while studying English for brief daily lessons. The immersion (experimental) group of students in the other eighteen schools is provided an alternative program with these main features: "comprehensible" English is used in the classroom as the language of instruction from the first day of school; reading and all other subjects are taught in English; Spanish language is taught only for about one hour daily and is occasionally used to explain a new concept being taught; English is not taught as a separate subject but is the medium for learning subject matter. The major results reported are these:

1. The immersion project students outscored students in the traditional bilingual education program at every grade level on tests of English reading and language arts.
2. Immersion students scored as high on the mathematics tests as

the control group and scored above average on state tests in science and social studies.

3. In grade three, 90 percent of the immersion students had mastered reading and writing skills in Spanish on a par with the students in the control group, even though the former had had a minimum of instruction in Spanish.

Interviews with school personnel yielded the following attitudes:

1. Teachers in the immersion project were much more optimistic about the effectiveness of their program in motivating their students to learn English.
2. Only one-third of the transitional bilingual program teachers believe that their students will successfully transfer to reading in English.
3. All the school principals who had experience with both programs expressed the opinion that the immersion program is a better approach to educating language minority students (Office of Research and Evaluation 1987, 51–59).

Since reading is so basic to most academic learning, and literacy in English is one of the stated goals of all bilingual programs in the United States, it is important to look at which successes language-minority students are achieving and to compare different teaching approaches. Until very recently, neither federal bilingual funds nor bilingual educators have supported the kind of experimentation described above, because of the strong political and ideological commitment to native-language reading.

There are a few other layers to the reading hypothesis. Even if it were clear that there is an advantage for Spanish speakers in learning to read first in their home language, does it follow that this will be true for speakers of languages that do not use the Roman alphabet? Is it logical to apply this principle to all the 145 languages in which bilingual education is currently provided? If children are to read first in Japanese, Mandarin, Farsi, or Khmer, for example, they would need to spend years mastering a large system of symbols before going on to read in English. Some of the languages or dialects represented in our programs do not presently have written-symbol systems (Hmong, Cape Verdean). Should written forms be created so that children can be taught to read an artificial script for which there are no existing texts and later transfer those skills to reading in English?

Another dimension to the reading controversy does focus mainly on Spanish-speaking children. The great majority of these children are not immigrants from other countries who may not know a word of English; rather, they are residents of the mainland United States or Puerto Rico. Living on the U.S. mainland or in Puerto Rico, it would be almost impossible to have had no exposure to the English language. Federal statistics show that up to 60 percent of the children in bilingual education programs are English dominant; that is, their English-language skills are stronger than their Spanish language skills (Baker and Rossell 1987). Indeed, for some unknown number of these children, teaching them to read in their "mother tongue" would be teaching them in a foreign language. It is obviously unsound educational practice to teach these students reading in Spanish on the grounds that it will help them learn English. In the Newton, Massachusetts; Berkeley, California; and Fairfax County, Virginia, public schools (the school districts I am most familiar with) we have taught limited-English students by the thousands to read in English first with a high degree of success.

Linguistic Interdependence Hypothesis

Canadian linguist Jim Cummins's theory suggests that learning successfully in a second language depends on prior learning in the first or native language; that children must be taught new concepts in their native language until the age of abstract reasoning (around eight years of age), or they will not be able to learn these notions in a second language; that language-minority children should be taught literacy skills and subject matter in their native tongue for a minimum of five to seven years if they are to attain their own individual highest level of proficiency. This idea, too, derives from the vernacular advantage theory.

This yet-unproven hypothesis has had a powerful influence on the bilingual education field, providing the basis for the transitional bilingual education model itself. Skutnabb-Kangas and Toukamaa cited it in a UNESCO report in which they concluded "that the migrant children whose mother tongue stopped developing before the abstract thinking phase was achieved thus easily remain on a lower level of educational capacity than they would originally have been able to achieve" (Skutnabb-Kangas and Toukomaa 1978, 27). This conclusion does not rest on any proven results but on an idea of what might have been and on a political attitude in favor of extended native-language instruction.

In the early 1970s when Cummins's hypothesis was first announced, the idea of using the home language to teach subject matter while students learned enough English for classroom work seemed humane and less frustrating for the students. It seemed obvious, too, that children could learn English for social, informal uses quickly but that it would take longer to develop the conceptual depth in English to learn academic subjects taught in that language. Since those early years we have discovered that there is no evidence to support this hypothesis. In fact, there is current research indicating no advantage to children in teaching them subject matter in their native language.

In directing the Newton Public Schools Bilingual Program for the past seven years, I have observed no difference in achievement in the mastery of subject matter between the children who are provided some native-language help in Spanish, Italian, Chinese, and the children from twenty-five other language backgrounds who are given no native-language support at all. We have not done a formal research study on this. I simply base my conclusions on the records of achievement according to these criteria: successful mainstreaming of bilingual students after two to three years in our program with good academic skills; positive attitude toward school and learning among bilingual students; strong expressions of satisfaction with student achievement from the parents; low level of absenteeism; less than 1 percent drop-out rate and a high proportion of bilingual students going on to some form of higher education.

Dade County, Florida, with one of the highest concentrations of Spanish speakers in the country, has just published the report of a three-year experiment entitled "The Dade County Bilingual Curriculum Content Pilot Project." This is a study of 508 limited-English students in twelve schools, grades K–2. Six of the schools were randomly assigned to provide content instruction (mathematics, science, and social studies) in Spanish; the other six schools provided the content instruction solely in English using a curriculum designed for limited-English students (a structured immersion approach). A nationally normed, standardized test was used to assess student progress.

After three years, the main finding of this study was that there was no difference in the pattern of achievement of students who were taught the subjects in the native language and those taught only in English. Students who were limited-English when they started kindergarten achieved similar degrees of academic success in first and second grade, with or without native language instruction.

Two other findings are noteworthy. Students who were in the classes receiving native-language instruction for only one year scored higher on the tests than students who were in native-language classes for two or three years. Teachers (all of whom are bilingual) rated student attitudes toward learning and toward school in general to be comparable for both groups. In other words, the children who were taught in English from the first day of school apparently did not suffer emotional distress or anomie (Rothfarb, Urrutia, and Ariza 1987, *ii*).

A special note is in order here as to the concern for language-minority students' development of a positive self-image and emotional well-being and the belief in some quarters that the best way to promote this is to have teachers of the same ethnic, linguistic, and racial background as the students. I do not believe that matching these elements between teachers and students guarantees a better self-concept or a better educational experience. What these students need even more are the most competent and sensitive teachers, regardless of ethnicity. They need teachers who have high expectations for them, and they need to experience success in their classroom work. Language-minority students have a strong need to feel included in the whole school community and appreciated — *that* will engender self-pride. There is also a great need for the presence of more minority people in skilled jobs, businesses, the professions, and higher levels of management, however; they need not all be steered into teaching. The successful role models need to be in the community as well as in the schools.

I have recently read an advance copy of a new research study on the achievement of Berkeley, California, bilingual students that reports similar results to the Dade County study (Rossell 1988, 33).

The Berkeley school system has had two programs for about fifteen years. One is a transitional bilingual education program for approximately two hundred Spanish-speaking children in grades K–6; The other is called an Individual Learning Program, which provides an intensive English program for four hundred children from twenty language backgrounds.

The researcher traced the achievement of all the limited-English students in grades K–6 for the past three years in English-language and other subjects. Both standardized test scores and scores on the California state tests in the subject areas were analyzed. The report shows that there is no difference in achievement between the two groups and no discernible advantage for teaching subject matter in the native language.

I believe that there is a degree of confusion in Cummins's hypothesis of linguistic interdependence, and that the two strands should be disentangled. On the issue of learning in a second language, it is my firm conviction, based on all my professional experience, that children are capable of learning subject matter very soon in a second language. Of course their understanding will be less than perfect at the beginning, but during the developmental phase they will become increasingly capable of learning through a second-language medium as their daily practice permits more complex language and subject matter to be learned simultaneously. This is a dynamic process consistent with current language-teaching theory.

The other strand of the hypothesis has to do with the development of second-language skills. It may, in fact, take several years for a second-language learner to achieve parity with a native speaker of English or to reach his own highest level of ability in the second language. That need not keep the student from studying subject matter in that language. Nor does it mean that the student who is making good progress in the use of a second language cannot be functioning fairly well in a classroom with native speakers. The goal of native-like proficiency in a second language is most likely attainable by children who begin early (three to five years old) and experience a great deal of contact with the second language both informally and in a well-designed school program.

The longer the use of the second language in daily classroom work is delayed and kept to a minimum, the slower will be the transition to high-level skills in the second language. This conclusion seems so obvious that one should not have to mention it. I observed the outcome of this delayed approach in my five years of teaching fifth- and sixth-grade children in Springfield, Massachusetts. These students, after five to seven years in bilingual classrooms, had not yet learned sufficient English to be mainstreamed. Nor were their reading, math, or writing skills up to grade level in Spanish. It was not that they were semi-lingual but that they were semi-educated. All the social factors that make academic success difficult for language-minority children — that is, poverty, uneducated parents, broken homes, a high degree of mobility — were compounded when they were also required to use two languages in school, year after year. These children, in my observation, need more structure, more time on task, and more enrichment in the target language, not less.

Transitional bilingual education is attempting to do too much and holds out the false promise that it can all be achieved without discomfort, delay, or sacrifice. Within the confines of the normal school schedule of five-and-one-half hours a day, 180 days a year, it is nearly impossible to develop literacy in a home language, literacy in a second language, content learning in first one language and then another, understanding of the history and culture of the native land and the United States, and participate in the various other activities that go on in the average American school. When we consider the fact that many Hispanic students may be limited in their knowledge of Spanish and use a nonstandard dialect, then the native language approach imposes additional remedial responsibilities.

Twenty years' experience tells us that it is time to sort out our priorities: locally, to respond to each community's aspirations, and nationally, to define our goals and how we will work towards the integration of our society on an equitable basis while promoting respect for our various linguistic and cultural components. Public policy decisions will need to be taken at the state and local level to support programs that respond to the expressed desires of the community — whether they include native-language teaching or not. It is not the proper role of U.S. public education to force one type of program on all language groups. That is the current practice in Massachusetts, for example, where the state law does not allow or fund any other option but transitional bilingual education. In the city of Lowell, which has received the greatest influx of Southeast Asian refugees in the past few years of any city in the region, a large number of families have expressly stated that they do not want bilingual programs for their children, to the embarrassment of state education officials who are scurrying to find adult speakers of Khmer, Lao, and Vietnamese to train for teaching positions.

It is time to consider that different communities may want to develop different degrees of bilingualism, and that local aid should support these efforts as much as possible. But these should be secondary goals, after the primary and more urgent business of providing equal access for language-minority children to succeed in the mainstream classroom, to complete a high-school education, and to be able to go on to higher education or to productive work. For the communities that have a strong desire to maintain their native language and to see their children develop dual literacy, there is the possibility of extending the school day or the school year, or of securing local support for voluntary language and culture schools such as those maintained by Chinese, Japanese, and Hebrew-speaking communities. In either case, it will take the initiative and persistence of the community to make these things happen. These programs are desirable but are not the legal responsibility of public education.

Two-way programs are beginning to sprout up around the country, providing a second language experience for English-speaking students. They are a wonderful vehicle for integrating language-minority and language-majority students, providing an enriching experience for all the children enrolled. However, they require the willingness of mainstream American families to enroll their children in an experimental program. And, no matter how successful, these programs can only accommodate a small percentage of the total school population. Again, these efforts are valuable, but they are not the first priority in the education of limited-English children.

It will not be an easy task to achieve a national consensus on what our goals for the long range should be as our linguistic and cultural diversity grows in this period of the greatest influx of immigrants in our history. Nor will it be easy to determine what are the best ways for reaching our agreed-on goals. Some believe that we need a set of common understandings if we are to remain a unified, integrated, cohesive society, while others are more concerned with the retention of their cultural distinctiveness and wish, most of all, not to become assimilated. It is time to consider which educational policies will promote the different goals.

If the primary goal of our society is to maintain the native tongue of language-minority children and to develop literacy in that language, even at a cost to the development of English skills, then the kind of program that provides early and long use of the native language in the classroom is appropriate. This policy would have the long-range goal of encouraging bilingualism on a larger scale. It could have the effect of promoting separate linguistic communities and limiting the access to an equal education and employment opportunities for limited-English children. This is to put the purported wishes of the group ahead of the needs of the individual.

If the primary goal of our society is to help children develop the highest level of English skills, with the possibility that there would be some loss of home-language proficiency, then programs that place greater emphasis on the early and intensive use of English are appropriate. These programs would promote greater integration of language-minority children in the majority society and more rapid access to higher education and employment opportunities.

If there is a genuine impulse to develop a bilingual society and to provide a balanced education in two languages not only for language-minority children but for all interested families, then a K–12 program with instruction in two languages all through the years of schooling is the optimal approach. We would have to determine whether one language (Spanish) should be paramount with English or whether to encourage regional bilingualism in the manner of the Russian republics, that is, Spanish/English in Texas, California, and Florida; Chinese/English in San Francisco; Armenian/English in Watertown, Massachusetts; Vietnamese/English in the gulf ports of Louisiana; and so on.

Not enough has yet been discussed publicly about the hard choices that these policies would entail, not to mention the resources to implement them. Bilingual education advocates suggest that we can have it all—learn English well, succeed in classroom work, even become balanced bilinguals—through the kinds of programs currently in place. This is simply not so, and many professionals in the field who see the outcomes of these programs every day cannot endorse this view. When even as strong an advocate as Carlos Yorio of Lehman College can say at a Massachusetts Conference on Bilingual Education in 1986, "Our detractors are not lying—our children are not learning English well," we know the situation is not good.

Challenging the assumptions on which bilingual education rests is a first step in opening the field to greater efforts at experimentation and innovation. The adherence to an ideology of vernacular advantage is slowly beginning to give way to more pragmatic approaches. School programs are changing in California, Texas, Florida, and Massachusetts, with or without the blessings of the state education bureaucracies. Because the old ways of bilingual education have not worked very well in many places, school districts are more and more opting for practical solutions and quietly rejecting the unsubstantiated theories.

Adapted from *Forked Tongue: The Politics of Bilingual Education*, by Rosalie Pedalino Porter. Copyright 1990 by Basic Books, Inc. Reprinted by permission of Basic Books, Inc., Publishers, New York.

References

Baker, Keith, and Adriana de Kanter. 1981. *Effectiveness of Bilingual Education: A Review of the Literature*. Washington, D.C.: U.S. Department of Education.

Baker, Keith, and Christine Rossell. 1987. "An Implementation Problem: Specifying the Target Group for Bilingual Education." *Educational Policy* 1(2):263.

Hakuta, Kenji. 1986. *Mirror of Language: The Debate on Bilingualism*. New York: Basic Books, Inc.

Mace-Matluck, Betty, ed. 1984. *Teaching Reading to Bilingual Children Study*. Austin, Tex.: Southwest Educational Development Laboratory.

Mathews, Alfredo Jr. 1977. "What Are the Perceived and Particular Problems and Needs of Students Whose Background Is Hispanic in the Desegregation Process?" Paper presented at the National Conference on Desegregation and Education Concerns of the Hispanic Community. Washington, D.C., 26–28 June.

National Advisory and Coordinating Council on Bilingual Education. 1987. *Eleventh Annual Report*. Washington, D.C.: U.S. Department of Education.

Office for Research and Evaluation. 1987. *Interim Report of the Five-Year Bilingual Education Pilot*. El Paso, Tex.: El Paso Independent School District.

Paulston, Christina Bratt. 1982. *Swedish Research and Debate about Bilingualism*. Stockholm: National Swedish Board of Education.

Rossell, Christine H. 1988. "The Effectiveness of Educational Alternatives for Limited English Proficient Children in the Berkeley Unified District." San Francisco, Calif.: A Report to the U.S. District Court in the case of *Teresa P. et al. v. the Berkeley Unified School District*.

Rothfarb, Silvia, C. Urrutia, and M. Ariza. 1987. *Evaluation of the Bilingual Curriculum Project: Final Report of a Three-Year Study*. Miami, Fla.: Dade County Public Schools.

Skutnabb-Kangas, Tove, and Pertti Toukamaa. 1978. "The Education of Migrant Workers and Their Families." *Educational Studies and Documents* no. 27. UNESCO Reports.

3

Social Purposes of Bilingual Education: *U.S. English*, the ELA, and Other Matters

John Edwards

Lying at the conjunction of academic research and writing, personal and group interest and commitment, and social policy, bilingual education often generates more heat than light.

I feel I should begin with a couple of personal observations. The first is that, although I have been labeled an opponent of maintenance bilingual education (Fishman 1981), I hope my position has been a cautionary one in an area that surely warrants such attention. While it is certainly true that I have some real reservations about this form of bilingual education, I regret an inability of many in the area to distinguish between a critical stance and a hostile one (see Edwards 1982). It is of course understandable that bilingual education arouses strong feelings, and is not a topic noted for dispassionate discussion; I have elsewhere drawn attention to treatments heavily laced with value judgments and opinion (Edwards 1980a, 1981). While a completely value-free stance is clearly impossible, there are presumably degrees of subjectivity. I have tried to present my own work as more objective than much of what I have read, but it has of course attracted criticism itself on grounds of bias and value. No doubt I have fallen prey to the view, common among writers, that one's own work gives a balanced account, while that of others is less judicious. Time will ultimately sort all this out.

I also want to put on record here my *personal* conviction that an ethnically diverse society may be more vibrant than a homogeneous one, that different cultures contribute to and enrich society through their varying linguistic perspectives on the world, that bilingualism (or multilingualism) is an asset rather than a disadvantage (and represents a state of affairs more common in the world than monolingualism), and that bilingual education, in at least some of its incarnations, need not be problematical. The fact that I have pointed to difficulties associated with ethnolinguistic pluralism, bilingualism, and bilingual education should not, therefore, be simply equated with an antipathetic stance.

What Is Bilingual Education?

In 1970, Andersson and Boyer defined bilingual education as "instruction in two languages and the use of those two languages as mediums of instruction for any part of or all of the school curriculum" (p. 12). This is very broad, and allows for many variations (see Fishman 1977; Gaarder 1967; Mackey 1970). In the United States, federally funded bilingual education has largely had a transitional tone—that is, the emphasis has been upon helping minority-language children achieve sufficient English proficiency to allow mainstreaming; there is typically, therefore, a large English as a Second Language (ESL) component, although this by itself would not justify the label of bilingual education. Although several hundred projects have catered to scores of language groups, most bilingual education programs have been directed towards Spanish-speaking children.

Although most of the programs funded under Title VII Elementary and Secondary Education Act (ESEA)—and most of the state-initiated ones as well—have had a compensatory flavor, the enabling act (passed in 1968 and subsequently amended) has been interpreted as elastic enough to permit considerable variation. Extracts from the act (cited in Grosjean 1982, 76–77), for example, include the following statements regarding educational directions for children of limited English-speaking ability:

> . . . instruction designed to enable them, while using their native language, to achieve competence in the English language . . .

[T]he term 'program of bilingual education' means . . . instruction given in, and study of, English and, to the extent necessary to allow a child to achieve competence in the English language, the native language . . . with appreciation for the cultural heritage of such children. . . .

[i]n order to prevent the segregation of children . . . a program of bilingual instruction may include the participation of children whose language is English . . . for the principal purpose of contributing to the achievement of that objective [that is, helping children of limited English-speaking ability to improve their English].

While the general tenor here is one of emphasis upon development of English skills — even the participation of English-speaking children is viewed mainly as a contribution to this — there clearly is a fairly flexible provision for the first language; the "extent necessary" could, one might argue, be rather considerable, leading to the possibility of bilingual education of some duration. Thus, while the transitional focus has dominated, reflected in the preponderance of bilingual education programs at the primary-school level only (see Edwards 1981), Grosjean (1982) notes that there remains enough scope for the argument that bilingual programs should help to maintain the language and culture of the minority-group child. Thus the stage is set, as it were, for not only a debate about whether bilingual education should exist at all, but also about the *form* it should take — transitional or maintenance.[1]

Within the academic community and elsewhere, there has been considerable opposition to the transitional philosophy (see Center for Applied Linguistics 1977–78, for a collection of views; see also Spener 1988). This is because many writers on bilingual education are proponents of an enduring cultural pluralism and ethnolinguistic diversity, and see transitional bilingual education as actually expediting the assimilation process (via mainstreaming). On the one hand, there is some satisfaction that bilingual education is mandated at all, but there is also frustration that it is not in a maintenance form, which would allow programs to act as servants to the cause of pluralism. There is, therefore, the hope that bilingual education can be changed in format (see also Edwards 1981).

The larger debate is over bilingual education per se. As I have noted elsewhere (Edwards 1980b), there has been extensive criticism from several quarters, extending back to the very beginnings of federally funded programs. The major arguments here have to do with

1. The scope of popular support for bilingual education
2. The process by which bilingual education was implemented (that is, as a "top-down" phenomenon, legislated into existence, and part of the war on poverty)
3. The degree to which a real change of attitude has occurred concerning the assimilation of minority groups
4. The social fragmentation, separatism, divisiveness, and balkanization of society implied by a thoroughgoing bilingual education (Here, comparison is often made to other countries.)[2]
5. The perceived negative and regressive consequences of promoting ethnicity and nationalism (a view endorsed by orthodox Marxism, though not associated with it alone)
6. The degree to which bilingual education may work against the successful socioeconomic progress of minority groups in mainstream society
7. Concern that what should be privately supported efforts are subsidized by government
8. Concern—in some cases a fear—that a familiar social status quo is being eroded or altered, that the perceived character of society is undergoing an unwelcome transformation

For me, and perhaps for many of us here, the arguments of most interest have to do with the social changes that, it is thought, bilingual education may contribute to. That is, bilingual education is seen as a reflection of a generalized support for diversity, helping to strengthen minority languages in the United States (particularly Spanish) and helping to weaken the position of English. Against this is the support for bilingual education that sees it as a force for an enduring ethnolinguistic diversity that means richness and strength for all without an erosion of English, and as a pillar of ethnic-group identities seen to be at risk of assimilation. This, I suggest, is the main battleground for the moment, and is the area upon which I wish to focus. Before doing this, however, I think it advisable to consider some pedagogical and cognitive matters related to bilingual education and bilingualism.

Cognitive and Developmental Aspects of Bilingualism and Bilingual Education

In the information sent to me by the organizers of this conference, three broad areas of evaluation were suggested as possibly appropriate for programs of bilingual education. The first involves measuring success in terms of pupils' linguistic proficiency and academic progress, the second involves children's sense of well-being and self-esteem, and the third suggests the importance of bilingual education as a promoter of social change, empowerment, and economic progress. We can look at each of these in turn.

Linguistic and Academic Proficiency

Before we ask about academic success in bilingual education, perhaps it would be useful to recall briefly the state of our knowledge about bilingualism and cognition. Baker (1988), Grosjean (1982), and others have noted that studies attempting to relate bilingualism to cognitive growth and intelligence have produced a variety of findings. Generally speaking, early studies found negative consequences of bilingualism, while later ones showed a positive relationship between bilingualism and cognition. There have, as well, been studies reporting no significant effects one way or the other. The study of bilingualism and intelligence by Peal and Lambert (1962) was something of a watershed here. The authors first criticized earlier work for faulty design and poor control of potentially confounding factors (socioeconomic status, to name one important one), then went on to claim that their study demonstrated positive associations between bilingualism and mental flexibility, interlanguage transfer, and intelligence. Such positive results have also been challenged, however (see, for example, MacNab 1979).

Some of the chief difficulties involved in attempting to show a relationship — positive or negative — between bilingualism and cognitive development, mental flexibility, intelligence, and so on involve these questions:

1. How do we adequately define bilingualism itself; do we require perfectly balanced bilinguals for the "best" contrast with mono-

linguals, and how do we measure bilingualism, balanced or otherwise (see Martin-Jones and Romaine 1984, for example)?
2. How do we define intelligence; relatedly, how do we know that IQ tests adequately assess this quantity (see Edwards 1989a)?
3. How do we ensure comparability between groups of bilinguals and monolinguals; controlling for age, sex and some other variables may not be difficult, but what about socioeconomic status? Most measures of this may not come to grips well enough with home differences of vital importance.[3]
4. How do we interpret any relationship found between bilingualism and intelligence, cognition et cetera. Is it a causal one, and, if so, in which direction? Does bilingualism lead to increased IQ, for example, or does a higher IQ increase the likelihood of functional bilingualism? In their own 1962 study, Peal and Lambert raise this matter.

These and other factors mean that strong conclusions about bilingualism and cognition are not warranted. Baker (1988) observes that there *may* be some link between the two, but also feels that any cognitive advantages attaching to bilingualism are rather slight. Paivio and Begg (1981) also express cautious optimism here, being mainly concerned to show that there is not a cognitive *price* for bilingualism. Grosjean (1982) feels that the appropriate view is that bilingualism has no major positive or negative effect on cognitive development; he cites McLaughlin:

> In short, almost no general statements are warranted by research on the effects of bilingualism. It has not been demonstrated that bilingualism has positive or negative consequences for intelligence, linguistic skills, educational attainment, emotional adjustment, or cognitive functioning. In almost every case, the findings of research are either contradicted by other research or can be questioned on methodological grounds. (1978, 206)

Grosjean also makes the apposite suggestion that social factors may be of great importance in accounting for contradictory reports about bilingualism and cognition. He notes that most positive findings come from studies of immersion children (where language attitudes are favorable), most negative ones from those "submersed" in second-language education (leading to so-called subtractive bilingualism).[4]

My own view is that being bilingual (or multilingual, for that matter) is unlikely to mean any significant increase in cognitive and intellectual skills, although it would also seem that bilingualism need not lead to decreased or weakened capacities. It would be perverse, however, to deny that bilingualism can represent another *dimension* of one's capacities, and in that sense be a repertoire expansion. I see nothing controversial about this, just as I would see nothing controversial in the statement that a number of years' devotion to the study of great literature can lead to a heightened, or at least altered, sensitivity to the human condition. I would emphasize, though, that all effects of bilingualism are importantly mediated by the social context.

Context seems to be the important feature in programs of bilingual education as well. Certainly, studies exist showing all sorts of effects. Measurement difficulties abound for all variables involved, and the sorts of controls necessary for fuller predictions are hard to put in place when the education of real children is at issue. This means that it is often difficult to know just what to attribute positive or negative effects to. An example here may be useful. Several writers have described the Rock Point (Arizona) program as a success story for bilingual education (in this case, Navajo-English; see, e.g., Cummins 1981; Donahue 1982; Rotberg 1984). Rotberg notes that when children receiving the bilingual instruction (with English reading introduced in second grade) were compared with children given ESL training (and taught in English), the bilingual-program children were superior in both English reading and mathematics. Attention to the actual reports from the program itself (Rosier and Farella 1976; Rosier and Holm 1980) is instructive, however. In 1963–64, an intensive ESL program was instituted for these Navajo children. This resulted in significant improvement, although the children still lagged behind national standardized-test norms. They were then enrolled in the bilingual program, after which further improvement was recorded. It is impossible to say, however, how much of this can be ascribed to bilingual education per se. It could, for example, be due to continued ESL training in a more supportive and pleasant atmosphere. (What *was* the atmosphere within which the prior ESL instruction occurred? What were the teaching styles? Were the teachers sympathetic to Indian-white cultural differences?)[5]

What I am suggesting here is that it may be quite possible, in bilingual programs reporting success, that that success is due to contextual factors rather than program specifics. In a French-English program I was involved with in Vermont some years ago (Edwards 1973, 1976), the presence of extra teachers, extra materials, and extra *attention* of a sympathetic kind was a formidable aspect of the success achieved.[6]

So far as linguistic proficiency goes, evidence suggests that, in bilingual education programs for minority-group children, "instruction through the *minority* language [that is, their first language] has been effective in promoting proficiency in *both* languages" (Cummins 1981, 139). Some have considered this type of assertion counterintuitive, feeling that any time taken away from ESL or instruction through English must necessarily lead to lessened English proficiency. However—and particularly in light of the contextual matters just noted—I don't think this is counterintuitive at all. Such an outcome presupposes, of course, considerable extra-educational exposure to English, and a clear message that English is a valuable and prestigious asset (Ekstrand 1983, for one, notes difficulties with mother-tongue instruction if such conditions are not met). It may also presuppose that the bilingual education experience lasts sufficiently long for positive effects to occur—that is, there is evidence that the very nature of the program may mean somewhat of a lag (though not a psychologically or educationally worrying one) in acquiring majority-language proficiency (see, for example, Cummins 1983). The outcome also suggests that there may well be a significant cross-language transfer of skills (the "common underlying proficiency" model of Cummins). A further suggestion is that children may succeed here because of higher motivation stimulated by, and associated with, the security deriving from learning in their maternal variety.

There will continue to be argument in some quarters for the old "submersion" approach. Submersion clearly works for minority-group children, but the psychological cost may be high and, more to the point, unnecessary. That is, some form of bilingual education may ease the passage of these children; presumably we do not wish to impose unwarranted hardship. Podhoretz (1985) notes his gratitude for being humiliated at school over his lack of English, since it proved a spur towards social mobility and success. But would it not be preferable to learn English without humiliation? Nunberg (1986) observes that learning English through submersion is neither an intrinsically ennobling experience nor a particularly efficient one.

Such success as has been reported for bilingual education in terms of academic and linguistic proficiency depends to a very large extent, I believe, on matters having very little to do with either bilingualism or education per se. Given the importance of context, of definitional problems, and of measurement, it is not surprising that negative or at least inconclusive effects have also been reported. Much-noted studies here include the surveys of Danoff et al. (1978), Baker and deKanter (1981, 1983), and Willig (1985; a good critique of bilingual education design and research). Paulston (cited in Rotberg 1984, 137) notes that research in bilingual education is characterized by "disparate findings and inconclusive results . . . a study can be found to support virtually every possible opinion."

Children's Well-Being and Self-Esteem

What I have already said would indicate that success in bilingual education may well be due to contextual features. These may well operate by increasing the participants' sense of well-being and self-worth. Similar arguments have been raised in connection with school programs and textbooks reflecting various nonstandard English varieties (see Edwards 1989a). The very fact of seeing one's maternal variety valued and legitimated in such an important setting as the school may have powerful positive consequences. An important point to ponder here: is bilingual education the only, or the best, way of providing positive atmospheres for minority-group children, or could the positive effects sometimes attributed to bilingual education be achieved in other ways?

The Empowerment of Minority-Group Children

Cummins has suggested that recent American educational interventions — including compensatory education and bilingual programs — have not succeeded in stemming the school failure of minority-group children. Their group language and values remain subordinate in the prevailing and continuing pattern of social power relationships and, consequently, they remain disabled; "the relationships between teachers and students and between schools and communities have remained essentially unchanged" (1986, 18), despite legislative and policy initiatives.

Similar sentiments have been expressed by Spener (1988). One also recalls Ogbu's (1978, 1982) observations about the "caste-like" status attaching to membership of some minority groups, a status that cannot be changed through school success. Criticism of existing school programs comes from McDermott and Gospodinoff (1981) with their observation that schools function to maintain ethnic boundaries (see also Edwards 1989b).

Cummins (1986) notes that schools empower or disable minority-group children to the extent to which they incorporate children's language and culture in the school program, encourage community participation in schooling, promote intrinsic motivation of language use and knowledge generation, and avoid locating "problems" in the children (rather than in the context). Sensitivity to these issues (and others; see Spener 1988) is undoubtedly part of good educational strategy, and I have touched on them elsewhere (Edwards 1985, 1989a). There are some potential difficulties here, however. First, it is possible to argue that too much adaptation of school to minority group may deprive the latter of needed social skills and knowledge. Spener, for example, has critical comments on the idea of a core curriculum and on the promotion of standard English — yet we know that minority-group parents are usually most concerned that their children gain access to things valued by the mainstream (Edwards 1985). Second, Spener concurs with Skutnabb-Kangas's idea of education intentionally reproducing an underclass to fill menial jobs and to act as an economic buffer (see Skutnabb-Kangas 1984). While I have reservations about the degree of conscious planning here, there certainly does exist the possibility, particularly for castelike minority groups, that school will not prove an avenue of empowerment.[7]

Spener's hope here is for maintenance bilingual education, but this, and other educational interventions, may not really empower children. This brings me to the third point, a general and important one. Schools by themselves have very little power if they are attempting to counter or to soften extra-educational currents. If minority-group members are relatively powerless, it is because of social attitudes and pressures — influences that make it very difficult for real empowerment to develop through education alone, even if that education is sensitive to the matters noted above. Traditionally and currently, too much reliance is placed upon the shoulders of the school as an active agent of social change.

Social Aspects of Bilingual Education

As I have emphasized elsewhere (Edwards 1981, 1982, 1984a), and as the preceding discussion indicates, the sociopolitical context is the major feature in understanding the results of bilingual education. It is also the arena within which the most vitriolic wrangling occurs. This is because, in addition to (or in spite of) the cognitive and pedagogical matters already noted, the more widespread concern is over larger issues having to do with social mobility, pluralism, ethnolinguistic diversity, assimilation — in short, with the face of society itself. Indeed, these issues are themselves intimately connected to cognitive and pedagogical ones, to the successes and failures of educational interventions. While I believe that cognitive matters should be discussed *alongside* social ones — and I will conclude this paper by attempting to bring them together — the two dimensions are often not jointly considered.

Certainly, the large social issues are extremely important. We find linguists themselves acknowledging that bilingual education is not primarily a linguistic matter. Thus, Ferguson observes that "social, political, psychological, economic and other factors must surely outweigh the purely linguistic factors in any analysis of bilingual education efforts and in any actual policy planning for bilingual education" (1977, 43). Paulston states that "I don't think the important questions about bilingual education come from a linguistic perspective" (1977, 88).

Socially based criticisms of bilingual education (see, for example, Edwards 1980b, 1985) have included, unsurprisingly, a large number of political and journalistic statements, and we might begin here by looking at some recent examples. Bickley (1980), Kirp (1983), and others have suggested that recent federal policy in the United States is essentially anti-bilingual education and pro-ESL, that bilingual education is thus on the way out, and that the force of new initiatives is for mainstreaming (see also Gray 1982a, 1982b, 1982c). In 1981, President Reagan stated that

> [I]t's absolutely wrong and against the American concept to have a bilingual program that is now openly, admittedly dedicated to preserving their native language and never getting them adequate in English so they can go out into the job market and participate. (Landry 1986, 136; Spener 1988, 150)[8]

In support of an English Language Amendment (ELA; see below) to the Constitution:

1. Senator Hayakawa said: "[A] common language can unify; separate languages can fracture and fragment a society." He also noted that learning English is the major task of each immigrant and the way to participate in the democracy (Marshall 1986a, 23).
2. Congressman Shumway observed: "[L]inguistic minority groups . . . must learn English if they are to become fully integrated into American society . . . we must not promote the segregation of the nation's immigrants by legislating bilingual programs." He also endorsed a view that bilingual education retards English acquisition (Marshall 1986a, 26).
3. Senator Huddleston noted: "[F]or the past 15 years, we have experienced a growing resistance to the acceptance of our historic language, an antagonistic questioning of the melting pot philosophy . . . thousands of immigrant and non-immigrant children are languishing in near-permanent bilingual/bicultural programs . . . [their parents are] given false hopes that their cultural traditions can be fully maintained in this country" (Marshall 1986a, 31). Senator Huddleston also quoted a view that Hispanic Americans are now demanding that the United States become a bilingual nation (see also Hayakawa 1987a).

Other related sentiments include those of

1. Secretary of Education Bennett, who noted that education in the United States has "lost sight of the goal of learning English

as the key to equal educational opportunity" (Combs and Lynch 1988, 38).

2. Senator Hayakawa: "[C]an we not unite on English as our national language by law as well as by custom so that our nation shall not be torn asunder in the decades and centuries to come" (U.S. English n.d.).

3. William A. Henry III. "[A] new bilingualism and biculturalism is being promulgated that would deliberately fragment the nation into separate, unassimilated groups . . . the new metaphor is not the melting pot but the salad bowl, with each element distinct. The biculturalists seek to use public services, particularly schools, not to Americanize the young but to heighten their consciousness of belonging to another heritage" (U.S. English n.d.).

Associated closely with such views, and with the ELA (first proposed by Senator Hayakawa in 1981), is the organization "U.S. English", established by Hayakawa in 1983 to support the amendment. (Actually, five amendments have been proposed, with two versions currently before Congress [Marshall 1986a; Combs and Lynch 1988]. Although there are variations in these, all have a first section stating that "the English language shall be the official language of the United States.") The idea of official English certainly has widespread appeal — as of mid-1988, fourteen states had established English as official, with legislation pending or initiatives made in as many as thirty others (Combs and Lynch 1988; U.S. English 1988).

If we look at the views held by both proponents and opponents of English-as-official-language, we will see in a nutshell the main social elements in the most recent debate over bilingual education and associated issues in America. In what follows, I gather together information from a number of sources so as to present the major arguments in summary form; after this, I will provide some comments.[9]

Arguments Made by Supporters of Official English

1. English, as a common language, is necessary for unity, political stability, and full participation in American society (U.S. English 1985a). It is a world medium of communication and,

in having English, the United States is spared the linguistic problems plaguing other countries (U.S. English n.d.). Sociolinguists call single-language countries impoverished, and multilingual ones enriched. In part, this reflects the amount of material multilingual countries provide for academic "amusement," but, more importantly, it shows a utopian ideal of a harmonious multilingual society (Imhoff 1987).

2. The ELA would not prohibit private-context use of other languages, language teaching, educational language requirements, or "foreign" languages for public convenience or safety (U.S. English 1985a).

3. Bilingual ballots should be opposed for economic and symbolic reasons (U.S. English 1985b). It is racist to suggest that these ballots are needed only for some language groups (Spanish Americans, American Indians, and Asian Americans) who must be perceived as not intelligent enough to learn English (Hayakawa 1987a).

4. The ELA would not prohibit short-term transitional bilingual education (U.S. English 1985a). However, bilingual education leads to a "prolonged state of identity confusion" and detracts from the rapid mastery of English (U.S. English 1984). School should help children of limited-English-speaking ability, but bilingual education has resegregated schools (Bikales 1983) and can isolate children for years (Bikales and Imhoff 1985). Bilingual education has become a "self-interested discipline" (Imhoff 1987).

5. Groups are now rejecting the melting-pot ideal, and see assimilation as a betrayal; they want funding to maintain diversity (U.S. English n.d.). Prominent here are those ethnic chauvinists claiming to speak for Hispanic Americans, who want to replace the melting pot with a "salad bowl" (Bikales and Imhoff 1985; Hayakawa 1987a).

6. Canada is an example of a country divided by language. In a letter to Canadian members of U.S. English, Hayakawa (1987b) notes that "no one knows better than a Canadian the pitfalls of a bilingual government and society."

7. The original framers of the Constitution were not supporters of a multilingual America, even though they did not enshrine English as official—perhaps because they wanted to encourage immigration, perhaps because they saw English dominance as self-evident (Bikales 1986; see also Imhoff 1987; Reed 1987).

8. Historically, American legislation has not blocked the societal participation of non-English speakers (Bikales 1986).
9. Making English official is a benign policy, which will not create social chaos (Bikales 1986; Imhoff 1987).
10. Most Americans support the melting-pot ideal, cultural pluralism is an unstable quantity, and there is a fine line between cultural enrichment and social chaos (Bikales and Imhoff 1985).

Arguments Made by Opponents of Official English

1. The ELA is unnecessary because English is not in danger in the United States, nor will the country become a generally bilingual one (Baetens Beardsmore and Willemyns 1986; Combs and Lynch 1988; Veltman, 1986).
2. The ELA and U.S. English really reflect an "English Only" sentiment. Support should be given to the concept of "English Plus" and a "Cultural Rights Amendment" to protect language and cultural diversity (Combs and Lynch 1988; Landry 1986).
3. The ELA tells ethnic-minority Americans that it is not good to be actively bilingual (Combs and Lynch 1988). It is thus potentially disruptive (Baetens Beardsmore and Willemyns 1986), liable to cause resentment (Marshall 1986a), and a "slap in the face" (Marshall 1986b).
4. The ELA puts bilingual education in jeopardy (Combs and Lynch 1988; Fishman 1988; Marshall, 1986b), despite the cognitive advantages it bestows (Marshall 1986b) and the fact that it is actually in the service of assimilation (Görlach 1986; Marshall 1986a; Veltman 1986). Additional points made concerning bilingual education: it was instituted because bilingualism was seen as a disadvantage (Clyne 1986), it means money and jobs (Veltman 1986), and children in bilingual education programs actually get *more* English instruction and training (Alatis 1986).
5. The ELA is primarily an anti-Spanish proposal, despite the fact that Spanish Americans *are* keen to learn English, and *are* shifting to it (Combs and Lynch 1988; Fishman 1988; Marshall 1986b). Related points: Clyne (1986) asks if language shift can be slowed, Landry (1986) feels that shift is not inevitable, and Veltman (1986) observes that spokesmen for the community often do not want to know or to recognize that rapid language shift is occurring.

6. The ELA really springs from insecurity, xenophobia, and intolerance (Donahue 1985; Fishman, 1988; Veltman 1986). The specific language issue masks a more general apprehension (Baetens Beardsmore and Willemyns 1986).
7. The framers of the Constitution were linguistically tolerant (Donahue 1985; Marshall 1986a; Milán 1986).
8. Pluralism and enrichment bilingual education are desirable per se; "the *unum* grows out of *pluribus* but does not replace it" (Fishman 1988, 138).
9. A laissez-faire approach here is more appropriate than compulsion (Baetens Beardsmore and Willemyns 1986; Clyne 1986; Marshall 1986a).
10. Canada is *not* an appropriate comparison-case (Maldoff 1986).

Summary Comments on Main Arguments

English *is* necessary for full participation in American life, and no one recognizes this more than minority groups themselves. "It is a reasonable assumption that most immigrants hope to find in their new country a way of life in which the rewards will repay the material and psychological costs of making the move" (Edwards 1981, 37) — and this will usually involve communicative language shift (see also Baetens Beardsmore and Willemyns 1986; Sibayan 1986; Veltman 1986). The general pattern here is one in which bilingualism is an unstable, bridging phenomenon, occurring as a way station on the road to English monolingualism by the third generation or so. Exceptions here include groups — usually religiously based — who engage in voluntary self-segregation, and those who, because of their concentrations and closeness to a homeland, may show a slightly less rapid rate of shift. The United States is not going to become a bilingual country, and the dominance of English rests firmly upon socioeconomic pillars unlikely to tumble. The direct answer, then, to proponents of the ELA is that it is simply unnecessary.

We might, therefore, consider the whole matter a nonissue. But, psychologists and others know very well that *perceptions* are the basis for actions, and there is no doubt that perceptions of U.S. English and the ELA lead to alarm in many quarters. Despite the disclaimers, a nativist sentiment is being projected, which has aroused anxieties among minority groups. It may well be that those most exercised here are group spokesmen (see below) who can sometimes be atypical of those for whom they presume to speak — but it really doesn't matter. To the extent to which anyone is negatively affected by an unnecessary course of action, then the latter should be discontinued. In this sense, the ELA is not a "benign" matter.

Does the United States have anything particular to fear from Spanish speakers? Again, and based upon patterns of language shift, the simple answer is no. Yet perceptions figure importantly once more, in this case perceptions of concentrations of Hispanic Americans, illegal immigration, and the "salad bowl" concept (see Combs and Lynch 1988). This clearly worries supporters of U.S. English. Bikales and Imhoff (1985), for example, cite data showing limited commitment by Mexican-American children to the "American political community," and indicating that Hispanic Americans think of themselves as Hispanic first, American second. To my mind, this suggests that the more subtle agenda behind the ELA is to maintain a social status quo, and reflects apprehension, insecurity, and — among some, perhaps — intolerance. Hispanic Americans, then, are symbols of unwanted change. External symbols, particularly the French speakers of Canada, are also employed here to bolster the view that linguistic diversity means conflict, even though the dynamics of the Canadian scene are quite dissimilar to those of America, and the French-English question there is quite unlike the Spanish-English question in the United States.

On the issue of bilingual ballots we again see symbolism at work. U.S. English (1985b) maintains that English-only ballots do not prevent anyone from voting, since interpreters can be brought into the voting booth — but this is surely using a hammer to kill a gnat and, besides, it might disturb the confidentiality supposed to characterize the voting process. Why not simply provide ballots in any language required, where at all possible, if it will ease things for bona fide voters? That bilingual ballots should cost six dollars, as opposed to two dollars for English ballots (U.S. English 1985b), seems incredible if true, and surely cannot be using economies of scale.[10]

Turning to bilingual education itself, it does seem as if, at first glance, opponents have overstated their case by saying that the

ELA puts it at risk; U.S. English states quite clearly that transitional bilingual education need not be affected, and the amendment itself makes provision for education in this format — although the intent here would seem to be for a too-short intervention. Indeed, both proponents and opponents of the ELA recognize that transitional bilingual education need not necessarily work against assimilation, and may perhaps even expedite it. The argument then made by U.S. English *against* bilingual education on the grounds of "identity confusion" and "resegregation" thus seems perverse, as well as unsubstantiated. If they are switching here to an attack on *maintenance* education, they should still be comforted by the thought that even that disputed format need not retard assimilation or English proficiency (Epstein 1977).[11] These U.S. English arguments against bilingual education, however, do give legitimate fears to supporters of the program, fears that a ripple effect may eventually engulf them (Fishman 1988). Indeed, it doesn't seem unreasonable to assume that proponents of U.S. English, who currently give at least a grudging nod in the direction of transitional bilingual education, would prefer a return to submersion or to ESL-only interventions.

Supporters of U.S. English have claimed that ethnic-minority groups are now rejecting the melting pot and asking for federal money to maintain an enduring ethnolinguistic diversity, even though most Americans favor assimilation (indeed, evidence suggests that most ethnic-group members themselves are largely assimilationist; see Edwards 1981). This is a thorny issue with at least two major aspects: how widespread is the call for enduring pluralism, and what should the government response be?

First, there is some reason to believe that the spokesmen for minority groups may be somewhat atypical of more ordinary group members (see Edwards 1981, 1984b) — a position held by such writers as Myrdal (see Mann 1979), Weinreich (1974), Higham (1975), Greeley (1978), and, more recently, by Veltman (1986). Incidentally, this need not mean at all that spokesmen are insincere, nor that they view themselves as anything other than valid leaders. The general sentiment in America, however, indicates an overall willingness to assimilate, in particular to acquiesce in communicative language shift. Thus, Veltman observes that most immigrant groups offer only "minimal resistance to the penetration of the English language into the household" (1986, 179). Relatedly, Heath (1981) notes that most Americans have not viewed current bilingual education as anything other than an aberration in educational and linguistic history.

Second, the appropriate government response to calls for active promotion of diversity, especially through educational intervention like maintenance bilingual education, is caution. In fact, I believe that the laissez-faire approach specifically advocated by opponents of the ELA can be usefully extended to many language and social matters. Mann (1979) has noted, for example, that matters of ethnicity are best left to those directly concerned, that the appropriate legislative response is none at all.

> Many see lack of government legislation as ignorance or discrimination. They fail to understand that, as Mann implies, lack of response (in legislative terms) is itself a government action. My contention is that a refusal to legislate on matters of ethnicity is a reasonable response . . . this presupposes, of course, a real tolerance (*this* may well be backed up in law) for groups to define themselves as they see fit. (Edwards 1984b, 299)

If it is thought that this approach fails to protect minorities at risk of assimilation in the United States, my response would be simply that such risk — where it exists due to social pressures — cannot be removed through legislation, unless that legislation were to be so draconian as to be counterproductive.

It might be appropriate here to say something about the history of language legislation in the United States. As noted above, opponents and proponents of official English differ over whether or not the framers of the U.S. Constitution were supporters of a multilingual society. We know that Franklin and others expressed anti-German sentiment (see Heath 1981), but we also know that the Constitution did not enshrine English. Why? It is important to recall that the English tradition was not, and has not been, one of language legislation. Heath and Mandabach (1983) speak of the United States inheriting the English reluctance to politically regulate language, and it is instructive to note that, perhaps alone among the great powers, neither England nor America produced a language academy (Edwards 1985).[12] This tolerance, and the allowance for social forces to settle language questions, was no doubt sustained by the thought that England dominance was obvious and unendangered. The antagonism to German demonstrates, perhaps, that if this assumption had not been generally met, legislation supporting English might well have occurred.[13]

The story of legislation restricting languages other than English is best described by Kloss (1977), but Heath (1981) and Heath and Mandabach (1983) make it clear that there has been a general tolerance for "foreign" languages, and that these and English have been more subject to socioeconomic pressures than to legal ones. The repressive language legislation early this century (often connected with war emotion) was relatively quickly dismissed as unconstitutional (Fishman 1988).[14]

Is the idea of a harmonious multilingual society a utopian one, a dream of "sociolinguists" and others, as Imhoff (1987) has claimed? Is cultural pluralism an inherently unstable quantity? In one sense the answer is no — multilingual and multicultural societies obviously exist. However, they often do suffer tensions. Pluralism also often tends to reduce itself over time, and it may involve an unwelcome Balkanization that keeps people enclosed within boundaries. I reproduce without further comment a quotation from Fishman:

> Stable bilingualism and biculturism cannot be maintained on the basis of open and unlimited interaction between minorities and majorities. Open economic access and unrestricted intergroup interaction may be fine for various practical and philosophical purposes. Indeed, they strike most of us as highly desirable legal and social principles; but they are destructive of minority ethnolinguistic continuity. (1980, 171)

We should also be aware that much special pleading is done for particular groups, under the guise of a general cultural pluralism (see Gleason 1979) that groups often "cloak their vested interests in appropriate ideological terms" (Veltman 1986, 180); and that bilingual education can, in some cases at least, be supported for self-interested reasons.[15]

Conclusions

The preceding comments have, I hope, made my position reasonably clear; it now remains for me to summarize the main matters.

The evidence shows that bilingual education can be pedagogically useful and, in its transitional format, has a common-sense appeal. Indeed, there are grounds for believing that transitional bilingual education should exist beyond a two- or three-year time span; there are very real issues concerning the most suitable point at which mainstreaming should occur (Edwards 1984b). All of this presupposes an environment in which the second language (English, in this case) is visible and valued. In these circumstances, transitional bilingual education seems appropriate, and we ought not to return to earlier submersion methods if they can be avoided. (One can imagine circumstances, of course, where they cannot — because of insufficient concentrations of non-English speakers, because of financial and other constraints.) In the transitional format, bilingual education can and should be endorsed by all who wish both to recognize minority-group children's language and to psychologically ease their way into English — bearing in mind, of course, the difficulties noted above attaching to definitional and evaluational matters in *all* forms of bilingual education, and in thus determining just what the active agents are in bilingual programs.

Of course, proponents of societal diversity and pluralism will object that such education actually expedites assimilation, and should be replaced with maintenance programs. Their major arguments are that maintenance bilingual education is necessary for the maximization of English proficiency (see Fishman 1988), and that it is required to halt assimilation and to act as a support for enduring diversity. There is, in fact, no compelling evidence for the necessity, on English-proficiency grounds, of maintenance education; rather, the evidence indicates that, in an environment where English dominates, mainstreaming may not itself be *necessary* for full English development (Edwards 1981). There are, however, other reasons why mainstreaming — which if done appropriately need not be psychologically or linguistically damaging — may be recommended. For example, maintenance programs may simply prove too costly to implement on a scale needed to satisfy all potential beneficiaries. Mainstreaming may be needed for the adequate provision of needed core curriculum features, to assist in social cohesion, advancement, and access.

This brings me to the second argument for maintenance education — as a support for ethnolinguistic pluralism and a force against assimilation. There are a number of things to be said in this connection. First, in a society like the United States, there is no evidence to suggest that many aspects of ethnicity (including language) can be significantly maintained through formal intervention unless the group concerned is a voluntarily self-segregating one. (If a group has segregation forced upon it — a morally indefensible situation — then intervention can be taken for granted.)[16] Language shift is essentially inevitable for most minority groups. It might be argued that intervention could slow the rate of language shift, but one could ask what long-term purposes this would serve.

Second, the intervention of maintenance bilingual education presumes an altogether too powerful role for the school. It is being asked to intervene often more or less in isolation from, or even in opposition to, strong social currents. When social pressures and historical developments have created a situation in which a community is seen to be at risk of language shift, we cannot expect schools to halt this.

Third, in line with what has already been mentioned, maintenance bilingual education can be seen as an inappropriate government involvement reflecting the idea that diversity is not only to be approved of in a tolerant fashion, but also to be promoted to the level of official policy. My view is that government should intervene as little as possible in matters of ethnic identity. Therefore, just as I see no value in legislation like the ELA, which might lead to resentment in some quarters, neither do I support legislation like the Cultural Rights Amendment.

Fourth, and relatedly, implementation of a program like maintenance bilingual education would presumably have the best chance of long-term success if it were able to build upon a general public sentiment in favor of diversity and pluralism, and of government support for ethnic-group interests. Veltman (1986) has argued that the general public is just as intolerant now as in the past, but that it is now aware of the negative connotations of appearing so, and consequently is likely to give socially desirable responses in interviews and questionnaires. Social desirability certainly does influence the results of attitude measurement of all kinds (see Crowne and Marlowe 1964), and a study by Sigall and Page (1971) has indicated that, when subjects were led to believe that their attitudes could be accurately measured by an electronic device (hence, there would be no use in attempting to cover up true feelings via socially desirable responses), their oral responses (in this case, concerning blacks) showed the old, familiar patterns of intolerance and prejudice.

It may be, however, that there is more tolerance nowadays for diversity. Allowing for the possible operation of social desirability, Canadian surveys like those of O'Bryan, Reitz, and Kuplowska (1976) and Berry, Kalin, and Taylor (1977) do reveal an awareness that "unofficial" languages and multiculturalism can be social strengths. However, this should be interpreted more as *passive* tolerance than as *active* commitment. Thus, Berry, Kalin, and Taylor (1977, 143) report that when "money and effort are at stake . . . respondents switch to neutrality and even rejection of multiculturalism." Similarly, Breton, Reitz, and Valentine observe that "the majority of Canadians tend to support multiculturalism as an ideal, so long as it does not affect their own lives, the sociocultural institutions in which they participate, or their pocketbook" (1980, 384). (See also Edwards and Chisholm 1987; Edwards and Doucette 1987.) I suggest that this passive tolerance for diversity — which clearly should not be equated to a more active quantity — also characterizes the American scene. It should also be noted that such levels of tolerance as currently exist cannot necessarily always be relied upon (Edwards 1984b).

Finally, it is worth asking what the result would be if maintenance bilingual education *were* widely implemented, for minority and majority groups alike. It is common to hear the argument made that this would capitalize on the linguistic richness in society, maintaining languages that otherwise would decline, and ensuring a full supply of language-competent individuals of great usefulness to the country. However, given the points already made, and particularly the overpowering dominance of English, it is doubtful if this approach is likely to produce these desirable effects. One of the best school language programs is Canadian immersion education, but even here the French produced by the English-speaking majority-group participants has been described as "somewhat artificial" (Mackey 1981), "Frenglish" (Hammerly 1987) and "fossilized interlanguage" (Lister 1987). Veltman has also observed that immersion graduates do not possess sufficient French to "look for a job, to pursue their education, to go to the movies or the theater. In short, these programs do not produce functional bilinguals" (1986, 180–81). More central here are Genesee's findings (1981) that the carryover between acquired competence in French (such as it is) and actual *use* is not great. Given that this applies even in a city like Montreal, where ample opportunities exist for intergroup communication, what is the implication for the production of active bilinguals in, say, Iowa? Continued use of language skills is presumably a large part of what the whole exercise is supposed to be about.

***

If I have parted company here with at least some of the opponents of the move to make English official in the United States, it has clearly not been in order to throw in with the other side. I think the matters under discussion here are too complex not to involve a considerable grey area between simple points of opposition. The middle ground is, as ever, a rewarding one to study.

Notes

1. Otheguy and Otto (1980) have indicated a distinction within maintenance bilingual education — is it to be a *static* program, where initial first-language competence is preserved, or a *developmental* one, where the goal includes growth in both first and second languages?
2. Gleason (1984) notes that *divisiveness* refers to forms of social differentiation one disapproves of; *pluralism* indicates differences one finds acceptable or good!
3. Baker (1988, 19) provides an apposite example here:

   Two children of the same sex and age living in the same village may have fathers who work side by side as underground miners. One family regularly attends Welsh chapel, eisteddfodau, and competes in penillion singing and poetry competitions at local and national eisteddfodau. The miner and his wife send their bilingual child to a designated bilingual secondary school. The culture of the second family concerns bingo, the Club, discos and pigeon racing. Their monolingual child attends a non-Welsh speaking school. For the quantitative researcher, the children are matched on socio-economic class. In reality the differences are great.

4. He also refers to Cummins's "threshold hypothesis" (see Cummins 1981, 1984).

5. Alatis (1986) has commented about children in bilingual education actually getting *more* English instruction than their counterparts in "regular" education. Also, Veltman (1986) points to Navajo as the one example where language transmission to the young is occurring (although, in 1983, he noted that new generations *are* increasingly anglicized).

6. The success or failure of bilingual programs may not always be accurately reflected in official reports. I well remember attending the 1973 Teachers of English to Speakers of Other Languages (TESOL) conference in Puerto Rico, where I met many directors of American projects. Their informal comments in the bar revealed difficulties with bilingual programs never documented in written accounts.

7. While radical criticism blames underachievement on the capitalist system's desire to reproduce an underclass, it may be incorrect in assuming an altogether too neat transmission of intent from power centers, through schools and teachers, to children. For really monolithic systems, we should look outside the capitalist world. Spener also implies the possibility of transitional bilingual education producing "semi-lingualism," and mentions Cummins's notions of basic interpersonal communicative skills (BICS) and cognitive academic learning proficiency (CALP). Discussion and criticism of these interesting matters, which I do not have time to deal with here, may be found in Ben-Zeev (1984), Cummins and Swain (1983), Edelsky et al. (1983), and Martin-Jones and Romaine (1984).

8. This is the same Reagan who Fishman (1981) cites as responding to or being part of a "truly popular basis" of bilingual education. Generally, Reagan's remarks (and those of other, like-minded contemporary figures) are not unlike remarks made much earlier. Teddy Roosevelt, for example, was a great believer in the American crucible, and Zangwill dedicated his play, *The Melting-Pot*, to him. In 1915, Roosevelt said that "there is no room in this country for hyphenated Americanism . . . [the foreign-born] must talk the language of its native-born fellow-citizens" (cited in Reitz 1980). He also observed, in a famous passage, that "we have room for but one language here, and that is the English language, for we intend to see that the crucible turns our people out as Americans, of American nationality, and not as dwellers in a polyglot boarding house" (cited in Bikales 1985).

9. For further details on the summary comments, see Edwards (1981, 1984a, 1984b, 1985).

10. In fact, even two dollars for a simple ballot seems exorbitant, unless I misunderstand something about the American voting process.

11. This note of Epstein's, occurring on page 4 of his monograph, is misreferenced by Marshall (1986a) as being on page 48.

12. They each had a famous dictionary maker, however (Johnson for England, Webster for the United States), who acted more or less as a one-man academy.

13. It seems somewhat naive for Donahue (1985) to claim that early American language tolerance can be equated to the tolerance implied in the Bilingual Education Act of 1968.
14. Glazer (cited in Grosjean, 1982) notes that languages that had flourished elsewhere, under adversity, succumbed to shift in the American "air of freedom."
15. Other interesting matters, for which I have no space here, include a consideration of whether language shift can be *slowed* through education (Clyne 1986), and whether bilingual education was instituted because bilingualism was seen as a disadvantage. Marshall (1986a) also provides some examples of questions apparently asked by U.S. English in a survey, questions that are poorly worded and, in fact, loaded; a general discussion of survey instruments might prove useful.
16. Some aspects of ethnicity, particularly symbolic and private ones, may remain for a long time, but they are not, by their nature, susceptible to formal sustaining efforts (see Edwards 1981, 1985).

References

Alatis, J. 1986. "Comment: The Question of Language Policy." *International Journal of the Sociology of Language* 60:197–200.

Andersson, T., and M. Boyer. 1970. *Bilingual Schooling in the United States*. Washington, D.C.: U.S. Government Printing Office.

Baetens Beardsmore, H., and R. Willemyns. 1986. "Comment." *International Journal of the Sociology of Language* 60:117–28.

Baker, C. 1988. *Key Issues in Bilingualism and Bilingual Education*. Clevedon, Avon: Multilingual Matters.

Baker, K., and A. de Kanter. 1981. *Effectiveness of Bilingual Education*. Washington, D.C.: U.S. Department of Education.

———. 1983. *Bilingual Education*. Lexington, Mass.: Lexington Books.

Ben-Zeev, S. 1984. "Bilingualism and Cognitive Development." In *Bilingualism and Language Disability*, edited by N. Miller, 55–80. London: Croom Helm.

Berry, J., R. Kalin, and D. Taylor 1977. *Multiculturalism and Ethnic Attitudes in Canada*. Ottawa: Supply and Services Canada.

Bickley, V. 1980. "English as a Language of Mediation." *English around the World* 23:1–5.

Bikales, G. 1983. "'Temporary' Bilingual Education Lives On." *Washington Times*, 18 Aug.

———. 1985. "Make English Official by Passing New Laws." *USA Today*, 10 Apr.

———. 1986. "Comment." *International Journal of the Sociology of Language* 60:77–85.

Bikales, G., and G. Imhoff. 1985. *A Kind of Discordant Harmony: Issues in Assimilation*. Washington, D.C.: U.S. English.

Breton, R., J. Reitz, and V. Valentine. 1980. *Cultural Boundaries and the Cohesion of Canada*. Montreal: The Institute for Research on Public Policy.

Center for Applied Linguistics, ed. 1977–78. *Bilingual Education: Current Perspectives*. 5 vol. Arlington, Virginia: C.A.L.

Clyne, M. 1986. "Comment from 'Down Under.'" *International Journal of the Sociology of Language* 60:139–43.

Combs, M., and L. Lynch. 1988. "English Plus." *English Today* 16:36–42.

Crowne, D., and D. Marlowe. 1964. *The Approval Motive*. New York: Wiley.

Cummins, J. 1981. "Biliteracy, Language Proficiency and Educational Programs." In *The Social Psychology of Reading*, edited by J. Edwards, 131–46. Silver Spring, Md.: Institute of Modern Languages.

_____. 1983. "Language Proficiency, Biliteracy and French Immersion." *Canadian Journal of Education* 8:117–38.

_____. 1984. *Bilingualism and Special Education: Issues in Assessment and Pedagogy*. Clevedon, Avon: Multilingual Matters.

_____. 1986. "Empowering Minority Students: A Framework for Intervention." *Harvard Educational Review* 56:18–36.

Cummins, J., and M. Swain. 1983. "Analysis-by-Rhetoric: Reading the Text or the Reader's Own Projections? A Reply to Edelsky et al." *Applied Linguistics* 4:23–41.

Danoff, M., G. Coles, D. McLaughlin, and D. Reynolds. 1978. *Evaluation of the Impact of ESEA Title VII Spanish/English Bilingual Education Programs*. Palo Alto, Calif.: American Institutes for Research.

Donahue, T. 1982. "Toward a Broadened Context for Modern Bilingual Education." *Journal of Multilingual and Multicultural Matters* 3:77–87.

_____. 1985. "'U.S. English': Its Life and Works." *International Journal of the Sociology of Language* 56:99–112.

Edelsky, C., S. Hudelson, B. Flores, F. Barkin, B. Altwerger, and K. Jilbert. (1983). "Semilingualism and Language Deficit." *Applied Linguistics* 4:1–22.

Edwards, J. 1973. *Growing up a Franco-American: The Social and Academic Effects of Bilingual Education in Northern Vermont*. Unpublished Ph.D. Thesis, McGill University.

_____. 1976. "Current Issues in Bilingual Education." *Ethnicity* 3:70–81.

_____. 1980a. "Bilingual Education: Facts and Values." *Canadian Modern Language Review* 37:123–27.

_____. 1980b. "Critics and Criticisms of Bilingual Education." *Modern Language Journal* 64:409–15.

_____. 1981. "The Context of Bilingual Education." *Journal of Multilingual and Multicultural Development* 2:25–44.

———. 1982. "Bilingual Education Revisited: A Reply to Donahue." *Journal of Multilingual and Multicultural Development* 3:89–101.

———. 1983. "Further Remarks on Bilingual Education." *Harvard Educational Review* 53:241–43.

———. 1984a. "The Social and Political Context of Bilingual Education." In *Multiculturalism in Canada: Social and Educational Perspectives*, edited by R. Samuda, J. Berry, and M. Laferrière, 184–200. Toronto: Allyn and Bacon.

———. 1984b. "Language, Diversity and Identity." In *Linguistic Minorities, Policies and Pluralism*, edited by J. Edwards, 277–310. London and New York: Academic Press.

———. 1985. *Language, Society and Identity*. Oxford: Blackwell.

———. 1989a. *Language and Disadvantage*. 2nd ed. London: Cole and Whurr.

———. 1989b. "Language in Education." In *Handbook of language and social psychology*, edited by H. Giles and W. P. Robinson. New York: Wiley.

Edwards, J., and J. Chisholm. 1987. "Language, Multiculturalism and Identity: A Canadian Study." *Journal of Multilingual and Multicultural Development* 8:391–408.

Edwards, J., and L. Doucette. 1987. "Ethnic Salience, Identity and Symbolic Ethnicity." *Canadian Ethnic Studies* 19:52–62.

Ekstrand, L. 1983. "Maintenance or Transition — or Both? A Review of Swedish Ideologies and Empirical Research." In *Multicultural and Multilingual Education in Immigrant Countries*, edited by T. Husén and S. Opper, 141–59. Oxford: Pergamon.

Epstein, N. 1977. *Language, Ethnicity and the Schools*. Washington, D.C.: Institute for Educational Leadership.

Ferguson, C. 1977. "Linguistic theory." In *Bilingual Education: Current Perspectives,* Center for Applied Linguistics, 43–52. Arlington, Virginia: C.A.L.

Fishman, J. 1977. *Bilingual Education*. Rowley, Mass.: Newbury.

———. 1980. "Minority Language Maintenance and the Ethnic Mother Tongue School." *Modern Language Journal* 64:167–72.

———. 1981. "In Defense of Learning English and Maintaining Other Languages (in the United States and Elsewhere Too). *English around the World* 25:1–3.

———. 1988. "'English Only': Its Ghosts, Myths, and Dangers." *International Journal of the Sociology of Language* 74:125–40.

Gaarder, A. 1967. "Organization of the Bilingual School." *Journal of Social Issues* 23(2):110–20.

Genesee, F. 1981. "Bilingualism and Biliteracy: A Study of Cross-Cultural Contact in a Bilingual Community." In *The Social Psychology of Reading*, edited by J. Edwards, 147–71. Silver Spring, Md.: Institute of Modern Languages.

Gleason, P. 1979. "Confusion Compounded: The Melting Pot in the 1960s and 1970s." *Ethnicity* 6:10–20.

_____. 1984. "Pluralism and Assimilation: A Conceptual History." In *Linguistic minorities, policies and pluralism*, edited by J. Edwards, 221–57. London and New York: Academic Press.

Görlach, M. 1986. "Comment." *International Journal of the Sociology of Language* 60:97–103.

Gray, T. 1982a. "Reaganomics and Education." *Linguistic Reporter* 24(6).

_____. 1982b. "And Debate Goes On . . . " *Linguistic Reporter* 24(7).

_____. 1982c. "Bilingual Program? What's That?" *Linguistic Reporter* 24(9).

Greeley, A. 1978. "After Ellis Island." *Harpers* 257(1542):27–30.

Grosjean, F. 1982. *Life with Two Languages*. Cambridge, Mass.: Harvard University Press.

Hammerly, H. 1987. "The Immersion Approach: Litmus Test of Second Language Acquisition through Classroom Communication." *Modern Language Journal* 71:395–401.

Hayakawa, S. 1987a. "One Nation . . . Indivisible?" In *Geolinguistic Perspectives*, edited by J. Levitt, L. Ashley and K. Rogers, 29–47. Lanham, Md.: University Press of America.

_____. 1987b. *Letter to Canadian Members of U.S. English*. 1 Sept.

Heath, S. 1981. "English in Our Language Heritage." In *Language in the U.S.A.*, edited by C. Ferguson and S. Heath, 6–20. Cambridge: Cambridge University Press.

Heath, S., and F. Mandabach. 1983. "Language Status Decisions and the Law in the United States." In *Progress in Language Planning*, edited by J. Cobarrubias and J. Fishman, 87–105. Berlin: Mouton.

Higham, J. 1975. *Send These to Me*. New York: Atheneum.

Imhoff, G. 1987. "Partisans of Language." *English Today* 11:37–40.

Kirp, D. (1983). "Elusive Equality: Race, Ethnicity, and Education in the American Experience." In *Ethnic Pluralism and Public Policy*, edited by N. Glazer and K. Young, 85–107. London: Heinemann.

Kloss, H. 1977. *The American Bilingual Tradition*. Rowley, Mass.: Newbury.

Landry, W. 1986. "Comment." *International Journal of the Sociology of Language* 60:129–38.

Lister, R. 1987. "Speaking Immersion." *Canadian Modern Language Review* 43:701–17.

Mackey, W. 1970. "A Typology of Bilingual Education." *Foreign Language Annals* 3:596–608.

_____. 1981. "Safeguarding Language in Schools." *Language and Society* (Ottawa) 4:10–14.

MacNab, G. 1979. "Cognition and Bilingualism: A Reanalysis of Studies." *Linguistics* 17:231–55.

Maldoff, E. 1986. "Comment: A Canadian Perspective." *International Journal of the Sociology of Language* 60:105–114.

Mann, A. 1979. *The One and the Many: Reflections on the American Identity*. Chicago: University of Chicago Press.

Marshall, D. 1986a. "The Question of an Official Language: Language Rights and the English Language Amendment." *International Journal of the Sociology of Language* 60:7-75.

_____. 1986b. "An Endangered Language?" *English Today* 6:21-24.

Martin-Jones, M., and S. Romaine. 1984. "Semilingualism: A Half-Baked Theory of Communicative Competence." Paper presented at the Fourth Nordic Symposium on Bilingualism, Uppsala.

McDermott, R., and K. Gospodinoff. 1981. "Social Contexts for Ethnic Borders and School Failure." In *Culture and the bilingual classroom*, edited by H. Trueba, G. Guthrie and K. Au, 212-30. Rowley, Mass.: Newbury.

McLaughlin, B. 1978. *Second-Language Acquisition in Childhood*. Hillsdale, N.J.: Erlbaum.

Milán, W. 1986. "Comment: Undressing the English Language Amendment." *International Journal of the Sociology of Language* 60:93-96.

Nunberg, G. 1986. "An Official Language for California?" *New York Times*, 2 Oct.

O'Bryan, K., J. Reitz, and O. Kuplowska. 1976. *Non-Official Languages: A Study in Canadian Multiculturalism*. Ottawa: Supply and Services Canada.

Ogbu, J. 1978. *Minority Education and Caste*. New York: Academic Press.

_____. 1982. "Societal Forces as a Context of Ghetto Children's School Failure." In *The Language of Children Reared in Poverty*, edited by L. Feagans and D. Farran, 117-38. New York: Academic Press.

Otheguy, R., and R. Otto. 1980. "The Myth of Static Maintenance in Bilingual Education." *Modern Language Journal* 64:350-56.

Paivio, A., and I. Begg. 1981. *Psychology of Language*. Englewood Cliffs, N.J.: Prentice-Hall.

Paulston, C. 1977. "Research." In *Bilingual Education: Current Perspectives*, Center for Applied Linguistics, 87-151. Arlington, Va: C.A.L.

Peal, E., and W. Lambert. 1962. "The Relationship of Bilingualism to Intelligence." *Psychological Monographs* 76(546).

Podhoretz, N. 1985. "Against Bilingual Education." *New York Post*, 8 Oct.

Reed, A. 1987. "The Embattled Dominance of English in the United States." In *Geolinguistic Perspectives* edited by J. Levitt, L. Ashley, and K. Rogers, 221-30. Lanham, Md.: University Press of America.

Reitz, J. 1980. *The Survival of Ethnic Groups*. Toronto: McGraw-Hill Ryerson.

Rosier, P., and M. Farella. 1976. "Bilingual Education at Rock Point—Some Early Results." *TESOL Quarterly* 10:379-88.

Rosier, P., and W. Holm. 1980. *The Rock Point Experience*. Arlington, Va.: C.A.L.

Rotberg, I. 1984. "Bilingual Education Policy in the United States." *Prospects* 14:133-47.

Sibayan, B. 1986. "Comment." *International Journal of the Sociology of Language* 60:163–68.

Sigall, H., and R. Page. 1971. "Current Stereotypes: A Little Fading, a Little Faking." *Journal of Personality and Social Psychology* 18:247–55.

Skutnabb-Kangas, T. 1984. "Children of Guest Workers and Immigrants: Linguistic and Educational Issues." In J. Edwards (Ed.), *Linguistic Minorities, Policies and Pluralism*, edited by J. Edwards, 17–48. London and New York: Academic Press.

Spener, D. 1988. "Transitional Bilingual Education and the Socialization of Immigrants." *Harvard Educational Review* 58:133–53.

U.S. English. 1984. *Talking Points*. Washington, D.C.: U.S. English.

_____. 1985a. *Fact Sheet: English Language Amendment*. Washington, D.C.: U.S. English.

_____. 1985b. *Fact Sheet: Bilingual Voting Ballots*. Washington, D.C.: U.S. English.

_____. 1988. *Update* 6(2).

_____. n.d. *In Defense of Our Common Language*. Washington, D.C.: U.S. English.

Veltman, C. 1983. *Language Shift in the United States*. Berlin: Mouton.

_____. 1986. "Comment." *International Journal of the Sociology of Language* 60:177–81.

Weinreich, U. 1974. *Languages in Contact*. The Hague: Mouton.

Willig, A. 1985. "A Meta-Analysis of Selected Studies on the Effectiveness of Bilingual Education." *Review of Educational Research* 55:269–317.

4

The Effectiveness of
Educational Alternatives for
Limited-English-Proficient
Children

Christine H. Rossell

Introduction

After a decade of rapid growth in federally funded bilingual education, questions are increasingly being asked about its purpose, its effectiveness, and its future. Indeed, as a result of the controversy and disagreement over the effectiveness of bilingual education, the 1984 Bilingual Education Act authorizes for the first time substantial federal funding of alternative English instruction programs for limited-English-proficient (LEP) children. This is an implicit acknowledgement by federal legislators that alternative educational programs for LEP children may be as effective as bilingual education. This paper addresses the effectiveness of alternative educational programs for limited-English-proficient children, first, by assessing the research evidence on policy alternatives for educating children who do not speak English; second, by evaluating alternative programs for the education of LEP children in the Berkeley Unified School District; third, by analyzing the post-reclassification progress of LEP children in Berkeley; and fourth, by comparing the educational achievement of LEP children in Berkeley to that of LEP children in two exemplary school districts. The legal suit brought against the Berkeley Unified School District by a group of Hispanic parents alleged that the school district had an inferior, and therefore unconstitutional, educational program for limited-English-proficient children because it did not employ sufficient native-tongue teachers, tutors, or materials, and because some teachers in its special language program did not hold specialized English as a Second Language (ESL) or bilingual credentials or degrees. These allegations embody the most common issues debated by critics and supporters of bilingual education.

Research on the Effectiveness of Bilingual Education

The plaintiffs' insistence on bilingual education — that is, native-tongue instruction — is evidenced throughout the complaint against the Berkeley Unified School District: *Teresa P. et al v. Berkeley Unified School District et al.* (724 F. Supp. 698, September 8, 1989) and is at the heart of the case. In particular, the plaintiffs were objecting to the fact that the bilingual education alternative ended at sixth grade. After that, students could only enroll in an English-language instruction program — ESL pullout or sheltered English classes. The Berkeley Plaintiffs' First Amended Complaints, 27 September 1987, alleged on p. 17 that "limited English proficient students in Berkeley need and are legally entitled to appropriate and adequate educational services including . . . instruction in the student's own primary language where appropriate."[1] Regarding the two types of programs the district has for LEP children — the Bilingual Program and the all-English Individual Learning Plan (ILP) — plaintiffs alleged that the bilingual program suffers from the failure "to provide a full time program of understandable instruction [that is, too much English is being used]."[2] They further asserted that "limited English proficient students placed in the District's [all-English] ILP program are denied understandable instruction" and that among the program's deficiencies are the following: "the failure to provide students instruction in academic subjects in the student's primary language sufficient to sustain academic achievement."[3] Similar complaints can be found in most other bilingual education cases.

It is thus relevant to discuss the research on bilingual education to determine whether greater primary-language instruction is the panacea claimed by the plaintiffs in this and other cases. The rationale underlying transitional bilingual education (TBE) differs depending on the age of the child. For very young children, the assumption is that learning to read in the native tongue first is a necessary condition for optimal reading ability in the second language. For all children, it is argued that learning a second language takes time, and children should not lose ground in other subject matters, particularly math, during that time period. Although most bilingual education advocates recommend late-exit TBE programs of a minimum of five years, the majority of elementary school programs are three-year programs. The Berkeley Unified School District's program, however, is of the type recommended by the experts in this field. In Berkeley, children are typically in the program for seven years, unless their parents request a transfer.

What does the research on bilingual education tell us about whether transitional bilingual education is the best educational program for dealing with the English-language problems of LEP children? Unfortunately, millions of dollars have been spent on evaluations of bilingual education programs that cannot answer this, and many other, important policy questions. As mentioned above, in order to determine whether a bilingual education program is successful, the research must have a "treatment" group subjected to the program and a "control" or comparison group, similar to the treatment group, that has not received that program. If students have not been randomly assigned to these two groups — those in the program and those not in the program — differences between the groups that existed prior to the program must be statistically eliminated. Differences between the groups after the program must be tested by means of an appropriate statistical analysis to determine if the differences are greater than could have been expected by chance. Unfortunately, many evaluators do not seem to understand how critical these elements are to an assessment of program success.

Those with no control group at all often rely on an invalid model designed by the U.S. Office of Evaluation called the "A-1 Evaluation Design." This model determines whether gains in achievement for students in bilingual education are significantly greater than would be predicted by comparing them to test scores derived from a national monolingual English-speaking sample. The model is invalid because there is no reason to assume that LEP students will experience cognitive growth that is anything like that of fluent-English-proficient (FEP) students. Whereas LEP students will typically exhibit large gains in "achievement" from year to year that are solely a function of their increased understanding of English, FEP students will have small or no increases in achievement from year to year. Thus, comparing the gains of LEP students to those of FEP students will almost always produce an invalid finding in favor of the program being examined. The real comparison should be to LEP students in alternative programs or no program at all.

Although many local evaluators, and some social scientists, argue that it is impossible to assemble a control group, that is, students similar to those receiving bilingual education except that they are not in a bilingual education program, they are usually wrong in this regard. Most schools with bilingual programs also have an ESL program for the "exotic" language groups, and virtually all school districts with bilingual programs have at least one ESL program in the district that could serve as a comparison group for the bilingual program. Therefore, there usually is no excuse for not having a control group in the program evaluations.

If we only consider the studies that assess alternative second-language programs and are of good methodological quality[4] — characterized by random assignment to a treatment and control group, or statistical control for pretreatment differences between groups where random assignment is not possible — there is no consistent research support for transitional bilingual education as a superior instructional practice for improving the English-language achievement of limited-English-proficient children. In thirty-six methodologically sound studies meeting the above criteria,[5] TBE is compared to (1) "submersion," that is, doing nothing, (2) ESL, and (3) structured immersion in terms of its effects on second-language (usually English) learning and mathematics.

Since most transitional bilingual education programs in this country are in grades 1–3, if learning to read first in your native tongue facilitates reading in the second language, as its advocates claim, then TBE should consistently produce results superior, and never inferior, to the results of doing nothing in second-language achievement. If learning content areas in your native tongue while you are learning a second language means that you do not lose ground in those areas as do those who immediately start learning them in "a language they do not understand," students in TBE should always be superior, and never inferior, in mathematics to those in submersion.

In fact, in second-language learning, 29 percent of the studies show transitional bilingual education to be superior, 21 percent show it to be inferior, and 50 percent show it to be no different from submersion—*doing nothing.* Altogether, 71 percent show TBE to be no different or worse than the supposedly discredited submersion technique.[6] In math, 7 percent of the studies show TBE to be superior, 27 percent show it to be inferior, and 67 percent show it to be no different from doing nothing. Altogether, 93 percent of the studies show it to be no different or worse than the supposedly discredited submersion technique in developing math proficiency.[7]

It is often contended by the plaintiffs in court cases that the issue is learning *in* a language, not learning a language. These data do not show TBE to be superior in either learning a language, or learning *in* a language—in this case, math. With regard to learning other subjects such as geography, social studies, and history (on which there is very little information), none of these subjects is more important than English and math. Students will be tested in English and math for the rest of their lives, and all kinds of placement decisions will be made on their scores in these two subject matters alone. Of what value is it to be at grade level in geography or social studies, if one's English and math scores are poor? Indeed, these math findings suggest an important problem: subject matter is taught in the student's first language (L1), but the student is tested for his or her understanding of that subject in *English.* It is possible that for many students the difficulty of having to translate what was learned in another language may be great enough that the subject matter lost in the translation may equal or surpass what is lost in submersion before the second language (L2) is mastered enough to understand subject content. This is why Saville and Troike, although otherwise advocates of bilingual education, recommended beginning mathematics in the second language (Saville and Troike, 1971).

Because the American Institutes for Research (AIR) study is a national survey of 8,900 students in thirty-eight Title VII projects, it should be given more weight than the others, which are of single school districts and student samples of between 25 and 300. The AIR study found TBE to be inferior to submersion in second language learning, and no different in math learning.[8]

Although many so-called submersion situations probably have an ESL program where the students are pulled out of the regular classroom and taught English for one or two periods a day, it is not specified in the evaluations described above. Thus, many of the studies classified above as submersion may in fact be ESL. Nevertheless, in the average ESL program, the student is still in the submersion situation for 80 percent of the day. Thus, even if the ESL component was ignored in some of these evaluations, the students were primarily in the submersion situation. In six studies, however, transitional bilingual education is specifically compared to ESL, with submersion in content areas.[9] Five studies show no significant difference between transitional bilingual education and ESL in second-language learning, and one shows TBE to be inferior. Of the three studies that examined math, one showed TBE to be superior, and two showed no significant difference.

This review is not the only one to conclude that there is no research support for transitional bilingual education. Engle (1975), Epstein (1977), Baker and de Kanter (1981), Venezky (1981), and Rotberg (1982) also concluded there was no research support for transitional bilingual education. Even supporters of bilingual education for ideological or political reasons have had to admit in recent years that the research evidence is simply not there. Hakuta,[10] in his 1986 review, *Mirror of Language* concludes:

> There is a sober truth that even the ardent advocate of bilingual education would not deny. Evaluation studies of the effectiveness of bilingual education in improving either English or math scores have not been overwhelmingly in favor of bilingual education. . . . An awkward tension blankets the lack of empirical demonstration of the success of bilingual education programs. Someone promised bacon, but it's not there. (p. 219)

Carter, despite being an advocate of bilingual education and an expert witness in several bilingual education cases over the last decade, begins a 1986 article with the question: "Regardless of the many roots of the debate, one issue is unresolved. Does bilingual education work?" (Carter and Chatfield 1986, 201).

Paulston, a linguist and advocate of bilingual education, makes some telling points in her 1982 report to the National Swedish Board of Education. With regard to transitional bilingual education in the U.S. as the best way to learn English, she notes:

> The rationale for bilingual programs are that they are more efficient in teaching English although there is not much hard data to support such a view; it has however been the standard argument. . . . The Canadians believe, *with justification*, [emphasis added] that fluent proficiency in the target language only occurs when the language is used as a medium of instruction. (1982, 47–48)

She also approvingly cites Toukamaa, another bilingual education advocate, who writes:

> [w]e wish to dissociate ourselves from those arguments, for teaching in the mother tongue, which attempt to frighten parents into choosing mother tongue–teaching by threatening emotional and intellectual under-development in those children who do not receive mother tongue-teaching. Teaching in the mother tongue does not seem to have the magical effect on the child's development, for good or for ill, which it has sometimes been ascribed. (Toukamaa 1980, 103; as cited in Paulston 1982, 49)

The Association for Supervision and Curriculum Development, an organization of ninety thousand principals, school superintendents, teachers, and other educational leaders, noted in their April 1987 report on bilingual education that "it is unclear which approach is better [teaching children in English or in their native tongue]" (Association 1987, 35). Despite this acknowledgement in several places in the report, they go on to recommend native-tongue instruction.

How are so many reviewers (see, for example, Dulay and Burt 1979; Troike 1978; Zappert and Cruz 1977) able to conclude that transitional bilingual education is a "superior" educational alternative? One technique, used by Zappert and Cruz, is to simply redefine the word. As they argue:

No significant difference should not be interpreted as a negative finding for bilingual education. . . . When one adds the fact that students
in bilingual education classrooms learn two languages, their native
language and a second language, one can conclude that a statistically
non-significant finding demonstrates the positive advantages of bilingual education. (1977, 8)

The main argument made for transitional bilingual education in
the court decisions, and the regulations, however, is that it
produces *greater* English-language achievement and content-area
mastery than doing nothing, not the same achievement. Doing
nothing is assumed to be a Fourteenth Amendment violation that
transitional bilingual education will *remedy*, not have no effect on.

The next technique used in research reviews to make transitional
bilingual education appear to be superior is to include performance in Spanish language arts as one of the research findings
demonstrating its superiority. Zappert and Cruz also do this.
Again, while I agree this is an important and desirable outcome, it
is not the goal of government policy nor of the court decisions. If
we examine the findings of the twelve studies reviewed by Zappert
and Cruz for their effect on *English* language achievement, 63
percent of the findings show no difference between transitional
bilingual education and doing nothing.

Willig's (1985) technique is more sophisticated. When her meta-
analysis found no difference between transitional bilingual education and doing nothing (submersion) or between transitional bilingual education/ESL and submersion/ESL, she used a regression
analysis adjustment to uncover a difference in favor of bilingual
education. The regression adjustment, however, is statistically invalid.[11]

Why is it that transitional bilingual education fares no better
than submersion/ESL if students learn to read better in a second
language after learning to read in their native tongue? The most
common answer offered by the plaintiffs in the court cases is that
the programs are "badly implemented." In fact, however, as Engle
concluded in 1975, there is absolutely no evidence that students
can learn a second language *better* if they learn to read in their
native tongue first (Engle 1975). Indeed, the Canadian experiments in immersion and bilingual education show just the opposite. The later-immersion English-Canadian students who had first

learned to read in English were ultimately surpassed in French, when compared to the French native speakers, by the early immersion students who had first learned to read in French (Swain 1974, 1978; Cziko 1976; Stern 1978). After reviewing the Canadian research, Swain concluded:

> The introduction of reading in the second language in early French immersion programs prior to the introduction of reading in the native language appears to foster rapid transfer of reading skills. The teaching of English reading [primary language] followed by the introduction of French reading appears to have negative effects on reading in both French and English. (1974, 127)

While Swain was discussing native English speakers learning French, I know of no educational theory that would suggest this process is cognitively different for native, non-English speakers learning English. In the United States, Cohen, Fathman, and Merino, whose earlier evaluation is often cited as evidence of the superiority of bilingual education, concluded after the six-year evaluation of the same Redwood City, California, six-year program where lower-class Hispanic students were taught bilingually:

> These findings suggest that reading taught bilingually may not facilitate reading in English; that instead, children who learn to read first and exclusively in English appear to do better in English reading over time. (Cohen, Fathman, and Merino 1976)

Paulston succinctly summarizes the research on Swedish bilingual education:

> The conclusions are fairly obvious. If you want students to maintain their home language at a level of proficiency as close as possible to national norms, but at a cost to Swedish, then home language classes is the choice. If you want Swedish proficiency, but at a probably increasing loss in home language proficiency, the ordinary Swedish classes is the choice.[12] Finally if you want bilingual students, combined classes is the choice. *There really are no contradictory data to these conclusions* [emphasis added]. (Paulston 1982, 50)

Hence, despite the fact that Swain was talking about learning French in an English-dominant country, Paulston was talking about learning Swedish in a Swedish-dominant country, and Cohen, Fathman, and Merino were talking about learning English in an English-dominant country, they all came to the same conclusion after reviewing a large body of research on bilingual education in each country. The highest level of proficiency in a second language is attained by being instructed in that language from the beginning of one's education.

Virtually every analyst of second-language learning is agreed that the length of time spent in language study is, all other things being equal, far and away the single greatest predictor of achievement in that language (Stern 1976; Edwards and Smythe 1976; Genessee 1978; Halpern 1976; Izzo 1981; Gray et al. 1984). The Ottawa immersion experiments are particularly instructive because they have tried a whole range of time provisions, from small daily amounts, to larger daily amounts of 40, 60, 90, and 150 minutes, to a full school day of 300 minutes of French immersion. The studies have shown that the language achievement of these different groups of students increases as the time increases (Stern et al. 1976).

After reviewing the alternatives to early-immersion programs for the acquisition of French as a Second Language, Edwards and Smythe conclude:

> The above findings suggest that, although a half and half bilingual program during the early grades is feasible and fully compatible with satisfactory progress in first language skills and major areas of curriculum, it nevertheless may not be comparable to full immersion programs with reference to the acquisition of French language skills, particularly French language comprehension. . . . Since, as a general rule, second language competence is proportional to the number of hours of second-language instruction, and since extended [bilingual] programs entail at best a total of 1,000 to 2,000 hours during elementary years, children enrolled in these programs do not reach the level of second-language mastery which has been observed with children who are the product of full elementary immersion programs. (Edwards and Smythe 1976)

Rarely, however, is any of the vast body of research and theory on second-language learning introduced into the bilingual education cases. The bilingual education advocates have, until the Berkeley case, been able to limit the focus of the testimony to compensatory education issues.

TBE versus Structured Immersion

No study has found transitional bilingual education to be superior to structured immersion (see Rossell and Ross 1986), and the
only one to show no difference between the two in second language
learning was conducted seventeen years ago in the Philippines (Ramos, Aguila, and Sibayan 1967). This study, and a study by Barik
and Swain (1975) also showed no difference in math. All studies
comparing bilingual education to structured immersion since then
have found the latter to produce greater achievement in the second
language than the former (Barik and Swain 1978; Genessee, Lambert and Tucker 1977; Barik, Swain, and Nwanunobi 1977; Pena-
Hughes and Solis 1980; Gersten 1985). All of the studies conducted in Canada of immersion and bilingual education (partial
French immersion) have shown that the middle-class and working-
class English-speaking students who were immersed in French in
kindergarten and first grade were almost the equal of native-speak-
ing French students until the curriculum became *bilingual* in second grade, at which point their French ability declined and continued to decline as English was increased.

Most bilingual education analysts do not see the applicability of
these studies to the United States. First, they argue that the studies
are not relevant to the U.S. immigrant experience because the immersion and bilingual education students are middle class. In fact,
however, the experiments were conducted with working- class children and produced the same or better results (Tucker, Lambert,
and d'Anglejan 1973; Bruck, Jakimik, and Tucker 1971; Cziko
1975; Genessee 1976). The "time-on-task" principle—that is, the
amount of time spent learning a subject is the greatest predictor of
achievement in that subject—holds across classes. This is not unex-
pected, since I know of no educational theory that would suggest
lower-class children need to spend less time learning a subject than
middle- and upper-class children. Yet, this unexamined assumption
underlies all court decisions ordering bilingual education within
the constraints of the normal school day.

A second argument made to dismiss the Canadian French-im-
mersion experiments as applicable to the United States is that the
Canadian students were self-selected, and their mother tongue was
the dominant language of the country. Yet, of the dozens of transi-

tional bilingual education advocates who have argued that the Canadian immersion experiments are not applicable to the United States, not a single one has come up with a theory to explain how the brain operates differently when one is "politically subordinate." The time-on-task principle would suggest structured immersion will work better in the United States than in Canada since students learning English here will get L2 reinforcement both inside and outside of school, unlike the Canadian students.

Time on Task and TBE

If time on task — the amount of time spent learning a subject — is such a good predictor of achievement, particularly for low-achieving students (Wiley 1976; Rosenshine 1979; Clauset and Gaynor 1980), then transitional bilingual education should always be inferior to submersion, or doing nothing, because submersion allows the student to sit in the regular classroom and hear English all day. This is not the case. Many methodologically sound research studies show TBE to be no different from submersion, and some even show it to be superior. In addition, several methodologically sound research studies show TBE to be no different from ESL/submersion, although none shows it to be superior.

One explanation for this is that initially, when English-language instruction is incomprehensible, bilingual education might be superior to submersion in the regular classroom. As students learn English, however, the submersion situation will surpass TBE. If the TBE program is short and uses a lot of English, the net effect could be no difference between submersion and transitional bilingual education.

Another possible explanation for the frequent lack of harm, and occasional benefit, of transitional bilingual education is that the program has important psychological effects that compensate for the reduced English-language learning time. That is to say, if students in submersion programs often feel alienated or inferior, and if a special program, regardless of its educational utility, makes school more enjoyable, then they may come to school more often, stay longer, and work harder. For such a student, the disadvantage of being taught in his or her native tongue may be offset by greater attendance and thus greater time on task, so that the net effect is no difference between transitional bilingual education and doing nothing.

The evidence substantiating this, however, is lacking. Some researchers have reported positive findings for students in bilingual programs, whereas others have found little difference in students' attitudes or behavior. Paulston (1977) and Fishman (1977) both found studies that reported positive effects in school attendance, attitudes, and self-concepts for students in bilingual programs in the United States and Canada. The AIR study, however, found no difference in attitudes toward school between students in and out of the bilingual program (Danoff et al. 1977; Danoff et al. 1978). A study of a bilingual/bicultural program in Edgewood, Texas, which had been specifically designed to increase students' psychological as well as cognitive development, found no difference between students in the bilingual/bicultural program and comparison students in attitudes, self-concept, motivation, social values, absenteeism, grade retention, and dropout rates (Jones and Davis 1977). Chapa also found no difference in self-concept between children in a bilingual program and a control group, while Oxman found that students from bilingual schools scored significantly higher on tests of alienation than did those in the limited bilingual or nonbilingual schools (cited in Paulston 1977).

Structural changes in the normal school day or year may compensate for reduced English-language learning time in transitional bilingual education. Some transitional bilingual education programs reduce the pupil-teacher ratio and the time spent on nonacademic subjects to produce greater academic English-language learning time, even though half the program is taught in another language. One program studied by McConnell (1980, 1982) had the migrant children not only going to school year round, but being taught on the bus while en route to their various seasonal locations. Thus, the children were more than compensated for the daily reduction in English-language learning time by the extended school year. Of course, an important policy question is how much greater would the effect on English-language achievement have been if this had been a structured immersion program taught 100 percent of the time in comprehensible English?

Another possible explanation for the frequent lack of harm and occasional benefit of TBE is that the TBE programs that are equal to or superior to submersion are actually more nearly structured immersion programs. Fillmore (1980), for example, studied different kinds of bilingual education classes and found that the teacher who was most successful in raising the English-language achievement of her Chinese students provided a structured learning environment in which the students were continually pushed and not allowed to go at their own pace, but instruction was almost entirely in English. Although she calls this bilingual education, a curriculum taught 90 percent in English is much closer to the structured immersion model than to the bilingual education model.

Similarly, the Austin Independent School District program (Carsrud and Curtis 1980) is cited by Baker and de Kanter (1981) as a study that showed TBE to be no different from, or superior, to submersion. Yet, the teachers in this program used English as the medium of instruction 82 percent of the time. Both Legaretta (1977) and Arocena and Curtis (1984) report that English was used 75 percent of the time in the TBE classes studied. Not surprisingly, Arocena and Curtis also found the class with twice as much formal instruction had the highest achievement.

Tickunoff's (1983) descriptive study of successful bilingual instruction (fifty-eight teachers from six nationally representative sites) identified the following characteristics of successful programs: (1) 80 percent of the time was allocated to academic learning tasks, (2) L1 was used by teachers primarily to clarify instructions, and (3) content areas such as math and social studies were taught in *English*. While Tickunoff does not say so, these are the characteristics of structured immersion, not of bilingual education.

Many teachers and administrators do not "cheat," however, and they teach the program as its advocates assume — bilingually for as long as possible within the constraints of a normal school day and school year, and the normal curriculum which includes nonacademic subjects. These may be the programs in which TBE students are shown to be inferior in achievement to students in regular classrooms (Danoff et al. 1978).

Bilingual Teachers

One issue of importance in the bilingual education court cases is the school district's provision of bilingual teachers for bilingual education programs. Although the plaintiffs have been successful in arguing on a "common sense" basis that bilingual teachers are necessary for teaching limited-English-proficient students, the empirical research does not support this if one's goal is the highest English-language achievement a child is capable of. Two studies of the achievement gains of limited-English-proficient children taught by bilingual and monolingual teachers (Curtis 1984; Ligon et al. 1974) found no difference between the two. Similarly, the AIR national survey of bilingual education also found no relationship between whether a teacher was bilingual and the performance of his/her students (Danoff et al. 1977; Danoff et al. 1978).

Even more amazing, Moore and Parr (1978) found that teachers in the bilingual education program who were rated as *less* competent had better student performance. This finding is not as strange as it sounds if, as seems likely for a bilingual education program, the competence rating is primarily an evaluation of the teacher's bilingual ability. If that is the case, this would suggest that the teachers who taught in English because they were not bilingual had better student performance than those who, because they were bilingual, taught bilingually. What all these studies suggest is that the psychological advantage one gains from having a bilingual, same-ethnic-group teacher may be offset by the tendency of these teachers to actually teach the transitional bilingual education program as its proponents intend it to be taught—bilingually. Thus, it may be more important that a teacher teach in English than that he or she be bilingual, if one's goal is the greatest English-language proficiency that a student is capable of within the constraints of the normal school day.

The Berkeley Unified School District's Programs for LEP Students

Comparing Current Students in the ILP Program to those in the Bilingual Program

The plaintiffs in *Teresa P.* argued, as have most plaintiffs in bilingual cases, that the Berkeley Unified School District needed to provide more primary-language instruction in order to guarantee the rights of limited-English-proficient children in the district. I assessed this allegation by comparing the achievement of LEP children in the two types of second-language acquisition programs offered by the district. These programs differ greatly in how much English is used in instruction. The ILP program offers all instruction in English in the regular classroom, with ESL pullout instruction at the elementary level and ESL or "sheltered" classes at the secondary level, as well as tutoring, some of it by bilingual tutors. Approximately 88 percent of instructional time for K–6 students in the ILP program is spent in the regular classroom (that is, the submersion situation). The bilingual program offers instruction that is approximately 30 to 50 percent in Spanish for LEP students.[13] Thus, a comparison of the achievement of students in these two programs is a test of the validity of the plaintiff's assertion that LEP students need more primary-language instruction.

There are two types of achievement data that are routinely collected by the district that can be statistically analyzed. The first of these is the IDEA Proficiency Test (IPT), which is administered annually to every student classified by the home-language survey as potentially LEP. For the vast majority of students, IPT testing occurs in the fall of each year. The second type of data collected by the district is the Comprehensive Test of Basic Skills (CTBS) achievement data in reading, language, and math. This test is administered in the spring of each year.

The IPT data is much more complete because it is administered annually to every potential or current LEP student every year in grades K–12, whereas the CTBS test is only administered to students in K–8 who score above a certain level on the IPT.[14] In addition, once a student is in the bilingual or ILP program, the classroom teacher determines who is ready to take the CTBS, and there are systematic differences between the two programs in terms of how proficient in English students are before they are allowed to take the test.[15] On other hand, the CTBS data are interval-level data that measure not only English proficiency, but achievement in math and language. The IPT data, by contrast, are ordinal-level data, with only seven data points, measuring only English-language proficiency.[16] Thus, there is a trade-off between more complete data on the IPT and better scaled, more comprehensive data on the CTBS.

Table 4.1 shows the change in IPT scores from Fall 1986 to Fall 1987 for 326 LEP students in grades K–12[17] in the two types of

TABLE 4.1
Change in IPT Scores,
Berkeley, Fall 1986–Fall 1987

Variable	Mean	b	Beta	SE b
IPT Change	1.141			
IPT 1986	3.621	−0.377*	−0.52	0.062
Father a professional	0.141	0.127	0.03	0.237
Asian	0.483	−0.047	−0.02	0.188
Grade	3.737	−0.043	−0.11	0.028
Years in program	2.608	0.142	0.20	0.076
In bilingual program	0.316	0.522	0.19	0.338
Grade X bilingual program	0.771	0.222	0.27	0.122
Years in program X bil. prog.	0.975	−0.218	0.30	0.140
Constant		2.180		
r^2		0.235		
N		326		

*Statistically significant at 0.05 or better.

programs in Berkeley controlling for variables that have been suggested as of theoretical interest in the literature — ethnicity, social class, age (that is, grade), and years in the program. The relationship between social class and achievement, as well as achievement gains, is well known and does not need to be explained further here.

The reason for including age (grade is a surrogate for age) and its interaction with enrollment in the bilingual program is that the research on second-language learning shows that older students learn a language faster than younger students. Therefore, a one-year change analysis should statistically control for age. In addition, one wants to know if this differs by program (the interaction effect between grade and bilingual program), because some researchers argue that older students can do quite well in ESL because they have greater knowledge of the context within which language learning will occur, but that younger students need bilingual education. Indeed, this is the rationale behind many elementary-only bilingual programs. The reason for including a student's years in the program and its interaction with bilingual program is that advocates of TBE argue that the longer a student stays in the bilingual program, the better they will do in comparison to the students in the English-only program.

The data in table 4.1 show *no significant difference between the bilingual program and the ILP program*.[18] These data also show that the students with the greatest increase in their IPT score are those with the lowest IPT scores in the previous year. This indicates that the many analyses that compare the gains of LEP students to those of fluent-English-proficient students are biased in favor of the program the LEP students are enrolled in, since the less English one knows, the more gain in English one will have.

Because the above analysis includes grades K–12, and the district only operates a bilingual program in grades K–6, equations were run comparing bilingual education to the ILP program for students in grade K–6. These findings are shown in table 4.2, with two additional variables—the Thousand Oaks school (ILP) and its bilingual program (the interaction variable, Thousand Oaks×bilingual program). The bilingual program at Thousand Oaks was cited in the plaintiffs' original complaint as a program that had too much emphasis on English. As a result of their emphasis on English prior to 1987, the students in the bilingual program at Thousand Oaks had an average increase in IPT scores of 2.2 compared to 1.3 for Jefferson, 1.1 for Cragmont, and 1.1 for Columbus. A t-test of the difference between the Thousand Oaks program and the others is statistically significant at the .05 level or better. Therefore, it is necessary to control for the Thousand Oaks English-emphasis bilingual program in an analysis of elementary schools. When this is done, the findings are very similar to those shown in

TABLE 4.2
Change in IPT Scores—Elementary Students,
Berkeley, Fall 1986–Fall 1987

Variable	Mean	b	Beta	SE b
IPT Change	1.316			
IPT 1986	3.530	−0.385*	−0.53	0.071
Father a professional	0.120	0.417	0.11	0.266
Asian	0.417	0.190	0.08	0.203
Grade	2.247	0.037	0.06	0.071
Years in program	2.535	0.127	0.18	0.110
In bilingual program	0.412	0.195	0.08	0.385
Grade X bilingual program	1.005	0.209	0.30	0.131
Years in program X bil. prog.	1.267	−0.176	−0.28	0.152
Thousand Oaks	0.212	0.206	0.07	0.345
Thousand Oaks X Bil. prog.	0.146	0.704	0.21	0.454
Constant		1.925		
r^2		0.270		
N		250		

*Statistically significant at 0.05 or better.

table 4.1. There is no relationship between students' English-language proficiency gains and the type of program they are enrolled in.

There is also no evidence in these data that older children gain more in all-English programs. Nor is there any evidence that children gain more in English-language achievement the longer they stay in the bilingual program. Therefore, there is no support for the often-made allegation that negative findings from bilingual education programs are a product of evaluations conducted too soon after enrollment.

Tables 4.3, 4.4, and 4.5 show the change in CTBS achievement (in normal curve equivalents [NCEs])[19] in reading, language, and math from Spring 1986 to Spring 1987 for 111 to 120 students in grades K–8 for which there is 1986 and 1987 data controlling for the same variables as in table 4.1.[20] *These data show no significant difference between the bilingual program and the ILP program.*[21] Of all these variables, only the previous year's achievement has a significant (negative) effect on change in achievement. It is interesting that social class (the dummy variable, father a professional) is related to the absolute level of achievement, but not to *change* in achievement. This is consistent with other research that shows that, while no school district has been successful in eliminating social-class differences in achievement, some school districts have

TABLE 4.3
Change in NCE CTBS Reading Scores[1],
Berkeley, Spring 1986–Spring 1987

Variable	Mean	b	Beta	SE b
NCE CTBS Reading Change	4.48			
NCE CTBS Reading 1986	22.20	− .491*	−0.43	0.140
Father a professional	0.14	2.307	0.06	4.685
Asian	0.48	2.933	0.10	3.708
Grade	3.37	0.074	0.02	0.559
Years in program	2.61	0.614	0.08	1.271
In bilingual program	0.32	−2.827	−0.09	6.625
Grade X bilingual program	0.77	−0.588	−0.07	2.379
Years in program X bil. prog.	2.61	1.667	0.21	2.698
Constant		11.471		
r^2		0.179		
N		111		

[1]Chance scores estimated for 1986 missing data with low score on IPT.
*Statistically significant at .05 or better.

TABLE 4.4
Change in NCE CTBS Language Scores[1],
Berkeley, Spring 1986–Spring 1987

Variable	Mean	b	Beta	SE b
NCE CTBS Language Change	8.06			
NCE CTBS Language 1986	22.85	−0.390*	−0.48	0.112
Father a professional	0.14	−7.316	−0.17	4.538
Asian	0.48	1.603	0.05	3.590
Grade	3.74	0.135	0.03	0.581
Years in program	2.61	−0.748	−0.09	1.311
In bilingual program	0.32	−1.650	−0.05	6.515
Grade X bilingual program	0.77	1.106	0.12	2.310
Years in program X bil. prog.	0.98	1.555	0.19	2.626
Constant		16.834		
r^2		0.270		
N		112		

[1]Chance scores estimated for 1986 missing data with low score on IPT.
*Statistically significant at .05 or better.

been able to eliminate social-class differences in *progress*, as the Berkeley Unified School District has done.

In 1987–88 the Berkeley Unified School District, under pressure from the California State Department of Education, increased the native-tongue instruction in its bilingual education programs, including the Thousand Oaks program. Tables 4.6, 4.7, and 4.8 show the change in CTBS achievement from 1987 to 1988 for 207 K–8 students on whom there is achievement data for both years.[22]

TABLE 4.5
Change in NCE CTBS Math Scores[1],
Berkeley, Spring 1986–Spring 1987

Variable	Mean	b	Beta	SE b
NCE CTBS Math Change	12.48			
MCE CTBS Math 1986	25.38	−0.830*	−0.85	0.102
Father a professional	0.14	−4.635	−0.07	5.767
Asian	0.48	6.221	0.13	4.606
Grade	3.74	0.862	0.11	0.754
Years in program	2.61	1.545	0.11	1.636
In bilingual program	0.32	3.848	0.07	8.483
Grade X bilingual program	0.77	2.359	0.15	2.936
Years in program X bil. prog.	0.98	−1.612	−0.12	3.366
Constant		22.472		
r^2		0.537		
N		120		

[1]Chance scores estimated for 1986 mising data with low score on IPT.
*Statistically significant at .05 or better.

TABLE 4.6
Change in NCE CTBS Reading Scores[1],
Berkeley, Spring 1987–Spring 1988

Variable	Mean	b	Beta	SE b
NCE CTBS Reading Change	5.71			
NCE CTBS Reading 1987	28.99	− 0.397*	−0.39	0.076
Father's occupation	30.54	0.113	0.13	0.064
Asian	0.48	1.508	0.05	2.787
Grade	3.74	− 1.632*	−0.32	0.404
Years in program	2.61	− 0.525	−0.06	0.869
In bilingual program	0.32	−11.949*	−0.34	4.981
Grade X bilingual program	0.77	3.613*	0.35	1.788
Years in program X bil. prog.	0.98	− 1.011	−0.11	2.024
Constant		22.421		
r[2]		0.320		
N		207		

[1]Chance scores estimated for 1987 missing data with low score on IPT.
*Statistically significant at .05 or better.

Unlike the previous analyses, *these equations show bilingual education to have a significant negative effect on achievement in reading, language, and math.* On the other hand, grade (in the ILP program) also has a negative effect on achievement. In other words, controlling for the number of years in the program, a first grader in the ILP program will have a greater increase in reading achievement than a sixth grader. This is consistent with research on compensatory education, which shows younger students experi-

TABLE 4.7
Change in NCE CTBS Language Scores[1],
Berkeley, Spring 1987–Spring 1988

Variable	Mean	b	Beta	SE b
NCE CTBS Language Change	5.19			
NCE CTBS Language 1987	33.64	− 0.512*	−0.57	0.067
Father's occupation	30.54	0.130	0.14	0.069
Asian	0.48	− 0.378	−0.01	2.989
Grade	3.74	− 1.157*	−0.20	0.431
Years in program	2.61	0.141	0.01	0.947
In bilingual program	0.32	−13.244*	−0.33	5.372
Grade X bilingual program	0.77	− 1.503	−0.13	1.908
Years in program X bil. prog.	0.98	2.914	0.28	2.161
Constant		25.099		
r[2]		0.460		
N		177		

[1]Chance scores estimated for 1987 missing data with low score in IPT.
*Statistically significant at .05 or better.

TABLE 4.8
Change in NCE CTBS Math Scores[1],
Berkeley, Spring 1987–Spring 1988

Variable	Mean	b	Beta	SE b
NCE CTBS Math Change	10.85			
NCE CTBS Math 1987	36.29	− 0.632*	−0.64	0.064
Father's occupation	30.54	0.011	0.01	0.078
Asian	0.48	7.059*	0.14	3.374
Grade	3.74	− 1.322*	−0.17	0.506
Years in program	2.61	− 1.214	−0.09	1.099
In bilingual program	0.32	−14.701*	−0.26	6.146
Grade X bilingual program	0.77	− 1.000	−0.06	2.164
Years in program X bil. prog.	0.98	3.315	0.23	2.461
Constant		40.160		
r^2		0.593		
N		208		

[1]Chance scores estimated for 1987 missing data with low score on IPT.
*Statistically significant at .05 or better.

encing greater gains, but it does not explain why this effect is not found in the bilingual education program. For the bilingual program, the two variables ("grade" and "grade×bilingual") cancel each other out for reading achievement and for language and math achievement; the interaction variable is simply insignificant. Thus, there is no relationship between age and achievement gains for children in the bilingual program, controlling for years in the program, and no relationship between years in the program and achievement gains for children in the bilingual program, controlling for age.

Another difference here from the previous year's findings is that Asians have a significantly greater gain in math achievement than Hispanic and European students. Thus, the Asian LEP students, almost all of whom are in the ILP program, are having no trouble keeping up with subject-matter content in English.

Solving the equation for all variables (using the mean for 1987 achievement and father's occupation)[23] and ignoring the fact that some of these variables are not statistically significant indicates that a third-grade Hispanic student can expect an increase of 2.2 in CTBS reading (normal curve equivalents) from one year to the next if he or she is in the bilingual program, and 7.4 if he or she is in the ILP program. The same student can expect an increase of 2.8 in CTBS language achievement (NCEs) from one year to the next if he or she is in the bilingual program, and 8.9 if he or she is in the ILP program. This student can also expect an increase of 4.3 in CTBS math achievement from one year to the next if he or she is in the bilingual program, and 8.8 if he or she is in the ILP program. In short, the all-English ILP program produces significantly greater achievement gains in LEP children than the bilingual education program, despite the fact that the ILP students are in the supposedly discredited submersion situation (that is, a regular classroom) for almost 90 percent of their instructional time. Moreover, all analyses using the CTBS as the outcome variable are biased in favor of the bilingual program because the students are in the program for a half-year longer, on average, than the ILP students before they first take the CTBS exam.

Bilingual Credentialed Teachers

The plaintiffs in *Teresa P.* also alleged that the rights of LEP children were violated because they were taught by teachers who did not have bilingual or ESL teaching credentials. Since the purpose of having a credentialed teacher is to improve children's educational achievement, we can empirically assess the necessity of having bilingual-credentialed teachers by examining the relationship between the achievement of students and the special certification of their teachers. There is no empirical validation in the literature for the notion that teachers with special credentials or more education produce children with higher achievement than teachers without these credentials. Hanushek's careful review of the literature (1986), including only methodologically sound studies, found that of 106 studies, only 6 showed a statistically positive relationship between teacher education and student achievement, 5 showed a *negative* relationship, and the rest showed no relationship. Tickunoff's Significant Bilingual Instructional Features study identified fifty-eight outstanding bilingual education teachers (Guthrie, Tickunoff, Fisher, and Gee 1981). The most common preparation for these outstanding teachers was attendance at in-service workshops. Only one of the fifty-eight teachers had passed a proficiency test in the non-English language. Only nine had ever taken any college courses in bilingual education. Only four had ever taken any course work in linguistics.

I tested the relationship between bilingual credentialing and student achievement in the Berkeley public schools. Five of the bilingual education teachers did not have bilingual certificates, although they were bilingual.[24] Tables 4.9, 4.10, and 4.11 demonstrate that there is no relationship between a child's achievement gain and whether or not their teacher had a bilingual certificate in the bilingual education program of the Berkeley public schools.[25] Thus, it does not matter whether a teacher has a bilingual credential if one's goal is the highest English-language achievement that a student is capable of.

Post-Reclassification Progress of LEP Students in Berkeley

As important as the achievement of students currently in the alternative second-language program is the achievement of students who have been reclassified. The plaintiffs' allegations implied that, not only were some of the sixteen named plaintiffs having academic difficulty after exiting one of the two Berkeley programs for LEP children, but so were other LEP students in the district. Figures 4.1, 4.2, and 4.3 show the CTBS achievement progress of Berkeley LEP students pre- and post-reclassification in both the bilingual program and the ILP. Two things stand out in these graphs. First, there is remarkable progress in reading, lan-

TABLE 4.9
Change in NCE CTBS Reading Scores[1],
by Certified Bilingual/Bicultural Teacher,
Berkeley, Spring 1987–Spring 1988
(bilingual program only)

Variable	Mean	b	Beta	SE b
NCE CTBS Reading Change	2.43			
NCE CTBS Reading 1987	28.33	−0.417*	−0.44	0.119
Father's occupation	22.29	0.099	0.08	0.153
Grade	2.44	2.465	0.33	1.666
Years in program	3.07	−1.454	−0.19	1.538
Certified bilingual teacher	0.71	2.072	0.06	5.428
Constant		9.015		
r^2		0.224		
N		77		

[1]Chance scores estimated for 1987 missing data with low score on IPT.
*Statistically significant at .05 or better.

TABLE 4.10
Change in NCE CTBS Language Scores[1],
by Certified Bilingual/Bicultural Teacher,
Berkeley, Spring 1987–Spring 1988
(bilingual program only)

Variable	Mean	b	Beta	SE b
NCE CTBS Language Change	-1.32			
NCE CTBS Language 1987	37.34	-0.355*	-0.53	0.093
Father's occupation	22.29	0.051	0.05	0.146
Grade	2.44	-0.804	-0.12	1.642
Years in program	3.07	2.081	0.31	1.528
Certified bilingual teacher	0.71	1.187	0.04	5.234
Constant		5.534		
r^2		0.256		
N		62		

[1]Chance scores estimated for 1987 missing data with low score on IPT.
*Statistically significant at .05 or better.

guage, and math over time both pre- and post-reclassification, although of course there is greater progress over time pre-reclassification when most of the students' progress is due to the large increases in their English-language proficiency. Second, there is very little difference between the two programs post-reclassification, and the only difference pre-reclassification is in math, where students in the ILP program have greater math achievement, probably because of the greater math achievement of Asian students.

TABLE 4.11
Change in NCE CTBS Math Scores[1],
by Certified Bilingual/Bicultural Teacher,
Berkeley, Spring 1987–Spring 1988
(bilingual program only)

Variable	Mean	b	Beta	SE b
NCE CTBS Math Change	2.67			
NCE CTBS Math 1987	40.21	-0.745*	-0.80	0.082
Father's occupation	22.29	0.139	0.07	0.169
Grade	2.44	-2.120	-0.18	1.850
Years in program	3.07	2.301	0.19	1.730
Certified bilingual teacher	0.71	-1.614	-0.03	5.985
Constant		28.790		
r^2		0.612		
N		78		

[1]Chance scores estimated for 1987 missing data with low score on IPT.
*Statistically significant at .05 or better.

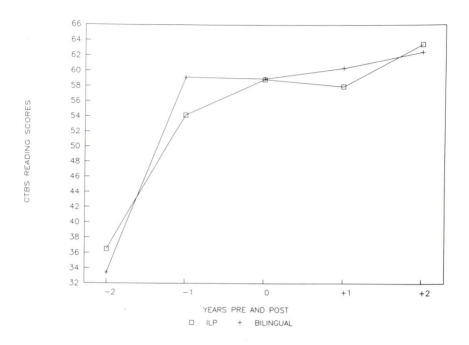

FIGURE 4.1
Pre- and Post-Reclassification CTBS Reading

Equally as impressive as the pre- and post-reclassification progress in CTBS achievement are the grades of these students shown in figures 4.4, 4.5, and 4.6. Although progress in grades seems less clearly positive than that of CTBS achievement, the line graph is somewhat misleading. The average post-reclassification grade varies from B+ to A− for high school students, or from E to S+ for elementary students, so small changes appear much larger than they are. For example, the apparently huge differences between the ILP and bilingual graduates in math in the second year after reclassification is the difference between a B+ average for the reclassified ILP students and an A− average for the reclassified bilingual students. Since bilingual students in grades 1–6 typically continue in the program when reclassified, the slightly higher average grade could also reflect the lesser competition in the bilingual classroom than in the regular classroom.

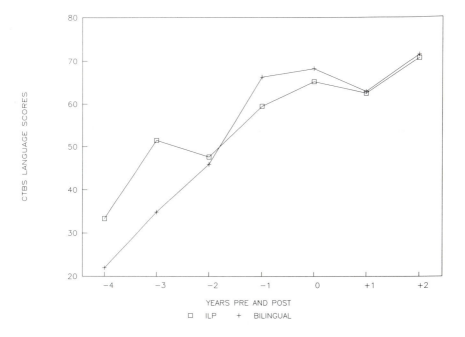

FIGURE 4.2
Pre- and Post-Classification CTBS Language

A pooled cross-sectional analysis[26] of all the post-reclassification reading, language, and math achievement data (in normal curve equivalents) for the years on which there is fairly complete data (through the second year after reclassification) is shown in tables 4.12, 4.13, and 4.14. *This analysis shows no significant difference between the bilingual program and the ILP program in post-reclassification achievement* controlling for pre-reclassification achievement. There is also statistically significant progress over time as indicated by the significant coefficient for time in reading, language, and math achievement.

The pooled cross-sectional analysis of reading, language, and math grades is shown in tables 4.15, 4.16, and 4.17. *There is no significant difference in student grades between the bilingual program and the ILP.* This analysis shows no significant progress over

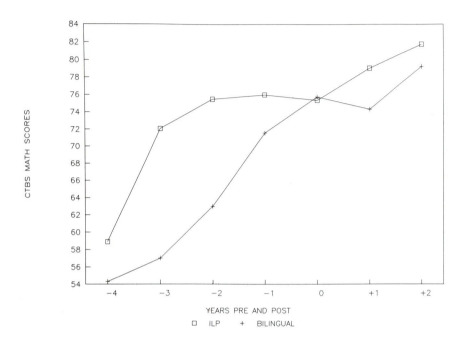

FIGURE 4.3
Pre- and Post-Reclassification CTBS Math

time, unlike the achievement data, because of the much smaller variance. The average grade for reclassified students is very high, and hence there is little room for progress. Thus, on the analysis of grades, the standard to keep in mind is that of the absolute level of achievement of these students.

All of these data show high levels of achievement on both standardized tests and grades for reclassified students in both programs. Thus, the plaintiffs' allegation that the Berkeley Unified School District is improperly reclassifying students is not borne out by the aggregate data presented here.

A Comparison with Other School Districts

The analysis presented above demonstrates (1) that students in programs with primary-language instruction have either the same or worse achievement than students in programs with little or no

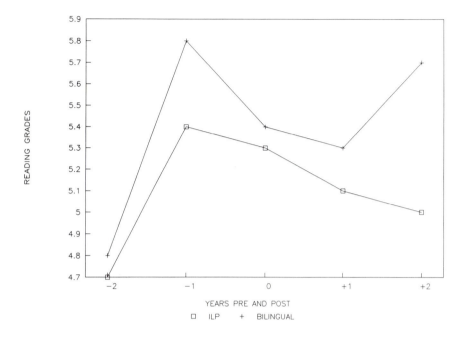

FIGURE 4.4
Pre- and Post-Reclassification Reading Scores

primary language instruction, and (2) that students in both types of programs who are reclassified do well in terms of progress on standardized achievement and grades both pre- and post-reclassification. When confronted with such evidence, however, supporters of bilingual education usually argue that the bilingual program did the same or worse than the English instruction program because the bilingual program is badly implemented.[27] A rebuttal to the allegation that any particular district runs poor programs is to compare that district to other school districts with highly regarded or exemplary programs.

Krashen[28] and Biber, in their book, *On Course* (1988), cite only two school districts in their entirety as having outstanding bilingual education programs—San Jose Unified School District and the Fremont Unified School District.[29] San Jose is considered exemplary because its bilingual program conforms to the three char-

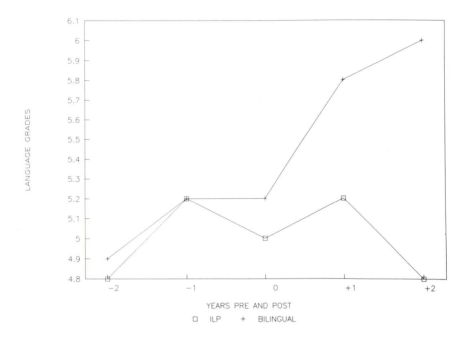

FIGURE 4.5
Pre- and Post-Reclassification Language Grades

acteristics of bilingual programs that Krashen considers necessary for success: (1) students receive subject-matter instruction in the primary language, without translation, (2) literacy is developed in the primary language, and (3) ESL instruction is provided, which includes comprehensible input-based methodology. Despite the fact that the bilingual program has these characteristics, however, students who graduate from the ILP program in San Jose have higher achievement.[30] Thus, all of the programs for LEP students in San Jose should be considered exemplary.

Fremont is considered exemplary for the same reason as San Jose—it has the three characteristics of successful bilingual programs. Not only is it considered outstanding by Krashen, but it has been identified by the California State Department of Education as an Exemplary Bilingual Education Program. However, in personal communication with the Director of Bilingual Education,

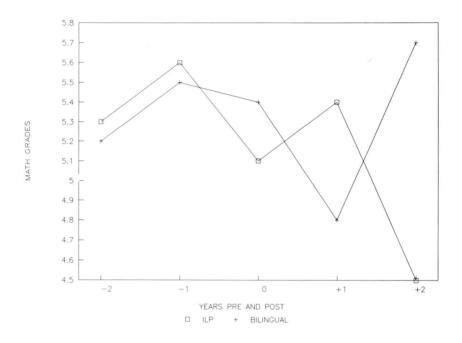

FIGURE 4.6
Pre- and Post-Reclassification Math Grades

Carmen Melendez, on 3 June 1988, I was informed that the Better
Communication through Bilingual Education (BCBE) Program
involves five additional treatments besides bilingual education.[31]

TABLE 4.12
NCE CTBS Reading Scores for Reclassified Students,
Berkeley, 1980–1987

Variable	Mean	b	Beta	SE b
NCE CTBS Reading Score	55.050			
NCE CTBS Reading, pre-reclass	52.987	0.324*	0.30	0.088
Grade at reclass	5.210	-0.700*	-0.19	0.341
Time	0.196	1.915*	0.18	0.864
In bilingual program	0.184	2.974	0.10	5.856
Years in program	2.502	-0.899	-0.10	0.803
Grade reclass X bilingual program	0.634	-1.642	-0.22	1.368
Time X bilingual program	0.044	-2.317	-0.10	1.979
Years X bilingual program	0.500	0.619	0.06	2.182
Constant		43.682		
r^2		0.239		
N		301		

*Statistically significant at 0.05 or better.

TABLE 4.13
NCE CTBS Language Scores for Reclassified Students,
Berkeley, 1980–1987

Variable	Mean	b	Beta	SE b
NCE CTBS Language Score	59.297			
NCE CTBS Language, pre-reclass	55.779	0.468*	0.45	0.081
Grade at reclass	5.210	-0.224	-0.05	0.410
Time	0.196	2.754*	0.21	1.082
In bilingual program	0.184	5.810	0.17	7.323
Years in program	2.502	-0.648	-0.06	1.018
Grade reclass X bilingual program	0.634	-2.748	-0.31	1.708
Time X bilingual program	0.044	-2.786	-0.10	2.460
Years X bilingual program	0.500	1.534	0.13	2.730
Constant		35.452		
r^2		0.247		
N		296		

*Statistically significant at 0.05 or better.

1. *Early intervention.* Children in the BCBE are asked to attend preschool, whereas that is not the case for the LEP students in other programs.
2. *Extended day.* Beginning with the second grade, students in the BCBE program go to school for an extra hour a day of reading in *English.*
3. *Parental outreach and involvement.* Parents agree to volunteer

TABLE 4.14
NCE CTBS Math Scores for Reclassified Students,
Berkeley, 1980–1987

Variable	Mean	b	Beta	SE b
NCE CTBS Math Score	69.613			
NCE CTBS Math, pre-reclass	67.668	0.555*	0.54	0.069
Grade at reclass	5.210	0.150	0.03	0.421
Time	0.196	2.260*	0.15	1.090
In bilingual program	0.184	12.218	0.30	7.416
Years in program	2.502	-1.220	-0.09	1.035
Grade reclass X bilingual program	0.634	-3.210	-0.31	1.732
Time X bilingual program	0.044	1.130	0.03	2.486
Years X bilingual program	0.500	-0.748	-0.05	2.768
Constant		33.961		
r^2		0.370		
N		302		

*Statistically significant at 0.05 or better.

TABLE 4.15
Reading Report Card Grades for Reclassified Students,
Berkeley, 1980–1987

Variable	Mean	b	Beta	SE b
Report card, reading	5.271			
Report card, pre-reclass	5.432	0.162	0.14	0.087
Grade at reclass	5.210	-0.126*	-0.22	0.047
Time	0.196	-0.168	-0.11	0.125
In bilingual program	0.184	1.298	0.30	0.847
Years in program	2.502	-0.178	-0.13	0.116
Grade reclass X bilingual program	0.634	-0.398*	-0.36	0.198
Time X bilingual program	0.044	0.025	0.00	0.287
Years X bilingual program	0.500	0.058	0.04	0.316
Constant		5.509		
r^2		0.189		
N		347		

*Statistically significant at 0.05 or better.

in the school and help their children with homework in the evening. The average parent-volunteer hours in the BCBE schools are 357 in kindergarten, 210 in the first grade, 105 in the second grade, 73 in the third grade and 54 in the fourth grade.

4. *Parental help with homework.* Parents are given a Home Study Guide and agree to participate in the early grades as tutors and in the upper grades as monitors of their children's homework.

5. *Focus on transferable skills.* The focus in the Spanish reading program is on those skills that will transfer readily to English, so ultimately with the extended day, the students are getting a double dose of reading.

TABLE 4.16
Language Report Card Grades For Reclassified Students,
Berkeley, 1980–1987

Variable	Mean	b	Beta	SE b
Report card, language	5.159			
Report card, pre-reclass	5.161	0.328*	0.28	0.092
Grade at reclass	5.210	-0.015	-0.03	0.048
Time	0.196	0.025	0.02	0.127
In bilingual program	0.184	1.030	0.26	0.864
Years in program	2.502	-0.234*	-0.19	0.118
Grade reclass X bilingual program	0.634	-0.305	-0.30	0.202
Time X bilingual program	0.044	0.132	0.04	0.291
Years X bilingual program	0.500	0.131	0.10	0.322
Constant		4.053		
r^2		0.153		
N		289		

*Statistically significant at 0.05 or better.

TABLE 4.17
Math Report Card Grades for Reclassified Students,
Berkeley, 1980–1987

Variable	Mean	b	Beta	SE b
Report card, math	5.384			
Report card, pre-reclass	5.598	0.409*	0.32	0.082
Grade at reclass	5.210	-0.215*	-0.34	0.047
Time	0.196	-0.238	-0.13	0.125
In bilingual program	0.184	0.052	0.01	0.849
Years in program	2.502	-0.073	-0.05	0.116
Grade reclass X bilingual program	0.634	-0.289	-0.24	0.199
Time X bilingual program	0.044	0.217	0.06	0.285
Years X bilingual program	0.500	0.223	0.14	0.317
Constant		4.493		
r^2		0.269		
N		354		

*Statistically significant at 0.05 or better.

The inclusion of these additional treatments, of course, significantly increases English-language and academic time on task. It also significantly increases the cost of bilingual education (almost a half-million dollars for two schools). As a result, the program has only been implemented in a few schools in Fremont and is unlikely to spread further. Nevertheless, Krashen and Biber cite this program as an example of the effectiveness of *bilingual* education and never mention the additional treatments. (One can only wonder how often this happens in the literature.)

It is possible to compare the reading and math achievement of LEP students in the Berkeley ILP and bilingual education programs with that of LEP students in these exemplary school districts because the state of California has a uniform testing program — the California Assessment Program (CAP) — for all school districts. The test scores are aggregated to the school level and classified into fluent-English and limited-English, but not into bilingual or ILP program. The analysis is biased in favor of Fremont because all schools on which CAP data is collected are included for San Jose and Berkeley, but only the three BCBE schools plus one ILP junior high school are analyzed in Fremont.

Table 4.18 compares CAP reading scores for LEP students in Berkeley to LEP students in San Jose and Fremont in a pooled cross-sectional analysis of three years, 1985–1987, and three grade levels, third, sixth, and eighth. This equation indicates that when

TABLE 4.18
CAP Reading Scores for LEP Students in Berkeley
Compared to Fremont and San Jose, 1985–1987

Variable	Mean	b	Beta	SE b
Reading CAP, LEP	180.17			
Berkeley	0.19	14.788	0.12	12.290
School has bilingual program	0.31	11.821	0.11	11.579
Reading CAP, FEP	270.11	0.106	0.06	0.168
Grade	4.91	-11.119*	-0.48	2.633
Percent on AFDC	16.07	- 1.479*	-0.34	0.514
Constant		223.512		
r^2		0.301		
N		108		

*Statistically significant at 0.05 or better.

Berkeley is compared to San Jose and Fremont, *there is no significant difference in LEP-student reading achievement* controlling for the percentage of students on Aid to Families with Dependent Children (AFDC) and the CAP reading of the FEP students.[32]

Table 4.19 compares CAP math scores for LEP students in Berkeley to San Jose and Fremont. This equation demonstrates that *Berkeley LEP students have significantly greater math achievement than LEP students in Fremont and San Jose.*

Thus, this analysis shows that when Berkeley is compared to two school districts that have been designated as having exemplary programs for limited-English-proficient students — one with expensive, additional treatments (Fremont) — it either does the same or better. There is no significant difference between the reading

TABLE 4.19
CAP Math Scores for LEP Students in Berkeley
Compared to Fremont and San Jose, 1985–1987

Variable	Mean	b	Beta	SE b
Math CAP, LEP	227.94			
Berkeley	0.19	43.616*	0.36	13.297
School has bilingual program	0.31	2.357	0.02	12.335
Math CAP, FEP	276.22	0.000	0.00	0.186
Grade	4.91	- 3.440	-0.15	2.638
Percent on AFDC	16.07	- 1.129*	-0.27	0.516
Constant		254.140		
r^2		0.129		
N		108		

*Statistically significant at 0.05 or better.

achievement of LEP students in Berkeley in comparison to Fremont and San Jose, and Berkeley LEP students have significantly higher math achievement. Thus, by one of the most important standards used in bilingual education court cases—does the program produce results—the Berkeley educational programs for limited-English-proficient students could be considered exemplary.

Conclusions

The research on bilingual education in other school districts and countries does not show primary-language instruction to be a unique solution to the provision of equal educational opportunity for immigrant children, as many of the experts in the field have increasingly acknowledged. Indeed, despite the general acceptance by the courts that submersion or doing nothing has failed, it fares no worse than transitional bilingual education. Thus, the failure to provide primary tongue instruction cannot be a violation of a child's equal educational opportunity if he or she has the same (or less) achievement with primary-language instruction as without. When bilingual programs with more primary-language instruction are compared to ESL programs with little or no primary-language instruction, there is either no significant difference in the achievement of students in the two programs, or the children in bilingual programs have lower achievement. Moreover, reclassified students are making significant progress over time, both pre- and post-reclassification in CTBS achievement, and their average grade is a B+. If the district is improperly reclassifying students, these data do not show it.

Thus, the all-English ILP program with all of its alleged faults is doing as well as or better than the bilingual education program. This analysis thus suggests that instruction in English must be an adequate pedagogical technique, contrary to the plaintiffs' allegations. This analysis also suggests that the Berkeley Unified School District's failure to provide in their ILP program what the plaintiffs consider to be sufficient primary-tongue tutors and materials and ESL certified teachers, and their use of paraprofessionals to provide help with ESL instruction, must be unimportant, or the ILP students would not have done as well as, or better than, the students in the bilingual program.

The comparison of Berkeley with two exemplary school districts — San Jose and Fremont — indicates that Berkeley LEP students have achievement as high as or higher than these other districts. Thus, there is no evidence that the students in the all-English-language instruction had the same or better achievement than the students in the bilingual program in Berkeley because the school district operates a poor bilingual program. Indeed, what evidence there is suggests that compared to other districts, the Berkeley Unified School District operates exemplary programs.

Policy Implications

When there are not enough LEP students to warrant a bilingual classroom with a full-time bilingual teacher, most school districts in the country operate an ESL pullout program identical to Berkeley's, with submersion in the regular classroom for 80 to 90 percent of the time. While an ESL pullout program is an acceptable and constitutional alternative, it is possible that the bilingual program in Berkeley often did no worse than the ESL program because ESL is *also* not the best way to teach LEP children English, although it appears to be better than bilingual education. The Canadian immersion studies suggest that there would be much greater differences in achievement between students in bilingual education programs and students in alternative English-language programs if the alternative English-language program were structured immersion rather than ESL pullout.

The ESL pullout program does not give students as much *effective* time on task in English as does a structured immersion program because in a structured immersion program LEP students are in one classroom taught *all day long* in an English geared to their level of understanding. In an ESL pullout program, LEP students may initially be taught in an English geared to their level of understanding only 10 to 20 percent of the day. As they gain English fluency, of course, this amount increases. But, a structured immersion program should ultimately be more effective than both ESL pullout and bilingual education because (1) instruction is in English, and (2) the English is *always* comprehensible. It thus provides more *effective* English-language time on task than either alternative. Structured immersion is also more cost-effective than transitional bilingual education because the teacher does not need to be fluent in another language and the classroom can be composed of students from different language groups. As with any remedial program, of course, there is the danger that students will be improperly selected for such programs and will not be exited (that is, mainstreamed) when they have learned enough English to function in the regular classroom. A committee of teachers should make these decisions, and standardized tests should be relied upon as little as possible (Rossell and Baker 1988). But, so long as such a program is not allowed to function as a remedial track for language-minority-background, fluent-English-proficient students who do not score well on tests, the available research suggests that, had the Berkeley school district operated such a program in the elementary grades, the students in such programs would have consistently done better than those in the bilingual programs. Unfortunately, the bilingual education advocates have prevented the adoption of structured immersion in the United States because it has usually been offered as an alternative to transitional bilingual education rather than as an alternative to ESL pullout.[33]

Thus, if one's goal is the highest English-language ability that a student is capable of, the research suggests that school districts should eliminate both their transitional bilingual education program and their ESL pullout program and replace them with a structured immersion program in which LEP children of different linguistic backgrounds are instructed entirely in English. For those parents who want a bilingual education for their children in order to maintain their native tongue—32 percent did so in Berkeley—the school district should offer a *voluntary* bilingual maintenance program from kindergarten through twelfth grade. But a bilingual maintenance program should be an *extended-day* program if the children enrolled are to achieve at a level of English-language ability that is comparable to students who are "specializing" in English. If the non-language instruction for LEP students were offered only in the after-school program, it would be similar to the native-tongue maintenance the Jews and the Chinese have often practiced, and it might have only a negligible negative effect in the LEP students' English. The ratio of non-English-language instruction to English-language-instruction should be tailored to each student's needs with the goal of producing the greatest English-language proficiency each student is capable of, as well as a functional bilingualism.

Parents should, however, be told the truth about bilingual education and its goals. A bilingual maintenance program is offered not because it is the best way to learn English, the objective of the federal and state legislation, but because it is a good way to become bilingual, and there are parents who want their children to be bilingual. Since being bilingual is a desirable characteristic, the demands of parents who want their children to be bilingual should be met. Thus, the case for bilingual education should not have to rest on its effectiveness in teaching children English, but on its effectiveness in making children bilingual. The bilingual education advocates have confused these two goals. In so doing, they have violated the civil rights of the 18 percent of parents (according to the Berkeley survey) who want their child in a bilingual program *only* because they believe it is the best way to learn English, and the unknown percentage of parents who would prefer their child to be in an all-English program, but who are coaxed or coerced into placing them in a bilingual education program by teachers and administrators (see, for example, Petersen 1990).

The policy alternatives I have outlined, by contrast, would protect the civil rights of *all* parents. It would do this by providing for consumer protection in the form of full disclosure, and by providing program alternatives that link means to goals based on the research evidence to date.

Postscript

On 14 February 1989, Judge D. Lowell Jensen issued a twenty-three-page decision concluding that Berkeley's program for limited-English-proficient children satisfied the federal statutory requirement that a school district "take appropriate action to overcome language barriers that impede equal participation by its students in its instructional programs" (20 U.S.C. 1703 [f]). This decision, which can be obtained from the defendants' attorneys, Celia Ruiz and Thomas Donovan,[34] relied heavily on the above research, and that of Randall Cognetta, in concluding that Berkeley's English-only program had no less efficacy than the native-language approach, and that bilingual credentialed teachers were not necessary to meet federal legal standards. Hence the plaintiffs had not proven their case.

This paper is a revised version of my report to the U.S. District Court, filed 29 July 1989, in *Teresa P. et al v. Berkeley Unified School District*.

APPENDIX 1[1]
Change in NCE CTBS Reading Scores,
Berkeley, Spring 1986–Spring 1987

Variable	Mean	b	Beta	SE b
NCE CTBS Reading Change	3.647			
NCE CTBS Reading 1986	29.360	−0.435*	−0.46	0.110
Father a professional	0.141	12.311*	0.33	4.358
Asian	0.483	1.920	0.07	3.462
Grade	3.737	−0.194	−0.05	0.511
Years in program	2.608	−0.327	−0.05	1.103
In bilingual program	0.316	1.896	0.07	6.102
Grade X bilingual program	0.771	−0.269	−0.03	2.213
Years in program X bil. prog.	0.975	0.515	0.07	2.496
Constant		14.450		
r^2		0.351		
N		85		

Change in NCE CTBS Language Scores

Variable	Mean	b	Beta	SE b
NCE CTBS Language Change	4.541			
NCE CTBS Language 1986	37.640	−0.282*	−0.33	0.110
Father a professional	0.141	1.118	0.03	4.801
Asian	0.483	0.732	0.03	3.604
Grade	3.737	0.281	0.07	0.538
Years in program	2.608	−0.757	−0.11	1.164
In bilingual program	0.316	6.916	0.25	6.394
Grade X bilingual program	0.771	1.287	0.16	2.323
Years in program X bil. prog.	0.975	0.119	0.02	2.619
Constant		12.274		
r^2		0.258		
N		85		

Change in NCE CTBS Math Scores

Variable	Mean	b	Beta	SE b
NCE CTBS Math Change	2.157			
NCE CTBS Math 1986	46.835	−0.534*	−0.63	0.090
Father a professional	0.141	4.981	0.10	5.425
Asian	0.483	7.184	0.21	4.328
Grade	3.737	0.507	0.10	0.646
Years in program	2.608	1.133	0.12	1.378
In bilingual program	0.316	5.280	0.14	7.673
Grade X bilingual program	0.771	1.902	0.18	2.758
Years in program X bil. prog.	0.975	−1.995	−0.21	3.122
Constant		16.971		
r^2		0.414		
N		89		

1. Tables in Appendix 1 omit the chance score estimated in Tables 4.3, 4.4, and 4.5. See footnote 61.
*Statistically significant at .05 or better.

APPENDIX 2[1]
Change in NCE CTBS Reading Scores,
Berkeley, Spring 1987–Spring 1988

Variable	Mean	b	Beta	SE b
NCE CTBS Reading Change	2.32			
NCE CTBS Reading 1987	35.17	−0.349*	−0.49	0.064
Father's occupation	30.54	0.060	0.10	0.057
Asian	0.48	−0.066	0.00	2.500
Grade	3.74	−0.382	−0.10	0.366
Years in program	2.61	−0.384	−0.06	0.781
In bilingual program	0.32	0.626	0.02	4.416
Grade X bilingual program	0.77	2.213	0.29	1.576
Years in program X bil. prog.	0.98	−2.306	−0.34	1.785
Constant		15.555		
r^2		0.267		
N		152		

Change in NCE CTBS Language Scores

Variable	Mean	b	Beta	SE b
NCE CTBS Language Change	0.95			
NCE CTBS Language 1987	41.48	−0.396*	−0.48	0.072
Father's occupation	30.54	0.117	0.16	0.065
Asian	0.48	−0.595	−0.02	2.868
Grade	3.74	0.205	0.05	0.413
Years in program	2.61	0.398	0.05	0.892
In bilingual program	0.32	−3.627	−0.12	4.995
Grade X bilingual program	0.77	−1.639	−0.19	1.793
Years in program X bil. prog.	0.98	1.140	0.15	2.031
Constant		13.577		
r^2		0.277		
N		152		

Change in NCE CTBS Math Scores

Variable	Mean	b	Beta	SE b
NCE CTBS Math Change	0.26			
NCE CTBS Math 1987	51.84	−0.468*	−0.60	0.061
Father's occupation	30.54	−0.062	−0.08	0.067
Asian	0.48	9.063*	0.28	2.954
Grade	3.74	0.386	0.79	0.427
Years in program	2.61	−0.405	−0.05	0.922
In bilingual program	0.32	−5.879	−0.17	5.167
Grade X bilingual program	0.77	−0.005	0.00	1.853
Years in program X bil. prog.	0.98	0.682	0.08	2.089
Constant		22.870		
r^2		0.406		
N		154		

1. Tables in Appendix 2 omit the chance score estimated in Tables 4.6, 4.7, and 4.8. See footnote 62.

*Statistically significant at .05 or better.

APPENDIX 3[1]
Change in NCE CTBS Reading Scores,
by Certified Bilingual/Bicultural Teacher,
Berkeley, Spring 1987–Spring 1988
(bilingual program only)

Variable	Mean	b	Beta	SE b
NCE CTBS Reading Change	3.15			
NCE CTBS Reading 1987	30.96	-0.451*	-0.59	0.092
Father's occupation	22.29	-0.037	-0.03	0.126
Grade	2.44	1.545	0.24	1.448
Years in program	3.07	-2.826*	-0.42	1.274
Certified bilingual teacher	0.71	-2.200	-0.08	4.750
Constant		24.399		
r^2		0.433		
N		61		

Change in NCE CTBS Language Scores

Variable	Mean	b	Beta	SE b
NCE CTBS Language Change	-1.61			
NCE CTBS Language 1987	40.23	-0.344*	-0.46	0.104
Father's occupation	22.29	0.009	0.00	0.147
Grade	2.44	-0.385	-0.06	1.658
Years in program	3.07	0.973	0.15	1.486
Certified bilingual teacher	0.71	-0.410	-0.02	5.520
Constant		10.266		
r^2		0.212		
N		61		

Change in NCE CTBS Math Scores

Variable	Mean	b	Beta	SE b
NCE CTBS Math Change	-4.13			
NCE CTBS Math 1987	50.25	-0.587*	-0.64	0.095
Father's occupation	22.29	0.023	0.01	0.159
Grade	2.44	3.786*	0.40	1.846
Years in program	3.07	-1.009	-0.10	1.616
Certified bilingual teacher	0.71	7.468	0.18	5.949
Constant		13.401		
r^2		0.570		
N		62		

1. Tables in Appendix 3 omit the estimated data in Tables 4.9, 4.10, and 4.11. See footnote 61.

*Statistically significant at .05 or better.

Notes

1. First Amended Complaint (Civil Rights Class Action), *Teresa P. et al v. Berkeley Unified School District*. U.S. District Court, Case no. C-37-2346 DLJ.
2. Id., at 21.
3. Id., at 22.
4. The initial list of studies on bilingual education was obtained from a search of ERIC documents, the Boston University, MIT, and the Boston Public Library card catalogues, Language and Language Behavior Abstracts, and the bibliographies of other reviews of the literature. The studies actually reviewed were those that could be obtained from (1) Educational Research and Information Center (ERIC); (2) University Microfilms International; (3) the journal and book holdings of Boston University, MIT, and the Boston Public Library; (4) the National Clearinghouse on Bilingual Education; (5) the Center for Applied Linguistics; or (6) the Department of Education. This is a fugitive literature, and not all studies are documented, nor could all documented studies be obtained.
5. These studies are listed in Rossell and Ross 1986. Two studies have been added here to the original list in that article. They are Yap, Enoki, and Ishitam 1988; and Rothfarb, Ariza, and Urrutnia 1987. Other recent studies have been rejected because of their inadequate research designs—the failure to assemble a control group or the failure to control for pretreatment differences between treatment groups.
6. This is slightly more negative than Baker and de Kanter's conclusion that 33 percent of the studies found TBE to be superior, 17 percent found it to be inferior, and 50 percent found it to be no different from submersion. Altogether, 67 percent of their studies found TBE to be no different from or worse than submersion (Baker and de Kanter 1981). Since Baker and de Kanter do not identify which studies are placed in each category in their table, I cannot explain why my conclusions differ slightly. The most likely explanation, of course, is that it is a function of my slightly different sample of studies.
7. This is also slightly more negative than Baker and de Kanter (1981). They concluded that 14 percent of the studies found TBE to be superior, 21 percent found it to be inferior, and 64 percent of the studies found TBE to be no different from submersion. Altogether, 85 percent of their studies found TBE to be no different from or worse than submersion.
8. Since there is no such thing as a perfect social science research study, all studies can be criticized on methodological grounds for political reasons. Accordingly, the AIR study (Danoff et al. 1977; Danoff et al. 1978) has been subjected to a barrage of criticism by advocates of TBE and beneficiaries of the federal support for it, who continue to create the impression that its findings have been rendered invalid. The

study, however, while not perfect, is good enough to draw policy conclusions regarding TBE as currently implemented. (See Berke 1981 for a discussion of its influence on Congress and the executive branch.) A U.S. Office of Education–sponsored review by a highly respected independent evaluation expert with no particular axe to grind concluded that the AIR conclusions were valid (Rossi 1979). Kenji Hakuta, an advocate of bilingual education, admits that "I have read the document quite thoroughly; it is technically a good, workmanlike job. . . . all in all, if I had been given the data to analyze, I probably would have derived the same conclusion" (Hakuta 1986, 220).

9. Two comparisons of ESL to bilingual education have been added to the original list in Rossell and Ross (1986). They are Yap, Enoki, and Ishitani 1988; and Rothfarb, Ariza, and Urrutia 1987.

10. Hakuta was one of the plaintiffs' experts in *Teresa P. v. Berkeley Unified School District.*

11. Adjusting for regression coefficients is invalid because it produces indeterminate results. In addition, the unadjusted mean answers the question we are interested in: what is the effect of bilingual education on English performance? If adjustment were statistically valid, it would only help us explain why we find this effect (Hedges 1986; Hedges 1981; Hedges and Olkin 1985).

12. With auxiliary teaching in Swedish.

13. Although the Jefferson Chinese bilingual program offers even less primary-language instruction — approximately 10–15 percent — there are so few LEP students in that program that it should not affect any analysis. In 1988, there were six students at Jefferson with pre and post data (or pre data that could be estimated) and in 1987 there was one student. In addition, individual LEP students receive more primary-language instruction than the class as a whole.

14. Students do not take the CTBS if they score A or B in grades K–2, A, B, or C in grades 3–6, or A in grades 7–12 on the IPT. In addition, the CTBS is not administered to high school students at all regardless of their English-language proficiency.

15. The bilingual education students are in their program for approximately a year more than the ILP students before they take the CTBS. When complete pre-post data is assembled, the differential is reduced to half a year.

16. The IPT scores are A, B, C, D, E, F, and M (mastery), with A being the lowest and M the highest.

17. The total sample is 565 but, as a result of transiency, only 362 had both 1987 and 1986 IPT data. Current ILP students who are former bilingual education students are excluded from all the analyses so as not to confound the effect of the two types of programs. When these students are excluded, the total sample size is reduced to 326. All analyses presented below exclude the bilingual education students now enrolled in ILP.

18. The main effect (i.e. the variable without the interaction) can be thought of as the effect of the ILP program and the same variable plus that variable multiplied times the bilingual program as the effect of the bilingual program.

19. Normal curve equivalent scores convert percentiles into normally distributed scores — that is, with most of the score in the middle and less at each tail. There is no difference in the findings of this study, however, regardless of whether percentiles or NCEs are used as the dependent variable.

20. There is no consistent difference in CTBS gains between the Thousand Oaks bilingual program and the other bilingual programs, and so that variable is not included in the equation.

21. A chance score was estimated for students who scored A or B in grades K–2, A, B, or C in grades 3–6, and A in grades 7–12 on the IPT the previous year, and who thus were ineligible to take the CTBS due to a lack of English proficiency. A chance score is the score a student would receive if he or she simply guessed. It is estimated by dividing the number of questions for each grade-level test by the number of items for each question. By estimating a chance score, the N is increased by approximately 30. The equations without the chance score are shown in Appendix 4.A. There is very little difference between the two, and still no significant difference between the bilingual program and the ILP.

22. In my 29 July 1988 report to the court, only elementary (K–6) students were analyzed in the 1987–88 analysis because the data for junior high school students were not available by the filing deadline for my report. There is no significant change in findings as a result of including seventh- and eighth-grade students. As with the 1987 analysis, a chance score was estimated if the previous year's score was missing but the student had taken the IPT and received a score that made them ineligible to take the CTBS. By estimating a chance score, the N is increased from 116 to 165. The equations without the chance score are shown in Appendix 4.B. There is a large difference between the two equations with no significant difference between the bilingual program and the ILP in the equation without estimated chance scores.

23. Father's occupation is a socioeconomic index derived from the 1980 census occupational classification scheme. See Stevens and Cho 1985.

24. The relationship could not be tested for the K–8 ESL students since none of the ESL teachers was ESL credentialed. Moreover, it is not clear what such an analysis means in a pullout program which only offers special instruction for three hours a week.

25. The analysis without the estimated data is shown in Appendix 4.C. It shows the same thing — no relationship between educational achievement and having a teacher with a bilingual credential.

26. A pooled cross-sectional analysis treats each year as a separate case. Thus, the N increases to a total of 301 cases when this is done.

27. In the Berkeley case, however, almost all criticism was focused on the ILP program by the time of trial.
28. Stephen Krashen was one of the plaintiffs' experts in *Teresa P.*
29. The others in the analysis include: a few schools in Baldwin Park (thirty-nine students in one analysis and eighty in another); one school in Los Angeles (Eastman Ave. Elementary); the two-way immersion schools in San Diego; one school in Calexico (Rockwood Elementary); and the Carpenteria Preschool Program in Carpenteria (Krashen and Biber 1988).
30. The Director of Bilingual Education speculates that this may be because the ILP students have higher social class than those in the bilingual program. Nobody has bothered to test this, however.
31. My suspicion was aroused by the evidence in the original evaluation that not only did the limited-English-proficient children in the program have significantly higher achievement than LEP children in other schools, but so did the *fluent*-English-proficient children. (This evidence, as well as the information on additional treatments, is omitted from Krashen and Biber's *On Course*.) Clearly, if FEP children in the program have significantly higher achievement than other FEP children in the district, the treatment effect is not solely, if at all, that of bilingual education. (See Herbert 1986.)
32. Berkeley has the lowest social class of the three school districts. The percentage of students on AFDC in Berkeley is 26 percent, in San Jose it is 14 percent and in Fremont, it is 5 percent for grade 3. Nevertheless, the same results were obtained when the regression equations were run without the control for AFDC and FEP achievement.
33. Some school districts may oppose structured immersion on philosophical grounds. The Berkeley Unified School District, for example, is opposed to such programs because they segregate students, albeit temporarily, by ethnicity and linguistic background. The bilingual education classes in Berkeley are able to enroll fluent-English-proficient students because they offer such students foreign-language instruction. A structured immersion classroom, by contrast, could not have fluent-English students in it because there is nothing special it could offer them.
34. Their address is Dinkelspiel, Donovan and Reder, No. 1 Embarcadero Center, 27th floor, San Francisco, CA 94111.

References

Arocena, M., and J. Curtis. 1984. "Same Bilingual Project, Different Gains: What Happened?" Paper presented at the annual meeting of the American Educational Research Association, New Orleans, La., Mar.

Association for Supervision and Curriculum Development. 1987. *Building an Indivisible Nation: Bilingual Education in Context*. Alexandria, Va.: Association for Supervision and Curriculum Development.

Baker, K., and A. de Kanter. 1981. *Effectiveness of Bilingual Education: A Review of the Literature*. Washington, D.C.: U.S. Department of Education.

Barik, H., and M. Swain. 1975. "Three Year Evaluation of a Large Scale Early Grade French Immersion Program: The Ottawa Study." *Language Learning* 25:1.

_____. 1978. *Evaluation of a Bilingual Education Program in Canada*. Switzerland: Commission Interuniversitaire Suisse de Linguistique Appliquée.

Barik, H., M. Swain, and E. Nwanunobi. 1977. "English-French Bilingual Education: The Elgin Study through Grade Five." *Canadian Modern Language Review* 33:459.

Berke, I. P. 1981. "Evaluation and Incrementalism: The AIR Report and ESEA Title VII." Paper presented at the annual meeting of the American Educational Research Association, New Orleans, La., Apr.

Bruck, M., J. Jakimik, and R. G. Tucker. 1971. "Are French Immersion Programs Suitable for Working-Class Children? A Follow-Up Investigation." *Word* 27:311.

Carsrud, K., and J. Curtis. 1980. *ESEA Title VII Bilingual Program: Final Report*. Austin Tex.: Austin Independent School District.

Carter, T. P., and M. L. Chatfield. 1986. "Effective Bilingual Schools: Implications for Policy and Practice." *American Journal of Education* 95 (November):201.

Clauset, K., and A. Gaynor. 1980. *Closing the Learning Gap: Effective Schooling for Initially Low Achievers*. Boston, Mass.: Boston University.

Cohen, A., A. Fathman, and B. Merino. 1976. *The Redwood City Bilingual Education Project, 1971–74: Spanish and English Proficiency, Mathematics and Language Use over Time*. Toronto, Ont.: Ontario Institute for Studies in Education.

Curtis, J. 1984. "Identification of Exemplary Teachers of LEP Students." Paper presented at the annual meeting of the American Educational Research Association, New Orleans, La., Apr.

Cziko, G. 1975. "The Effects of Different French Immersion Programs on the Language and Academic Skills of Children from Various Socioeconomic Backgrounds." Unpublished M.A. thesis, McGill University.

_____. 1976. "The Effects of Language Sequencing on the Development of Bilingual Reading Skills." *Canadian Modern Language Review* 32: 534.

Danoff, M. 1977. *Evaluation of the Impact of ESEA Title VII Spanish/English Bilingual Education Program*. Palo Alto, Calif.: American Institutes for Research.

Danoff, M., G. Coles, D. McLaughlin, and D. Reynolds. 1978. *Evaluation of the Impact of ESEA Title VII Spanish/English Bilingual Education Program*. Vol. 3: *Year Two Impact Data*. Palo Alto, Calif.: American Institutes for Research.

Dulay, H., and M. Burt., 1979. "Bilingual Education: A Close Look at Its Effects." *NCBE Focus* 1:1.

Edwards, H., and F. Smythe. 1976. "Alternatives to Early Immersion Programs for the Acquisition of French as a Second Language." *Canadian Modern Language Review* 32:24.

Engle, P. 1975. "Language Medium in Early School Years for Minority Language Groups." *Review of Educational Research* 45:283.

Epstein, N. 1977. *Language, Ethnicity, and the Schools: Policy Alternatives for Bilingual-Bicultural Education*. Washington, D.C.: Institute for Educational Leadership.

Fillmore, L. 1980. "Learning a Second Language: Chinese Children in the American Classroom." In *Georgetown University Round Table on Language and Linguistics*, edited by J. Alatis. Washington, DC.: Georgetown University Press.

Fishman, J. 1977. "The Social Science Perspective." In *Bilingual Education: Current Perspectives/Linguistics II*. Arlington, Va.: Center for Applied Linguistics.

Genesee, F. 1976. "The Suitability of Immersion Programs for All Children." *Canadian Modern Language Review* 32:494.

_____. 1978. "Individual Differences in Second Language Learning." *Canadian Modern Language Review* 34:490.

Genesee, F., W. Lambert, and G. Tucker. 1977. *An Experiment in Trilingual Education*. Montreal: McGill University.

Gersten, R. 1985. "Structured Immersion for Language Minority Students: Results of a Longitudinal Evaluation." *Educational Evaluation and Policy Analysis* 7:187.

Gray, T., R. Campbell, N. Rhodes, and M. Snow. 1984. "Foreign Language Learning in the Elementary Schools: A Comparison of Three Language Programs." Paper presented at the annual meeting of the American Educational Research Association, New Orleans, La., June.

Guthrie, E. A., W. J. Tickunoff, C. W. Fisher, and E. W. Gee. 1981. *Significant Bilingual Instructional Features Study*: Part 1, vol., 1: *Introduction and Overview of the SBIF*. San Francisco, Calif.: Far West Laboratory.

Hakuta, Kenji. 1986. *Mirror of Language: The Debate on Bilingualism*. New York: Basic Books.

Halpern, G. 1976. "An Evaluation of French Learning Alternatives." *Canadian Modern Language Review* 33:162.

Hanushek, E. A. 1986. "The Economics of Schooling: Production and Efficiency in Public Schools." *Journal of Economic Literature* 24:1, 141.

Hedges, L. V. 1986. "Issues in Meta-Analysis." In *Review of Research in*

Education 13, edited by E. Rothkopf, 353–98. Washington, D.C.: American Educational Research Association.

———. 1981. "Distribution Theory for Glass's Estimator of Effect Size and Related Estimators." *Journal of Educational Statistics* 6:107.

Hedges, L. V., and I. Olkin. 1985. *Statistical Methods for Meta-Analysis*. New York: Academic Press.

Herbert, C. 1986. *Better Communication through Bilingual Education*, Submittal Form. San Bernardino, Calif.: CHECpoint Systems, Inc.

Izzo, S. 1981. *Second Language Learning: A Review of Related Studies*. Rosslyn, Va.: National Clearinghouse of Bilingual Education.

Jones, E., and P. Davis, eds. 1977. *Final Summary Report on the Experimental Schools Project, Edgewood Independent School District*. San Antonio, Tex.: Development Associates.

Krashen, S., and D. Biber. 1988. *On Course: Bilingual Education's Success in California*. Sacramento, Calif.: California Association for Bilingual Education.

Legarretta, D. 1977. "Language Choice in Bilingual Classrooms." *TESOL Quarterly* 11:9.

Ligon, G. 1974. *ESAA Bilingual/Bicultural Project: 1973–74: Evaluation Report*. Austin Tex.: Austin Independent School District.

McConnell, B. 1980. "Effectiveness of Individual Bilingual Instruction for Migrant Students." Unpublished Ph.D. thesis, Washington State University.

———. 1982. "Evaluating Bilingual Education Using a Time Series Design." In *Applications of Time Series Analysis to Evaluation*, edited by G. Forehand. San Francisco: Jossey Bass.

Moore, F., and G. Parr. 1978. "Models of Bilingual Education." *Elementary School Journal* 79:93.

Paulston, C. Bratt. 1977. "Research." In *Bilingual Education: Current Perspectives/Linguistics II*. Arlington, Va.: Center for Applied Linguistics.

———. 1982. *Swedish Research and Debate about Bilingualism: A Critical Review of the Swedish Research and Debate about Bilingualism and Bilingual Education in Sweden from an International Perspective*. Report to the National Swedish Board of Education.

Pena-Hughes, E., and J. Solis. 1980. *ABCs*. McAllen, Tex.: McAllen Independent School District.

Peterson, S. 1990. "A Practicing Teacher's Views on Bilingual Education: The Need for Reform." In this volume.

Ramos, M., J. Aguila, and B. Sibayan. 1967. *The Determination and Implementation of Language Policy*. Cuezon City, Philippines, Phoenix Press, distributed by Oceania Publications, Dobbs Ferry, N.Y.

Rosenshine, B. 1979. "Content, Time, and Direct Instruction." In *Research on Teaching: Concepts, Findings, and Implications*, edited by P. Peterson and H. Walberg. Berkeley, Ca.: McCutchen Pub.

Rossell, C., and K. Baker. 1988. "Selecting and Exiting Students in Bilingual Education Programs." *Journal of Law and Education* 17:589–623.

Rossell, C. H., and J. M. Ross. 1986. *The Social Science Evidence on Bilingual Education*. Appendix 1. Journal of Law and Education 15:385.

Rossi, P. 1979. "Comments on Title VII Evaluation." Amherst, Mass.: University of Massachusetts.

Rotberg, I. 1982. "Some Legal and Research Considerations in Establishing Federal Policy in Bilingual Education." *Harvard Education Review* 52:149.

Rothfarb. S., M. Ariza, and R. Urrutia. 1987. *Evaluation of the Bilingual Curriculum Content (BCC) Pilot Project: A Three Year Study, Final Report*. Miami, Fla.: Dade County Public Schools.

Saville, M., and R. Troike. 1971. *A Handbook of Bilingual Education*. Washington, D.C.: Teachers of English to Speakers of Other Languages.

Stern, H. 1976. "The Ottawa-Carleton French Project: Issues, Conclusions, and Policy Implications." *Canadian Modern Language Review* 33:216.

_____. 1978. "Bilingual Schooling and Foreign Language Education: Some Implications of Canadian Experiments in French Immersion." In *Georgetown University Round Table on Language and Linguistics*, edited by J. E. Alatis. Washington, D.C.: Georgetown University Press.

Stern, H., M. Swain, L. McLean, R. Friedman, B. Harley, and S. Lapkin. 1976. *Three Approaches to Teaching French: Evaluation and Overview of Studies Related to Federally Funded Extensions of the Second Language Learning (French) Programs in the Carleton and Ottowa School Boards*. Toronto, Ont.: Ontario Ministry of Education.

Stevens, G., and J. Cho. 1985. "Socioeconomic Indexes and the New 1980 Census Occupational Classification Scheme." *Social Science Research* 42:142.

Swain, M. 1974. "French Immersion Programs across Canada: Research Findings." *Modern Language Review* 31:117.

_____. 1978. "Bilingual Education for the English-Speaking Canadian." In *Georgetown University Round Table on Language and Linguistics*, edited by J. E. Alatis. Washington, D.C.: Georgetown University Press.

Tickunoff, W. 1983. *An Emergency Description of Successful Bilingual Instruction: Executive Summary of Part I of the SBIF Study*. San Francisco, Calif.: Far West Laboratory for Educational Research and Development.

Toukamaa, P. 1980. *"Education through the Medium of the Mother Tongue of Finnish Immigrant Children in Sweden."* Bilingual Education. RELC Anthology Series No. 6. SEAMED Regional Language Centre. Singapore. University Press.

Troike, R. 1978. "Research Evidence for the Effectiveness of Bilingual Education." *NABE Journal* 3:13.

Tucker, G., W. Lambert, and A. d'Anglejan. 1973. "French Immersion Programs: A Pilot Investigation." *Language Sciences* 25:19.

Venezky, R. 1981. "Non-Standard Language and Reading—Ten Years Later." In *The Social Psychology of Reading*, edited by J. Edwards. Silver Spring, Md.: Institute of Modern Language.

Wiley, D. 1976. "Another Hour, Another Day: Quantity of Schooling, a Potent Path for Society." In *Schooling and Achievement in American Society*, edited by W. Sewell, R. Hauser, and D. Featherman. N.Y.: Academic Press.

Willig, A. 1985. "A Meta-Analysis of Selected Studies on the Effectiveness of Bilingual Education." *Review of Educational Research* 55(3): 269–317.

Yap, K., D. Enoki, and P. Ishitani. 1988. "SLEP Student Achievement: Some Pertinent Variables and Policy Implications." Paper presented at the annual meeting of the American Educational Research Association, New Orleans, La., April.

Zappert, L., and B. Cruz. 1977. *Bilingual Education: An Appraisal of Empirical Research*. Berkeley, Calif.: Berkeley Unified School District.

5

The Role of Culture
in the Acquisition of
English Literacy by
Minority School Children

Henry T. Trueba

America continues to attract many immigrants and refugees who, in search of a free, rich, and happy life, endure hardships and drastic social and cultural changes. They buy into American ideals of mass education, political participation, and economic opportunity equally accessible to all. Indeed, they learn that the very foundations of our democratic institutions are linked to ethnolinguistic diversity and the eager dedication to succeed exhibited by newcomers (Spindler 1977; Spindler and Spindler 1983, 1987a, 1987b).

The adjustment of immigrant and refugee families depends much on their ability to overcome the conflicts associated with drastic cultural changes: the new beliefs, the codes of behavior, the miscommunication, the stress, and often the prejudices they face on account of their differences. It is precisely in this context that the work of educators takes special significance (Trueba 1983, 1987a, 1987b, 1988, 1989a). Teachers are not only the key persons responsible for transmitting objective academic knowledge to all students. Teachers are the role models of American democracy, in charge of helping all children internalize cultural knowledge and values that are congruent with our social institutions.

Because refugee and immigrant children cannot succeed in our society without a high level of literacy in English, the acquisition

of the English language is crucial for them. Their overall adjustment to the new values and their participation in academic learning activities depends on how well they speak and write English.
The question is, therefore: How can one expedite the acquisition of
English? What instructional and language policies, what educational philosophy and classroom organization can maximize the
learning of English by newcomers? This question has been addressed by recent researchers (Trueba 1987a, 1987b, 1988, 1989a;
Goldman and Trueba 1987; Trueba and Delgado-Gaitan 1988; and
many others).

Persistent low literacy levels in English cannot be explained by
"linguistic deficiencies" or "cultural incongruities" only. Sociocultural, demographic, and economic factors do affect English-
literacy acquisition. Some schools, for example, have become over-
whelmed under the rapid influx of linguistic-minority children
without a tangible increase in financial resources. School administrators, teachers, and psychologists agree that English literacy is
the most critical problem in American education today (Spindler
1974, 1982; Spindler and Spindler 1983, 1987a, 1987b; Giroux and
McLaren 1986; Shulman 1987a, 1987b; Sockett 1987).

The Social Context of English Literacy

The rate of assimilation of some immigrant children is slowed
down by the trauma associated with being suddenly uprooted and
by the home values and skills that do not necessarily enhance the
literacy and other academic values stressed in this country. If we
examine the demographic distribution of language-minority
groups given in the 1980 Census data, as well as advance analysis
of recent demographic data (U.S. Bureau of the Census 1984; U.S.
Department of Commerce, 1987), we find that linguistic-minority
enrollment in our public schools will increase dramatically in the
last decade of this century and in the following years. Therefore,
the issues of cultural understanding and compassion become issues
of the survival and protection of the American dream, because the
future of our technological development, economic power, and
military power will be to a large extent in the hands of children
whose mother tongue is other than English.

As table 5.1 shows, there are approximately thirty-five million

TABLE 5.1

Estimated Numbers of Language Minority People in the United States, by Age Group, English or Non-English Language Spoken at Home, and Language, 1980

| Language | Total | Children[2] | People living in language minority families[1] | | | | | | Other home speakers of NEL's |
| | | | Aged 5-17 | | | Aged 18 and older | | | |
			Total	Speak English	Speak NEL	Total	Speak English	Speak NEL	
Total	34,637	2,562	7,948	3.466	4,482	20,616	5,549	15,067	3,511
Spanish	15,548	1,537	4,164	1,284	2,879	8,472	1,610	6,862	1,375
French	2,937	147	685	468	218	1,776	772	1,004	328
German	2,834	120	594	401	193	1,773	727	1,046	348
Italian	2,627	86	437	285	152	1,871	637	1,233	233
Polish	1,285	31	166	123	43	916	310	606	172
Chinese languages	769	58	152	37	115	476	44	432	84
Filipino languages	713	70	168	104	63	423	64	359	52
Greek	548	33	108	42	66	361	71	290	46
Japanese	542	26	98	65	33	358	114	244	59
American Indian or Alaska Native languages	512	54	155	66	89	262	59	203	41
Portuguese	480	34	103	36	67	307	57	249	35
Yiddish	430	16	41	22	20	290	76	214	83
Korean	384	40	95	36	60	224	42	182	25
Asian Indian languages	321	41	67	24	43	188	12	175	25
Arabic	312	32	64	26	38	179	37	142	38
Hungarian	266	8	37	24	12	186	55	131	36
Dutch	252	13	52	36	16	159	54	105	27
Vietnamese	250	27	75	14	61	122	15	107	27
Russian	232	10	34	15	20	152	34	117	36
Serbo-Croatian	211	10	35	16	19	146	35	110	21
Czech	194	5	26	21	5	134	46	87	29
Norwegian	814	5	26	19	7	120	48	72	34
Ukrainian	168	6	22	12	10	121	28	92	19
Swedish	163	5	22	15	7	103	43	60	33
Slovak	141	2	15	12	3	106	40	66	19
Armenian	127	6	20	7	13	89	14	75	12
Persian	138	10	24	7	17	76	14	63	28
Thai	127	17	31	11	21	66	14	52	13
Finnish	111	3	16	13	3	74	26	48	19
Lithuanian	104	2	11	8	3	73	21	52	17
Other languages	1,726	108	404	216	188	1,015	428	587	198

Source: 1980 Census of Population (Census 1984).

Note: Numbers are in thousands. Detail may not add to total because of rounding.

[1]Families in which one or more family members speak a non-English language at home.

[2]Children one or both of whose parents speak a language other than English at home.

NEL = a non-English Language.

persons in the United States who speak a language other than English at home, of whom about twenty million are not fluent in English. Almost eleven million of them are school-age children. Almost 50 percent of this linguistic-minority population (about 16 million) are Spanish-speaking. Together, French-, German-, and Italian-speaking linguistic minorities make up 24.2 percent (8.4 million). The Spanish-speaking population is concentrated in the southwestern states of California (7 million), Texas (3.8 million), Arizona (727,000), New Mexico (618,000), and Colorado (475,000) (U.S. Bureau of the Census 1984; U.S. Department of Commerce 1987).

School is a microcosm of the larger society, and as such reflects the same biases and prejudicial attitudes that become a barrier to democratic ideals of equity and educational opportunity for all. A few pseudoscientists (see, for example, Jensen 1981, and Dunn 1987) have argued that genetic differences (from a perspective of biological determinism) explain the low achievement of blacks and Hispanics. For the most part, these individuals are not taken seriously. Nevertheless, the devastating implications of their prejudicial position for instructional policy and practice has been felt in some circles. Their misunderstanding of what tests mean and in what ways they measure cultural differences rather than intelligence seems to bias their findings.

From a cultural perspective (Spindler 1977; Spindler and Spindler 1983, 1987a; Cummins 1986; Trueba 1989a) intelligence is the ability to pursue individual and group cultural goals through activities perceived as enhancing the values of the home culture. Intelligence is definitely not the ability to achieve high scores in tests constructed by individuals from a foreign culture, based on narrowly defined literacy and problem-solving settings. Cultural anthropologists (including DeVos 1983; DeVos and Wagatsuma 1966; Wagatsuma and DeVos 1984; Obgu 1974, 1978, 1987) have documented the differential performances of ethnic groups who, immigrating to diverse countries, are collectively low-achieving in one country, but high-achieving in another. The Koreans, for example, are considered outcast in Japan, yet they get recognition as outstanding students in the continental United States, Hawaii, and Europe.

Many immigrant and refugee children conduct a life of poverty and rural isolation in crowded dwellings where they lack privacy, toilet and shower facilities, comfort, and basic medical attention. In some cases migrant life for children means abuse, malnutrition, poor health, ignorance, and neglect. There is also cultural and linguistic isolation that results in cognitive underdevelopment, educational neglect, late exposure to literacy, and low school achievement, often leading to stereotypic classification into learning-disability groups.

Both lack of appreciation for one's own culture and lack of self-esteem are intimately related to the above factors, and they can also result in low aspirations and social and economic dependence on low-paying jobs. Added to this complex process of social stratification is the painful experience of incompetence and shock in dealing with mainstream persons representing social institutions such as banks, hospitals, stores, recreation facilities, churches, businesses, and service agencies. Consequently, adults who often face serious difficulties in written and oral English communication with mainstream persons depend on their children who are partially bilingual for translation. The children are forced into a position of adult responsibility relative to making economic, social, medical, and other difficult personal decisions. In this context, we can better understand the deep frustration of some Mexican-American parents in day-to-day interaction with mainstream people, and their suspicion of unfair treatment or even racism. It is tragic that these parents' feelings and views may create in children some hostility towards and misconception of mainstream values.

This initial phase of assimilation does not equally affect all of the children in the family. Older migrant children have burdens and responsibilities that younger children rarely face. Older children often describe in stronger terms their experiences working in the fields, moving around the country, living in unsanitary conditions, and feeling humiliated in schools. Some children remember when their hair was washed with kerosene or was cut in front of their peers — an inhumane attempt to solve the lice problem of children living in unsanitary conditions. Others remember their peers' calling them names or covering their noses because "Mexican kids smell and dress awful" — as some mainstream children commented.

Previous studies suggest that the differential, often minimal, participation patterns can be reduced to three main patterns:

1. Hypo-participation, or extreme efforts to be inconspicuous and to be left alone
2. Hyper-participation, which is characterized by anxious, superficial, and unproductive activities attempting to imitate others
3. Hostile/selective participation, characterized by desperate and destructive efforts to delay or prevent unpleasant participation in school activities

In a recent study (Trueba 1988, 130–42), for example, a third-grade Hmong child, Chou, and a fourth-grade Mexican child, Rosita, tended to keep their heads down on the desk the entire class period, or would just sit quietly, daydreaming as if they had completely given up attempting to cope with the world around them. Some minority children, including children from migrant families, go from a state of deep depression and psychological isolation to a state of anxiety. This is shown in their decreasing attempts to participate, or respond to questions and in their inability to focus on simple activities familiar to them. Other signs of emotional turmoil they exhibit are fear, physical restlessness, changing gaze, uncontrolled feet and hand movements, and bowel movements. These signs may increase during times of obligatory public performance if serious embarrassment is expected to result from poor performance, especially when children are reprimanded for not doing well.

While oral proficiency in English seems to persuade teachers that these language-minority children are making normal progress in school, the opposite, children's inability to rapidly acquire English-literacy skills, may lead to the classification (or misclassification) of children as "learning disabled" and ultimately may result in the drop-out phenomena (Rueda 1987).

Studies have consistently shown that linguistic-minority children's learning problems are manifested in three forms: (1) lack of overall participation in whole class activities, (2) lack of academic productivity in school and at home, and (3) the presence of vague and pervasive stress, fear, confusion, and other signs of ongoing emotional turmoil.

The following examples can illustrate our findings.

Research on linguistic-minority students' academic failures has attracted more attention than research on their successes (Ogbu

1974, 1978, 1987; McDermott 1987a; Trueba 1983). The close relationship between language, culture and cognition, and the significance of socially and culturally based theories of cognitive development and academic achievement are proposed by the socio-historical school of psychology (Vygotsky 1962, 1978; Wertsch 1985; Scribner and Cole 1981; Diaz, Moll, and Mehan 1986). The focus of efforts has been to explore how to create a culturally appropriate learning environment (congruent with the values of home culture) in order to maximize the cognitive development of children. Thus, we must face two important issues: the role of language in instruction (first and/or second language, vis-à-vis the purpose and nature of instruction), and the role of language and culture in the acquisition of English-literacy skills:

1. What is the most effective use of language in the classroom, if the primary goal of instruction is to foster cognitive growth in children?
2. If some of the literacy problems faced by limited-English proficiency (LEP) children are related to their different experiences, cultural knowledge, values, and overall background, could the use of the native language facilitate the cultural adjustment of children to school?

The English-only movement reflects the political clouds that have obscured the discussion of fundamental pedagogical principles applicable to all children. These principles suggest that cultural differences may often interfere with children's learning if the instruction ignores such differences. We all must go through cognitive processes such as automatization, encoding, cognitive construction strategies, internalization of mental procedures, and others that require a culturally congruent learning environment. In order to understand contextual clues and the nature of a cognitive task, children from other cultural and linguistic backgrounds must be given the opportunity to capitalize on what they know.

These principles must be stated and applied, even if political pressure and racial prejudice become an obstacle. One is prompted to ask: What has historically been behind such strong political movements, which attempt to curtail the use of non-English languages in educational and other public institutions? From the early 1880s, when Connecticut, Massachusetts, Rhode Island, New York, Wisconsin, and other states declared English as the mandatory school language, to the late 1960s, when the Bilingual Education Act was approved, there have been important changes. Yet the memory of jailing and subsequent trials for speaking other languages is still fresh for some older minority persons.

The education of linguistic minorities is primarily intended to help students acquire high levels of literacy so they can process information and develop their cognitive skills. Cognitive skills (the ability to structure learning tasks and knowledge itself effectively) can be best acquired through the native language and can then be easily transferred to a second language. Use of the native language to the extent that it is possible in the school setting facilitates children's ability to develop critical thinking skills. The reason is that cognitive structuring is conditioned by linguistic and cultural knowledge and experiences that children usually obtain in the home and bring with them to school (Cummins 1986; Goldman and Trueba 1987; Trueba and Delgado-Gaitan 1988; Trueba 1989b). Unfortunately, schools do not always have the resources to instruct children in their own languages; but the use of tutors and peers can help significantly.

The nature of the literacy problems faced by linguistic minorities is deeply related to their lack of such cultural knowledge that is presumed by the instructors and writers of textbook materials. Additional knowledge of children's culture and genuine respect for their home life-style can help school personnel and textbook writers to make lesson content more accessible and meaningful for minorities, prevent negative stereotypes, and raise awareness of children's learning potential.

We need to pursue a systematic socialization of students and school personnel whose main purpose is to construct a positive learning environment, to facilitate the cultural adjustment of children, and resolve the cultural conflicts arising in school. To develop such a learning environment, teachers and children need to learn a great deal more about each other, to understand each other's actual home-cultural background and previous experiences, and to engage in cooperative activities that guarantee academic success. Table 5.2 illustrates some such activities and their outcomes.

TABLE 5.2
Learning to Succeed:
Interactional Contexts and Stages of Socialization

		STAGES OF SOCIALIZATION	
		CONSTRUCTION OF SUCCESS	OUTCOMES
INTERACTIONAL CONTEXTS	COMMUNITY	Community-based counseling, legal and mental health services, basic exposure to public institutions (banks, schools, hospitals, etc.) through literacy classes. Message: "America is multicultural and your ethnic community is part of America."	Selective assimilation patterns through active participation in interethnic public activities. Collective presence in various institutional positions and roles.
	SCHOOL	Use of peer group to reinterpret degradation events and to create a climate of acceptance for cultural differences. Message: "Minority students belong here and can achieve with peer support."	Acceptance of potential success of minority students on the part of school personnel and peer groups. Increasing influence of interethnic peer groups in support of academic success.
	HOME	Reach-out efforts to help parents become strong school allies. Friendly communication for the purpose of creating a support system for the minority student. Message: "You and your child belong in our school."	Selective adult support for students. Reorganization of home life style to help students engage in academic work and provide emotional support. Knowledge of the function of school and roles of school personnel.
	SELF	On a one-to-one basis, reinterpret past experiences, overcome impact of degradation events, and engage in learning activities through personal relationships with teachers and peers. Discover actual and potential academic skills. Message: "You can succeed if you are willing to seek help."	Redefinition of and acceptance of self. Control over stress and commitment to academic work. Increased cognitive and linguistic skills to articulate abstract thought. Social skills to handle academic problems and engage in learning relationships.

We may need extra time and flexibility to place ourselves in a new cultural environment in which behavior can have different interpretations and in which the experiences we face daily in the home, school, and community have different meaning and value. Children and their teachers may come to realize that their own intra-psychological processes are linked to their "home" interpretations of events and behaviors not shared with other persons in school. Thus, in order to help children make the transition, reduce stress to tolerable levels, and participate actively in school learning activities, teachers themselves need a guarantee of academic success. Because children's adjustment to school is often impacted profoundly by the pre-arrival experiences they face, the loss and separation from relatives, and the feeling of guilt associated with this loss and separation, as well as by the many degrading and traumatic incidents (DeVos 1984) experienced by many refugees and low-status immigrants, teachers should not blame themselves for the slow progress shown by some children. Pleasant school encounters may easily lead to healing and may result in feelings of self-worth, personal safety, and happiness so that children are enabled to learn effectively.

In each of the four main interactional contexts (see table 5.2) teachers can have an impact by creating positive success experiences in children's school life, even if the success is minimum or in seemingly "nonacademic" or nonliteracy tasks. Teachers must maintain a great deal of faith in children's potential and a positive outlook on their incremental accomplishments. Consequently, teachers should have a great deal more latitude in parceling the curriculum tasks over a period of time, and in searching for strategies to maximize children's engagement in and experience of success.

Because the acquisition of academic knowledge, particularly toward the end of elementary school, requires a very sophisticated use of language, children's learning must be grounded in culturally based experiences (integral to the theory of learning postulated by the sociohistorical school of psychology led by Vygotsky—McDermott 1987a, 1987b; Goldman and McDermott 1987; Ogbu 1978, 1987; Trueba and Delgado-Gaitan 1988; Trueba 1987a, 1987b, 1989a). Consequently, the learner must play an active role in determining the whats and hows of the learning process. Naturally, the application of this theoretical position to daily practice requires a great deal of creativity and self-confidence on the part of the teacher, but the desired outcomes will occur.

Conclusion

Effective instruction for linguistic-minority children in cultural transition should be conducted in their mother tongue, and even if it must be conducted in a language not well understood by these children (English), it should be tailored to children's cultural knowledge and experiences. Furthermore, it can be conducted within a flexible organizational structure, in which teachers have a great deal more control of the instructional strategies and activities, as well as ability to take advantage of school instructional resources that increase comprehensibility (tutors; translators; parental groups; audio-visual, computer, and other technological packages; etc.).

Learning to succeed in social interactional contexts has powerful implications for success in other contexts, including strictly academic and psychological activities. Academic success helps children acquire personality integration and positive self-concept during the difficult transitional period from the home to the school culture.

In brief, school socialization for success would seem to require strategies such as the following:

1. Place students in learning environments that guarantee success, minimally at the social level, hopefully in specific academic tasks, thus converting potential failure into actual opportunities for healing, cognitive growth, and positive self-concept.
2. Identify learning strengths, skill level, and domain-specific preferences and motivation to learn, in order to make learning activities "culturally congruent" and to obtain maximum involvement of students.
3. Experiment with diverse instructional settings, experiences, and strategies, and periodically record children's responses and productivity, flexibly negotiating the level and content of what they want to learn.
4. Upon identifying a successful setting, maintain consistent, successful instructional strategies and clearly reiterate its goals, thus helping children internalize both the social norms for operating in class and the mental procedures for approaching a task.
5. Develop a creative reward system covering all ranges of guaranteed success in children's performance, taking into consideration different cultural norms and reward systems in the home.
6. Develop small groups of teachers who become colleagues and effective supporters of innovative approaches. When the academic tasks become potentially demoralizing, this group should keep teachers' morale at a high level.

The strategies outlined above, as means to engage the entire school in the process of socialization for the success of minority children, are designed to break the vicious cycle of stress, poor performance, embarrassment, and depression. Stress is minimized by guaranteeing success. When good performance is within the reach of the student's skill, there is no embarrassment, only pride and happiness, and learning becomes gratifying in itself as well as rewarding socially, taking the form of stronger personal relationships with peers and teachers. One final observation — confirmed by other studies (Trueba, 1989) — is that the development of a personal relationship between the teacher and the student is necessary to develop truly cooperative working relationships. These relationships seem to give children and teachers the perception of lowering the risks of failing and of enhancing the rewards of succeeding.

Nothing will contribute more to doing away with racial prejudice in schools, whether conscious or not, than the proof of academic success in minority children. Success attacks prejudice in its fundamental root which is the assumption that minorities are academically incompetent for reasons that keep them in that condition regardless of what teachers do. The concept itself of "learning disability," as applied to culturally different persons, must be revised in the face of demonstrated success by teachers and their students.

If, indeed, cultural conflict is at the heart of illiteracy among minority students, and if illiterate minority students have been socialized to fail by an insensitive educational system, the above strategies will help (1) sensitize the school system to develop culturally based instructional models that are effective for minorities and (2) socialize minority students to succeed academically.

References

Cummins, J. 1986. "Empowering Minority Students: A Framework for Intervention." *Harvard Educational Review* 56(1):18–53.

DeVos, G. 1983. "Ethnic Identity and Minority Status: Some Psycho-Cultural Considerations." In *Identity: Personal and Socio-Cultural* edited by A. Jacobson-Widding, 90–113. Upsala: Almquist and Wiksell Tryckeri AB.

_____. 1984. "Ethnic Persistence and Role Degradation: An Illustration from Japan." Paper read at the American-Soviet Symposium on Contemporary Ethnic Processes in the U.S.S.R., New Orleans, La., Apr.

DeVos, G., and H. Wagatsuma. 1966. *Japan's Invisible Race: Caste in Culture and Personality*. Berkeley, Calif.: University of California Press.

Diaz, S., L. Moll, and H. Mehan. 1986. "Sociocultural Resources in Instruction: A Context-Specific Approach." In *Beyond Language: Social and Cultural Factors in Schooling Language Minority Students*, 187–230. Sacramento, Calif.: Bilingual Education Office, California State Department of Education.

Dunn, L. M. 1987. *Bilingual Hispanic Children on the U.S. Mainland: A Review of Research on Their Cognitive, Linguistic, and Scholastic Development*. Circle Pines, Minnesota: American Guidance Service.

Durkheim, E. 1961. *Moral Education*. Glencoe, Ill.: Free Press.

Giroux, H., and P. McLaren. 1986. "Teacher Education and the Politics of Engagement: The Case for Democratic Schooling." *Harvard Educational Review* 26(3):213–38.

Goldman, S., and R. McDermott. 1987. "The Culture of Competition in American Schools." In *Education and Cultural Process: Anthropological Approaches*, 2nd ed., edited by G. Spindler, 282–89. Prospect Heights, Ill.: Waveland Press, Inc.

Goldman, S., and H. Trueba, eds. 1987. *Becoming Literate in English as a Second Language: Advances in Research and Theory*. Norwood, N.J.: Ablex Corporation.

Jenson, A. R. 1981. Straight Talk about Mental Tests. N.Y.: Free Press.

McDermott, R. 1987a. "Achieving School Failure: An Anthropological Approach to Illiteracy and Social Stratification." In *Education and Cultural Process: Anthropological Approaches*, 2nd ed., edited by G. Spindler, 173–209. Prospects Heights, Ill.: Waveland Press, Inc.

_____. 1987b. "The Explanation of Minority School Failure, Again." *Anthropology and Education Quarterly* 18(4):361–64.

Ogbu, J. 1974. *The Next Generation: An Ethnography of Education in an Urban Neighborhood*. New York: Academic Press.

_____. 1978. *Minority Education and Caste: The American System in Cross-Cultural Perspective*. New York: Academic Press.

_____. 1987. "Variability in Minority Responses to Schooling: Nonimmigrants vs. Immigrants." In *Interpretive Ethnography of Education: At Home and Abroad*, edited by G. Spindler and L. Spindler, 255–78. Hillsdale, N.J.: Lawrence Erlbaum Associates, Publishers.

Rueda, R. 1987. "Social and Communicative Aspects of Language Proficiency in Low-Achieving Language Minority Students." In *Success or Failure: Linguistic Minority Children at Home and in School*, edited by H. Trueba, 185–97. New York: Harper and Row.

Scribner, S. and M. Cole. 1981. *The Psychology of Literacy*. Cambridge, Mass.: Harvard University Press.

Shulman, L. 1987a. "Knowledge and Teaching: Foundations of the New Reform." *Harvard Educational Review* 57(1):1–24.

_____. 1987b. "Sounding an Alarm: A Reply to Sockett." *Harvard Educational Review* 57(4):473–82.

Sockett, H. 1987. "Has Shulman Got the Strategy Right?" *Harvard Educational Review* 57(2):208–19.

Spindler, G. 1974. "Schooling in Schoenhausen: A Study of Cultural Transmission and Instrumental Adaptation in an Urbanizing German Village." In *Education and Cultural Process: Toward an Anthropology of Education*, edited by G. Spindler, 230–71. New York: Holt, Rinehart and Winston, Inc.

_____. 1977. "Change and Continuity in American Core Cultural Values: An Anthropological Perspective." In *We the People: American Character and Social Change*, edited by G. D. DeRenzo, 20–40. Westport: Greenwood.

_____. 1982. *Doing the Ethnography of Schooling: Educational Anthropology in Action*. New York: Holt, Rinehart and Winston.

Spindler, G., and L. Spindler. 1983. "Anthropologists' View of American Culture." *Annual Review of Anthropology* 12:49–78.

_____. 1987a. *The Interpretive Ethnography of Education: At Home and Abroad*. Hillsdale, N.J.: Lawrence Erlbaum Associates.

_____. 1987b. "Cultural Dialogue and Schooling in Schoenhausen and Roseville: A Comparative Analysis." *Anthropology and Education Quarterly* 18(1):3–16.

Trueba, H. 1983. "Adjustment Problems of Mexican American Children: An Anthropological Study." *Learning Disabilities Quarterly* 6(4):8–15.

_____. 1987a. *Success or Failure? Learning and the Language Minority Student*. New York: Newbury/Harper and Row.

_____. 1987b. "Organizing Classroom Instruction in Specific Sociocultural Contexts: Teaching Mexican Youth to Write in English." In Goldman and Trueba 1987.

_____. 1988. "English Literacy Acquisition: From Cultural Trauma to Learning Disabilities in Minority Students." *Journal of Linguistics and Education* I:125–152.

_____. 1989a. *Raising Silent Voices: Educating Linguistic Minorities for the 21st Century*. New York: Harper and Row.

_____. 1989b. "Rethinking Dropouts: Culture and Literacy for Minority Student Empowerment." In *What Do Anthropologists Have to Say About Dropouts?* edited by H. Trueba, G. Spindler, and L. Spindler, 27–42. London: Falmer Press.

Trueba, H., and C. Delgado-Gaitan, eds. 1988. *School and Society: Learning Content through Culture*. New York: Praeger Publishers.

U.S. Bureau of the Census. 1984. *1980 U.S. Census*. Current Populations Report. Washington, D.C.: U.S. Government Printing Office.

U.S. Department of Commerce. 1987. "The Hispanic Population in the United States: March 1986 and 1987 (Advance Report)." Washington, D.C.: U.S. Government Printing Office.

Vygotsky, L. S. 1962. *Thought and Language*. Cambridge, Mass.: MIT Press.

_____. 1978. *Mind in Society: The Development of Higher Psychological Processes*, edited by M. Cole, V. John-Teiner, S. Scribner, and E. Souberman. Cambridge, Mass.: Harvard University Press.

Wagatsuma, H., and G. DeVos. 1984. *Heritage of Endurance: Family Patterns and Delinquency Formation in Urban Japan*. Berkeley, University of California Press.

Wertsch, J. 1985. *Vygotsky and the Social Formation of the Mind*. Cambridge, Mass.: Harvard University Press.

6

Promoting English Literacy

Herbert J. Walberg

Americans have aimed at universal literacy, but we have yet to succeed. How serious is the shortcoming? And what can we do about it? A 1980 survey of a cross section of workers showed that nearly all read each day, and they averaged about two hours at it. With about half the workers now in the "knowledge" industries, the capacity to communicate, especially to read, determines in part the welfare of the nation (Walberg 1987). Yet, as Miller (1988) pointed out, "semi-literacy" is a way of life for millions of Americans. Many are unable to read, follow directions, fill out job applications, and have confidence in everyday affairs. Their children, moreover, may not gain early language competencies to succeed at school, college, and work.

The literacy problem is generally more extensive among the poor and among immigrants from countries in which English is not the primary language. Semi-literacy rates are higher among blacks and Hispanics than whites, even though the number of semi-literate whites is highest.

Background

Achievement of English Literacy

In many English-speaking homes, children and youth experience vernacular language and culture that impede their progress in school and middle-class society (Miller 1988). From the 1974–75 to the 1983–84 school year, for example, reading proficiency rose slightly for nine-, thirteen-, and seventeen-year-olds. Whites, however, continued to excel; and blacks lagged behind Hispanics. Only about 39 percent of all seventeen-year-olds for the later period were able to "find, understand, summarize, and explain relatively complicated literary and informational material." Only about 5 percent were able to "understand the links between ideas . . . when not explicitly stated and to make appropriate generalizations . . . when texts lack clear introductions and explanations" (Miller 1988, 1,294).

Many young adults, aged twenty-one to twenty-five, lacked practical literacy: 44 percent lacked the ability required to locate information in a news article or almanac; 43 percent lacked the ability to follow directions to travel from one location to another using a map; and 44 percent lacked the ability to enter deposits and checks, and to balance a checkbook (Walberg 1989b).

International Comparisons

Citizens know about such language problems among large groups of children and youth. Educators refer to them as disadvantaged, limited-English-proficiency (LEP), language handicapped, and at risk. However, until the publication of the National Commission for Excellence in Education's (1983) *A Nation at Risk*, few Americans knew that the achievement of most of our students was very low by international standards in mathematics and science—the subjects most reasonable to compare. More recent test scores offer even more gloomy prospects. Of average eighth-grade students in twenty countries and provinces, those in the United States ranked twelfth in algebra, sixteenth in geometry, and eighteenth (above Swaziland and Nigeria) in measurement. Of twelfth graders in fifteen countries, those in the United States scored fourteenth in advanced algebra and twelfth in elementary functions and calculus.

Among the top 1 percent of twelfth graders in each of the fifteen countries, U.S. students scored worst in algebra. They exceeded in functions and calculus only British Columbia—a province that omits these subjects in high school. These findings are consistent with the conclusion that 1.5 million American seventeen-year-olds are unable to reason mathematically (National Assessment of Educational Progress 1988).

Consider science achievement: although near the international average at grades four and five, U.S. students exceed only those in the Philippines and Singapore among seventeen countries at grades eight and nine. Among advanced twelfth-grade students in fourteen countries, those in the United States ranked last in biology, eleventh in chemistry, and ninth in physics. As suggested by recent studies, the short school year, the lack of curriculum rigor and uniformity, inefficient and repetitive teaching, little homework, and a lack of parental involvement seem to be the major causes of meager U.S. achievement by international standards (Walberg 1989b).

Conditions of Youth Literacy

The conditions that affect youth language present a mixed and changing picture (Walberg 1989a). For example, the average per-pupil expenditures (in 1985–86 dollars) of public schooling rose 2.7 times, from $1,571 in 1955–56 to $4,206 in 1986–87. During the same period, pupil/teacher ratios declined from thirty to nineteen in elementary schools and twenty-one to sixteen in secondary schools.

Despite rising educational resources, family conditions for literacy deteriorated from 1950 to 1985; for example, the number of divorces per thousand married women doubled from ten to twenty-two. Several indicators of family difficulties roughly tripled: the percentage of children (under eighteen) whose families underwent a divorce during the year rose from .6 to 1.7 percent. The percentage of children in single-parent families rose from 7.1 to 21.0 percent. By group, the most recent percentages were 52 for blacks, 26 for Hispanics, and 16 for whites.

For the period 1950 through 1986, however, median family income doubled from $15,117 to $29,458 (in 1986 dollars). At the end of the period, median income was $17,604 for blacks, $19,995 for Hispanics, and $30,809 for whites.

From 1950 to 1985 the rates of serious diseases affecting youth changed remarkably: polio was conquered; measles and syphilis declined sharply. Gonorrhea, however, rose substantially from a high rate, and AIDS incidence about doubled from 1985 to 1986 (from a minuscule base rate).

The percent of high school students drinking alcohol within the past month varied from a substantial 65 to 72 percent and showed little variation from 1975 to 1986. By the same criterion, marijuana use showed rates of 23 to 34 percent during that period, and peaked in 1980. Although heroin use remained less than .5 percent, cocaine use rose from about 2 to 6 percent (from 1975 to the 1986 classes). LSD use declined from above 2 percent to below 2 percent; and PCP use remained at around 1.5 percent.

The annual number of crimes committed against youth aged sixteen through nineteen was sixty-eight per thousand: fifty-four were assaulted, eleven were robbed, and two were raped. Rates of assault and robbery were generally higher for males than females and for blacks than whites.

From 1950 to 1985, arrest rates per thousand under-eighteen-year-olds multiplied thirty times, from 4 to 119. In 1985, the most frequent causes for arrest for fourteen- to seventeen-year-olds were (in order) burglary, alcohol and weapons violations, assaults (other than aggravated), vehicle thefts, disorderly conduct, and drug abuse.

These grim numbers suggest that several conditions that affect literacy among children and youth have declined. Even the additional resources for education probably made little difference, since expenditures and class sizes are unlinked to the quality of education and learning.

The Case for English Literacy

Why should we worry? Several arguments seem reasonable and persuasive. First, parents most affected by language policies in schools strongly desire English mastery for their children (Educational Testing Service 1988). This national survey, of parents of school-aged Asian, Puerto Rican, Mexican-American, and Cuban elementary and secondary school students, concluded:

> "All parents first and foremost want their children to achieve in school and learn English. . . . Asian and Hispanic parents all overwhelmingly agree on the responsibility of the school to teach children English language skills. (p. *i*)

"A large majority of parents," moreover, "believe that it is the family's [rather than the school's] responsibility to teach children about the history and tradition of their ancestors" (p. *ii*).

Public education, moreover, is "a public good." Citizens pay for it because it presumably benefits not only students but society as a whole. Citizens expect a common core of culture, knowledge, and language to be taught. Individuals and groups are free to pursue special interests as electives or at their own expense; but all are expected to master the usual school subjects, which require English-language skills, namely, speaking, listening, reading, and writing. English vocabulary, moreover, constitutes the most pervasive factor in U.S. intelligence tests; and these tests are the best predictors of academic accomplishment in civics, science, and other subjects, probably because mastering a subject requires mastering its vocabulary.

Some historians believe, in addition, that we need to enlarge students' knowledge of American culture, geography, history, and literature to remain a cohesive nation. Students who remain culturally illiterate or ignorant of our national language and heritage may be unable to participate in civic life (Hirsch 1987; Ravitch and Finn 1988).

American youth themselves have raised their sights to intellectually demanding careers that demand English mastery both to acquire knowledge and to advance professionally. In 1977, for example, girls most often expected to become (in order of frequency) a secretary, teacher, nurse, medical technician, or model. Today, the professions — medicine, business, and law — lead girls' lists. In 1977, boys expected to become a skilled worker, engineer, lawyer, teacher, or athlete. Today, computers and electronics, business, skilled worker, medicine, engineering, law, and military service are boys' leading expectations (Walberg 1989a).

Those youth likely to advance themselves through education believe English mastery is critical: of high school students who plan to go to college, three-fourths strongly agree that good writing and communication skills are necessary for almost any job. Half similarly agree that top jobs in business go to people with a well-rounded education.

Given that citizens, educators, parents, and students themselves subscribe to the goal of promoting learning in general and English mastery in particular, how can they best go about it?

Promoting Learning: Nine Factors

In recent years, several breakthroughs have occurred in the analyses of large-scale educational surveys and in the syntheses of thousands of educational research results. In 1979, several psychologists wrote an article called "The Quiet Revolution in Educational Research" (Walberg, Schiller, and Haerterl 1979). Five years later, the results of nearly three thousand studies could be analyzed and reported (Walberg 1984). Recently, an Australian–U.S. team assessed 134 reviews of 7,827 field studies and several large-scale U.S. and international surveys of learning.

Recently published was a compact summary of these plus the findings of several hundred still more recent studies (Walberg 1989c). It begins with the effects of the psychological elements of teaching and discusses methods and patterns of teaching—all of which can be accomplished by a single teacher without unusual arrangements and equipment. It then turns to systems of instruction that require special planning, student grouping, and materials. Next described are effects that are unique to reading, writing, science, and mathematics. These findings show that nine factors increase learning. Potent, consistent, and widely generalizable, these nine factors fall into the three groups shown in table 6.1.

Collectively, the various studies suggest that the nine factors are powerful and consistent in influencing learning. These factors are the chief influences on academic achievement and, more broadly, school related cognitive, affective, and behavioral learning (Walberg 1984). Many aspects of these factors, especially the amount and quality of instruction, can be altered by educators; these deserve attention in improving opportunities for at-risk youth. The most recent compilation of results of some eight thousand studies supports the idea that some instructional methods and techniques work much better than others (Walberg 1989c). Educators are in a much better position today to select methods and techniques that have the largest and most consistent effects on students' learning.

Each of the first five factors—prior achievement, development, motivation, and the quantity and quality of instruction—appears necessary for learning in school; without at least a small amount of each, the student can learn little. High degrees of ability, for example, may count for little if students are unmotivated.

TABLE 6.1
Nine Educational Productivity Factors

Student Aptitude

1) **Ability** or preferably **prior achievement** as measured by the usual achievement tests

2) **Development** as indexed by chronological age or level of maturation

3) **Motivation** or self concept as indicated by personality tests or the student's willingness to persevere intensively learning tasks

Instruction

4) the **amount** of time students engage in learning

5) the **quality** of the instructional experience including method (psychological) and curricular (content) aspects

Psychological Environments

6) the **"curriculum of the home"**

7) the **morale** of classroom social group

8) the **peer group** outside school

9) minimum leisure-time **television viewing**

Quality of Instruction

The quality or method of instruction may be the most obvious factor for improvement, and it is worthwhile knowing how the usual practice, sometimes called "direct teaching," can excel. Since it has evolved for decades from school classes, direct teaching is relatively easy to carry out and it does not disrupt conventional institutions and expectations. It can, moreover, incorporate many psychological elements and methods. Early reviews of research suggested the psychological traits and behaviors of direct teachers: clarity, task orientation, enthusiasm, and flexibility. From later research, six activities of such teaching could be identified:

1. Daily review, homework check, and if necessary, reteaching
2. Rapid presentation of new content and skills in small steps
3. Guided student practice with close teacher monitoring
4. Corrective feedback and instructional reinforcement
5. Independent practice in seatwork and homework with a high, more than 90 percent, success rate
6. Weekly and monthly review.

A newer method, "comprehension teaching," values two-way interactive teaching and devolving autonomy to the learner. Using this method, teachers work within "a zone of proximal development" extending from what learners can do independently to the maximum they can do with the teacher's help. Accordingly, such teachers set up "scaffolding" for building knowledge but remove it when it becomes unnecessary. In mathematics, for example, the teacher can give hints and examples, foster independent use, and then remove support. This approach is similar to the "prompting" and "fading" of the behavioral cues and to common sense, but it sufficed to revive interest in transferring increased control over the learning process to learners themselves.

The 1980s cognitive research on teaching sought ways to encourage self-monitoring, self-teaching, or "metacognition" to foster independence. Skills were important, but the learner's monitoring and management of them have primacy; planning, allocating time, and review were partly transferred to learners. One scheme, for example, outlined three phases: (1) modeling, where the teacher exhibits the desired behavior; (2) guided practice, where the student performs with help from the teacher; and (3) application, where the student performs independently of the teacher. "Reciprocal teaching," as a further example, fosters comprehension by having students take turns in leading dialogues on pertinent features of the text. By assuming planning and executive control ordinarily exercised by teachers, students learn planning, structuring, and self-management. Perhaps that is why tutors learn from teaching, and why we say that to learn something well, teach it.

Comprehension teaching encourages readers to measure their progress toward explicit goals. If necessary, they can reallocate time for different activities. In this way, self-awareness, personal control, and positive self-evaluation can be enlarged.

Quantity of Instruction

From a curriculum standpoint, time, or amount of instruction, is the central and irreducible ingredient among the alterable factors in learning: the acquisition of a chunk or item of information requires an estimated five to ten seconds, relating it "meaningfully" to already-assimilated information requires additional seconds, and problem solving or discovery by trial-and-error combinations of chunks may take minutes, hours, days, or years.

Students may have the ability and motivation to acquire all basic human knowledge and to master dozens of languages. In principle, we may also be able to teach all this. What is lacking is time — a finite resource. Educators must choose a very limited part of all human knowledge and of the world's language to convey. Even this may be difficult since, as indicated above, many young adults wind up ill-informed and semi-literate even in their home language.

Moreover, only part of the time allocated for learning in school and outside study is employed efficiently. Quality of instruction, for example, can be understood as providing optimal cues, correctives, and reinforcement to ensure the fruitfulness of engaged time. Diagnosis and tutoring can help provide instruction suitable to the individual student. Inspired teaching can enhance motivation to keep students persevering. Quality of instruction, then, may be considered as efficient enhancement of allocated or engaged learning time.

Similarly, the four psychological environments can enlarge and enhance learning time. Good classroom morale may reflect a good match of the lesson to student aptitude, the socially stimulating properties of the academic group, or, in general, the degree to which students are concentrating on learning rather diverting their energies because of unconstructive social climates. Constructive peer groups outside school and stimulating home environments can help by enlarging learning time and enhancing its efficiency; students can both learn in these environments as well as become more able to learn in formal schooling.

Finally, television can displace homework, leisure reading, and other stimulating activities, and it may dull the student's keenness for academic work. For instance, some of the average of twenty-eight hours a week spent viewing television by high school students might usefully be added to the mere four or five weekly hours of homework they report.

Matthew Effects

Students who are behind at the beginning of schooling or who are slow to start often learn at a slower rate, and those that start ahead gain at a faster rate, which results in what has been called "Matthew effects" of the academically rich getting richer, originally noted in the Bible[1] (Walberg and Tsai 1983). This effect characterizes school learning, family, influences on development, and socioeconomic advantages in communication among adults as well as the development of reading comprehension and verbal literacy (Stanovich 1986). Ironically, although improved instructional programs may benefit all students, they may confer greater advantages on those who are initially advantaged. For this reason, the first six years of life and the "curriculum of the home" are decisive influences on academic achievement (Walberg 1984; U.S. Department of Education 1986).

A paper in *Science* by Stevenson, Lee, and Stigler (1986) provides a striking illustration of the Matthew effect. They carefully observed and tested Japanese, Taiwanese, and U.S. students in elementary school mathematics classes. Cross-nationally calibrated IQ tests showed that all three groups were equally able at the start of schooling; but with each year, Asian students drew further ahead in achievement. A small achievement advantage at the end of the first grade grew ever larger, so that by fifth grade, the worst Asian class in the sample exceeded the best American class.

The Asian students had a far more rigorous curriculum and worked at a faster pace. They studied far more at school and, with their parents' encouragement, at home. In the United States, success was more often attributed to ability; in Asia, to hard work. Like the dangers of racial, ethnic, and special-education classifications, ability tests may encourage a belief in educational predestination rather than effort as the key to achievement.

Content Counts

The amount of time spent on learning can be indexed (albeit imprecisely) by how many courses students take in a given subject and the number of items of content their teachers cover during a course or year. Studies in the United States and in other countries show that such indexes are strongly associated with how much students learn. Since time is finite, it must be carefully allocated to be sure that students master English and other essentials.

The International Association for the Evaluation of Educational Achievement (IEA) first showed compellingly the powerful effects of content exposure on learning. Although such exposure may not vary much within countries, especially within those with strong central ministries of education such as France and Japan, it varies widely among countries. The IEA group measured such content exposure in various ways, such as number of courses, hours of lessons during the year, standards, and test items covered in classes. These exposure indexes were among the most strong and consistent correlates of learning within and across countries. Even controlled for other productivity factors, such indexes typically yielded significant effects; such results were demonstrated in civics, English and French as foreign languages, literature, mathematics, reading comprehension, and science (Postlethwaite 1975, 28–29).

Within the United States, the National Assessment of Educational Progress (NAEP) offers further evidence of the powerful effects of content exposure. Although the effects emerge in analyses of data at several age levels in reading, social studies, and science (Walberg 1986), they can be most clearly seen in high school mathematics, since there is reasonable consensus about the subject matter (for example, trigonometry in contrast to Western history of English literature). On the NAEP mathematics test for seventeen-year-olds, for example, the scores correlated directly and strongly with the rated rigor of the highest course taken (ranging from consumer mathematics to calculus) and with the number of mathematics courses completed (.63 and .62). Dreeban and Barr's (1987) studies of the impact of word coverage on vocabulary acquisition and reading comprehension also showed strong associations.

Language Learning

Considerable research has been carried out on language learning, particularly oral comprehension and reading. Several well-established points have implications for teaching English and other subjects to ordinary and to limited-English-proficient students. These are discussed in this section.

Time and Learning

If students vary only slightly in their exposure to subject matter or language exposure, say, fifty versus fifty-two hours or weeks, we expect to find only minor, perhaps undetectable variations in their performance associated with the amount of time spent. If exposure varies substantially, however, we expect to find big differences in how well they do. Think of the differences among students with a few weeks versus those with four years of high school French, or a few days versus a year living in Paris with a French family; time then will appear as a large determinant of learning.

Consider also how long it might take us to master Japanese, Swahili, or Urdu. Yet all normal children in their cultures master these languages with apparently effortless ease. Why? Because of the amount and intensity of full-day exposure, day upon day over a period of years, and also because of the motivation to understand and be understood by family, peers, and significant others.

Consider students' usual exposure to language in school: the twelve years of 180 six-hour days in elementary and secondary school add up to about 13 percent of the waking time during the first eighteen years of life under the following assumptions and calculations:

- 18 years × 365 days × 24 hours = 157,680 total hours
- 18 years × 365 days × 9 hours = 59,130 sleeping hours
- 157,680 total hours − 59,130 sleeping hours = 98,550 waking hours
- 12 years × 180 days × 6 hours = 12,960 school hours

Schooling is 12,960 ÷ 157,680 or 8.2 percent of all hours and schooling is 59,130 ÷ 98,550 or 13.2 percent of waking hours.

Not all this school time, however, is used effectively for learning, since some allocated time is wasted on absences, lateness, inattentiveness, disruptions, noninstructional activities, and lessons that are too easy, too hard, or otherwise unsuitable. Thus, both lengthening school time and making it more efficient seem likely to benefit learning.

Through the formative years, however, until the end of high school, parents nominally control 87 percent of the student's waking time. Not only is this by far the largest fraction of the student's time, but it strongly influences the productivity of the small fraction of time spent in school.

From the start, students with limited-English-proficiency (LEP) have several disadvantages: by definition, when they start school, they know less oral (and written) English; they are often from larger families of lower socioeconomic status that speak little or no English—all factors that have been shown to impede learning (see evidence cited below). Specifically, this initial handicap in listening and speaking vocabulary is likely to impede their acquisition of "decoding" (figuring out the meaning of written words by their apparent sounds). This inability, in turn, impedes growth in their reading vocabulary and comprehension, and their achievement in all school subjects including social studies, science, and even mathematics, since they are mediated by language.

Since LEP children are handicapped at the start, they are likely to fall further behind because they are less efficient at acquisition. Unless they can soon catch up, they are likely to be subject to discouraging Matthew effects, that is, cumulative or ever-widening deficits. As noted above, this effect has been repeatedly demonstrated in education in general and in reading in particular.

Even during the school years, say, ages six to eighteen (or nineteen), LEP children are likely to have further handicaps with respect to the amount and quality of English exposure. For example, if their parents and neighborhood peers speak less English or speak it less well, they will have even less opportunity to practice and improve their verbal knowledge and skill. If their parents listen and watch primary-language radio and television programs, they and their children will make less progress. If they are unaware of the child's schoolwork or are unable to give full encouragement and support for academic effort, the child will have still more limited opportunity. Finally, if less English is spoken in all these extramural settings, LEP children will have still less rational reason to master English as a practical everyday skill. For all these reasons, to deny LEP children maximum English exposure in school would be a great disservice and injustice against their best interests.

Development of Language Skills

How do American children ordinarily learn English? Jeanne Chall (1983) of Harvard University has carefully documented several stages in developing listening and reading skills:

- In "prereading," birth to age six, the child learns to listen and comprehend oral language.
- In "initial reading," ages six to seven, the child learns "decoding," or the realization and memorization of letter-sound correspondences.
- In "fluency," the child begins to focus on content and develop speed and "automatization" in decoding.
- In "reading to learn" (in contrast to learning to read) reading becomes the procedure no longer to be learned but developed further in terms of vocabulary, comprehension, and speed and also to learn content of academic subjects and to use in everyday life.

In recognition of need for early oral mastery, public and private agencies spend millions of dollars on preschool, prereading programs to enlarge at-risk children's oral vocabulary and comprehension of oral language. The purpose of this vast effort is to facilitate the acquisition of the higher levels of language ability, reading in particular. Reading, of course, is the main way that children acquire knowledge in school. By seventh grade, most students can comprehend more by reading than listening. For those that acquire proficiency, moreover, reading is three or four times faster than listening (Sticht and James 1984).

Poor Readers

Poor children on average start off behind in oral skills and later read less well than those from middle-class families. The discrepancy, moreover, increases with age. Middle-class homes are more likely to have books, magazines, well-chosen toys, and other objects that stimulate intellectual and language growth. In addition, middle-class parents more often have high performance expectations for their children that develop the motivation to achieve well with words and in school. Many studies, including those of Chicano children, show that this "curriculum of the home" positively affects academic progress.

Lower socioeconomic-status (SES) parents, moreover, often take over for their children rather than letting them independently carry out their own tasks. Lower-socioeconomic status parents more often view the school as a distant, rather formidable institution over which they have little control. They engage in less-effective teaching strategies and lack confidence in their childrens' school performance. From such conditions children can acquire "learned helplessness," feelings of insufficiency, and anxiety (Wigfield and Asher 1984).

Such feelings may distract children from time on task in school. When processes such as decoding are inefficient, they require too much direct attention or too much working-memory capacity; the mental resources available for other processes may be insufficient. Word recognition tasks, for example, may interfere with the comprehension of meaning.

Feelings of either frustration or satisfaction may have enormous consequences for how much time children read and develop their skills further. Anderson, Wilson, and Fielding (1986), for example, in a study of daily time logs of fifth graders, reported large differences in amounts of daily reading among children: The number of minutes of reading varied from 0 to 71 minutes per day (2nd and 98th percentiles) with a median of 11.1; the number of words read per year varied from 8 to 4,700,000, with a median of 601,000. These enormous variations in reading, of course, lead to large differences in childrens' vocabularies and comprehension abilities.

Time and practice, however, can compensate for or remedy initial disadvantages. Given sufficient exposure or instruction, children, and even adults, can make rapid progress in learning difficult languages. "'Immersion' methods, for example, can bring about striking rates of acquisition. The Army Language School set 1,300 hours of instruction as a standard for an adult to achieve near native competence in Vietnamese. A child who spends about ten hours a day in school, in play, and with media in English might gain comparable, though seemingly natural and effortless, experience in 130 days" (Walberg, Hase, and Rasher 1978, 428).

In addition to natural exposure, sustained effort can also produce impressive results. Simon's (1954) "Berlitz model" of learning a foreign language assumes that an individual can choose the amount of practice, that practice makes the language activity easier, that ease increases the pleasantness of the activity, and that pleasantness increases practice. He hypothesizes that excessive difficulty slows practice because it is unpleasant; but if practice persists through temporary difficulty, it will become pleasant and the student will persist to achieve mastery.

All natural languages, moreover, apparently have an inherent characteristic that makes them easy to learn at the start: a very small number of different words (usually small ones such as *is, am, be,* and *the* in English) comprise most of the oral and written discourse. (Basic English and other easier-to-learn schemes are based on this principle). The word *the* comprises 7 percent of the words in a sample of five million in school textbooks. About a hundred different words comprise half of all the words; and about a tenth of the different words comprise about 95 percent of all words.

The letters of alphabets are also skewed (*e* is many times more frequent than *q* and *z*). Word parts also follow "the higher, the fewer" principle, as reported by the frequency of "ngrams" (initial and final clusters of letters in words). The tabulations of the highly skewed ngrams can be used to select frequent ones, such as *th,* for teaching oral recognition, phonics, and word recognition.

Word associations, possibly indicative of common thought patterns, are also skewed. A typical pattern is the association response to the word *on* among fourth-grade boys: in order of frequency, eighty-eight boys responded *off*; twenty-one *top*; and so on to such words as *bed* and *time,* which were each given once by separate boys (Walberg, Strykowski, Rovai, and Hung 1984).

Such distributions mean that children, after they acquire a few words, will be able to recognize many words in oral and written language. Children, nonetheless, must be constantly exposed to new and more-difficult words. Although they learn in part by repetition, after thorough mastery they need to be challenged with ever-more-difficult words and concepts. Families, peer groups, and schools are the chief agencies for exposure and deliberate instruction. They powerfully influence what children and youth learn. In large part, their content and language determine what children and youth learn. To the extent that they expose students to large amounts of English and increase the rigor of vocabulary in accordance with childrens' abilities, they promote English mastery.

Second Language Learning

Immigrant children have a difficult time in school, but much of their difficulty is attributable to lower socioeconomic origins. The Paris-based Organization for Economic Cooperation and Development (1987) carried out the most extensive study of this problem. Its aim was to assess, as objectively as possible, the progress of 2.5 million immigrant children in seven European countries — Belgium, France, Germany, Luxembourg, the Netherlands, Sweden, and Switzerland — and two non-European countries — Australia and Canada.

These children were overrepresented in special education, constituting 6 percent of foreign pupils versus 2.8 percent of nationals in special primary education in four comparable countries. More young foreigners than nationals were in shorter or less-difficult tracks of secondary education. A high percentage of foreign students failed to acquire a solid general school grounding. Differences in educational performance by nationals and foreigners were not so great where the foreign children's families had been resident in the host country for a long time.

The major conclusions about the reasons for foreign students' problems were these:

> Social background is the major explanatory factor in under-achievement. Children who belong to a disadvantaged social class, whether they are foreigners or not, whether they belong to an ethnic minority group or to the majority, tend to be low achievers or failures at school and obtain results that are on average lower than those of children belonging to the middle or upper classes. Social background is a more a determinant factor in under-achievement than nationality. (p. 10)

Moreover,

> It was found that, out of all the variables tested, social background understood as the socioeconomic category of the head of household, with all that implied for the child's environment and quality of life, was the most convincing explanatory factor. The effect of socioeconomic category was, moreover, enhanced when combined with other, frequently related, characteristics, such as family size and the degree of education of the parents. (p. 184)

Finally,

> The figures show that when there are a number of alternative streams available, the enrollment rate of foreign children is always higher than that of nationals in those streams or cycles which either require only minimal qualifications or provide only a short course of instruction. (p. 33)

Similar conclusions have been reached about immigrant students to the United States, particularly the currently largest group, Hispanics. The National Assessment of Educational Progress surveys illustrate the pattern. Applebee, Langer, and Mullis (1987) summarize as follows:

- "High schools graduate 700,000 functionally illiterate young people every year, and another 700,000 drop out. In 16 states, dropout rates range from 26 percent to 42 percent, and most big cities are on the high end" (p. 3).
- "Today, 9 out of ten colleges offer noncredit remedial courses in English and math to their incoming freshmen. The U.S. Department of Education says that as many as three out of five high school graduates who enter college require remedial work" (p. 4).
- "At all three grade levels, Hispanic and Black students read and write less well than their White classmates [grades 4, 8, and 11]" (p. 20).
- "As a group, Black and Hispanic students are well behind White students by grade 4, and the difference is not made up even for those who attend college" (p. 22).
- "Most young adults feel that their literacy skills are appropriate for their present jobs, but many Black and Hispanic young adults also recognize the importance of improving these literacy skills if they are to obtain better jobs" (p. 22).
- "The national assessments of the performance of children in school have also examined a few general aspects of their educational experience, such as the amount of homework they have completed recently, the number of pages of reading they have done for school, and the number of writing assignments completed. . . . The findings indicate a consistent, positive relationship between the amount of schoolwork and achievement in both reading and writing" (pp. 29–30).
- "Children of at-risk minorities and of the urban disadvantaged continue to be caught in a pattern of poor achievement that cannot be broken without more effective efforts at home and school" (p. 43).

Does Bilingual Education Work?

A controversial program for solving the problems of non-English-proficient immigrant children and youth is (transitional) bilingual education. The idea is to teach English as a second language for some fraction of the school day and use the home or first language as the medium for instruction for the substantive school subjects such as civics and science until students master English.

Such programs are or would be costly to provide and administer. If designed according to such first principles, for example, they would require for each subject such as physics and auto shop as many teachers as there are home languages such as Vietnamese and Swedish spoken in a district (as many as 130). Students themselves would pay a heavy penalty, since they would be segregated from the mainstream of school life.

Because entrance criteria for such programs are so lax or nondiscriminating, moreover, as many as a third of students whose home language is English-only would be classified for bilingual programs. Since exit criteria are set so high — higher, for example, than many monolingual English-speaking children could attain — it is nearly impossible, once a child is classified for some programs, to enter regular school programs.

All this might be tolerated if it could be shown that bilingual programs teach English better, which is the central problem they are intended to solve. Or, at least, that is the central problem as seen by most citizens and educators, as well as most immigrant parents and children. Unfortunately, little consistent evidence can be cited.

Much of the research has been done by advocates of bilingual programs who stand to benefit from their continuation and expansion. Besides, as Rossell (1988) has documented, much of the research is flawed in ways that appear to make bilingual education more effective than it actually is. The chief flaw is to analyze the English progress of children in bilingual programs without examining the gains of comparable children in control groups that might have made similar or better progress. Another flaw is the inclusion of additional special instructional procedures in the bilingual program which, if used in the control group, would lead to superior results.

Nearly all reviews of rigorous controlled studies show no advantage of bilingual programs over other alternatives. Rossell and Ross's (1986) review of thirty-six studies contrasted the results of bilingual education with three other approaches: (1) "English as a second language," in which children are taught English part of the day and participate in regular classes the rest of the day; (2) "structured immersion," in which instruction is in English but the teacher knows the child's home language; and (3) "submersion," in which students are placed in regular classes with no special treatment.

The results showed no consistent superiority of bilingual education over the other programs. Seventy-one percent of the language-gain comparisons, for example, showed bilingual education to be no different or worse than submersion, that is, doing nothing. In mathematics, 93 percent of the comparisons showed bilingual education to be equal to or worse than submersion. Other reviews[2] by disinterested researchers have reached similar conclusions (Engle 1975; Epstein 1977; Baker and de Kanter 1981; Venezky 1981; and Rotberg 1982).

Educational research in general would suggest such negative results from bilingual education. To the extent that standard school subjects are taught in the home language, bilingual education deprives non-English-proficient children of the very things they need — exposure and practice in English, and the major reasons to learn English, that is, do well in school and to communicate with others. It also deprives them of what helps their English-proficient classmates: subject-matter vocabulary development in English and exposure to increasingly demanding English language in general.

To the extent also that bilingual programs foster language isolation, they segregate students from the mainstream of school and extramural affairs conducted in English. In sum, bilingual education can be expected to impair or vitiate several of the nine determinants of academic success, namely: ability and motivation; quality and quantity of instruction; and home, classroom, peer-group, and media environments.

Conclusion

By the time they reach high school, U.S. students achieve poorly in academic subjects by the standards of other nations and by the demands of new technology and the "information society." In particular, they do poorly on measures of English literacy, mathematics, and science. Young people and their parents, however, realize that their school and life success depends on their English-language mastery.

An enormous amount of U.S. research shows that nine factors (table 6.1) promote academic learning, including language learning and English mastery. The alterable factors include the amount and quality of instruction and constructively stimulating classrooms, homes, peer groups, and mass-media exposure. Experiments show that these factors can be altered to improve learning by substantial amounts, and they deserve more widespread use.

For many immigrant children who are not proficient in English, the problems of second-language and academic learning are more acute largely because they come from deprived socioeconomic backgrounds. More than others, these children need maximum exposure to English in school in order to learn it, because they may be deprived of such exposure at home and in their neighborhoods. Because bilingual education deters the very factors that promote English mastery and other academic accomplishments, it can hardly be held out as their hope.

Notes

1. From Matthew 25:29: "For unto every one that hath shall be given, and he shall have abundance; but from him that hath not shall be taken away even that which he hath."
2. The exception is Willig (1985) who omitted two-thirds of the methodologically adequate studies and employed mistaken statistical adjustments of the estimates (Baker 1987; Rossell 1988).

References

Anderson, R. C., P. T. Wilson, and L. G. Fielding. 1986. *Growth in Reading and How Children Spend Their Time Outside of School.* Urbana, Ill.: University of Illinois Center for the Study of Reading.

Applebee, A. N., J. A. Langer, and I. Mullis. 1987. *Learning to be Literate in America.* Princeton, N.J.: National Assessment of Educational Progress, Educational Testing Service.

Baker, K. 1987. "Comment on Willig's 'A Meta-Analysis of Selected Studies of the Effectiveness of Bilingual Education.'" *Review of Educational Research* 57(3):351–62.

Baker, K., and A. de Kanter. 1981. *Effectiveness of Bilingual Education.* Washington, D.C.: U.S. Department of Education.

Chall, J. S. 1983. *Stages of Reading Development.* New York: McGraw-Hill.

_____. 1987. "Two Vocabularies of Reading: Recognition and Meaning."

In *The Nature of Vocabulary Acquisition*, edited by M. G. McKeown and M. E. Curtis. Hillsdale, N.J.: Lawrence Earlbaum Associates.

Dreeban, R., and R. Barr. 1987. "An Organizational Analysis of Curriculum and Instruction." In *Social Organization of Schools*, edited by M. T. Hallinan. New York: Plenum Press.

Educational Testing Service. 1988. *Parent Preference Study*. Princeton, N.J.: Educational Testing Service.

Engle, P. 1975. "Language Medium in Early School Years for Minority Language Groups." *Review of Educational Research* 45:283–301.

Epstein, N. 1977. *Language, Ethnicity, and the Schools: Policy Alternatives for Bilingual-Bicultural Education*. Washington, D.C.: Institute for Educational Leadership.

Fraser, B. J., H. J. Walberg, W. W. Welch, and J. A. Hattie. 1987. "Syntheses of Educational Productivity Research." *International Journal of Educational Research* 11(2):73–145 (whole issue).

Hirsch, Jr., E. D. 1987. *Cultural Literacy: What Every American Needs to Know*. Boston, Mass.: Vintage.

Miller, G. A. 1988. "The Challenge of Universal Literacy." *Science*, 9 Sept., 1,293–1,299.

National Assessment of Educational Progress. 1988. *Mathematics: Are We Measuring Up?* Princeton, N.J.: Educational Testing Service.

National Commission for Excellence in Education. 1983. *A Nation at Risk: The Imperative for School Reform*. Washington, D.C.: U.S. Government Printing Office.

Organization for Economic Cooperation and Development, Center for Educational Research and Development. 1987. *Immigrants' Children at School*. Paris, France.

Peterson, P. L., and H. J. Walberg, eds. 1979. *Research on Teaching*. Berkeley, Calif.: McCutchan.

Postlethwaite, T. N. 1975. *School Organization and Student Achievement*. Stockholm, Sweden: Almqvist and Wissell.

Ravitch, D., and C. E. Finn, Jr. 1988. *What Do Our Seventeen Year Olds Know?* New York, N.Y.: Harper and Row.

Rossell, C. 1988. "The Effectiveness of Educational Alternatives for Limited English Proficient Children in the Berkeley Unified School District. A Report to the U.S. District Court in the case of *Teresa P. et al. v. the Berkeley Unified School District*, July 29, 1988." Boston, Mass.: Boston University.

Rossell, C., and J. M. Ross. 1986. "The Social Science Evidence on Bilingual Education." *Journal of Law and Education* 15:380–95.

Rotberg, I. 1982. "Some Legal and Research Considerations in Establishing Federal Policy in Bilingual Education." *Harvard Educational Review* 52:149–62.

Simon, H. A. 1954. "Some Strategic Considerations in the Construction of Social Science Models." In *Mathematical Thinking in the Social Sciences*, edited by P. Lazarsfeld. Glencoe, Ill.: Free Press.

Stanovich, K. E. 1986. "Matthew Effects in Reading." *Reading Research Quarterly* 21:360–407.

Stevenson, H. W., S.-L. Lee, and J. W. Stigler. 1986. "Mathematics Achievement of Chinese, Japanese, and American Children," *Science* 231:693–699.

Sticht, T. G., and J. H. James. 1984. "Listening and Reading." In *Handbook of Reading Research*, edited by P. D. Pearson. New York, N.Y.: Longman.

U.S. Department of Education. 1986. *Japanese Education Today*. Washington, D.C.: U.S. Government Printing Office.

Venezky, R. 1981. "Non-Standard Language and Reading—Ten Years Later." In *The Social Psychology of Reading*, edited by J. Edwards. Silver Spring, Md.: Institute of Modern Language.

Walberg, H. W. 1984. "Improving the Productivity of America's Schools." *Educational Leadership* 41(8):19–27.

Walberg, H. I. 1986. "Synthesis of Research on Teaching." In *Handbook of Research on Teaching*, edited by M. C. Whittrock. N.Y.: Macmillan.

_____. 1987. "Learning over the Life Course." In *Cognitive Functioning and Social Structure over the Life Course*, edited by Carmi Schooler and K. W. Schaie. Norwood, N.J.: Ablex Publishing Company.

_____. 1989a. "American Youth: Ideals and Reality." Unpublished paper. University of Illinois at Chicago.

_____. 1989b. "Mathematics, Science, and National Welfare: Retrospective and Prospective Achievement." In *International Perspectives on Educational Reform*, edited by A. Purves. Alexandria, Va.: Association for Supervision and Curriculum Development.

_____. 1989c. "Productive Teaching and Instruction: Assessing the Knowledge Base." *Kappan*, in press.

Walberg, H. I., and S.-L. Tsai. 1983. "The Matthew Effect in Education," *American Educational Research Journal* 20:359–73.

Walberg, H. J., K. Hase, and S. P. Rasher. 1978. "English Mastery as a Diminishing Function of Time." *TESOL Quarterly* 12(4):427–37.

Walberg, H. J., D. Schiller, and G. D. Haertel. 1979. "The Quiet Revolution in Educational Research." *Phi Delta Kappan* 61(3):179–83.

Walberg, H. J., B. F. Strykowski, E. Rovai, and S. S. Hung. 1984."Exceptional Performance." *Review of Educational Research* 54:87–112.

Wigfield, A., and S. R. Asher. 1984. "Social and Motivational Influences on Reading." In *Handbook of Reading Research*, edited by P. D. Pearson. New York, N.Y.: Longman.

Willig, A. 1985. "A Meta-Analysis of Selected Studies on the Effectiveness of Bilingual Education." *Review of Educational Research* 55(3): 269–317.

7

Political Goals
of Language Policies

Brian Weinstein

States generally make choices of language to reach final political goals rather than for linguistic or communicative goals. This is particularly true of status choices, such as deciding that one language will be official and another will not, but even some corpus decisions, such as puristic removing of nonnative and nonstandard words from a language, are motivated by political goals. These two types of selection are political — even though there is an immediate communicative problem to be solved — because they influence the identity of the political system and society by symbolically defining who is in and who is out. Second, they influence patterns of participation by opening or closing access to power, wealth, and prestige insofar as they facilitate or obstruct comprehension, employment, and influence.

Behind what may be termed political goals are interests and ideologies. The state itself has interests and ideologies in part because it is composed of human beings: the state is not some dehumanized entity, an assemblage of bloodless institutions; it is composed of individuals who consciously perceive problems and interests in their role as the state and perhaps less consciously from the point of view of the other groups within the society to which they perceive they belong. In the language of political science, the state is "all those individuals who occupy offices that authorize them, and them alone, to make and apply decisions that are binding upon any and all parts of a territorially circumscribed population" (Nordlinger 1987, 362).

The state defends its own interests, which include maintaining order in the society and assuring the legitimacy of its institutions, methods, and personnel in the minds of the society. It also strives to extract resources from the society; it tries to resolve perceived internal problems; and it tries to protect its independence. Groups within the society, led by their own elites, perceive that they have interests and ideologies, some of which can be satisfied — or must be satisfied — by state action. They wish to facilitate their own access to desirable goals, possibly while preventing other groups from the same access; they may wish to alter the identity of the whole society, in accordance with their own vision, even by separating from it; or they wish to strengthen what exists depending on their perception of what they gain and lose. Both the state and the societal groups justify and explain their choices by an ideology appealing to universalistic values of solidarity, democracy, liberty, and so forth. In a few cases, there are no tangible interests behind these appeals. The ideology may then be a goal in and of itself.

As important as language choice or policy may be for state elites and societal elites, it cannot be autonomous from other policies in the economic and political domains if it is to be accepted and efficacious. The action of officializing a language is unlikely to affect identity and patterns of participation by itself; nor can supporters of officialization expect immediate acceptance of a previously nonofficial language unless certain linguistic, economic, and political changes have occurred in the society and state. Officialization of Hebrew in Israel would not have been feasible without the flourishing of Jewish nationalism or Zionism, the independence of the State of Israel, the planned modernization of the corpus of Hebrew by special institutions and by writers, and the influx of immigrants speaking different languages and in need of a lingua franca, as well as the restructuring of the society motivated by a strong desire to change personal lives and some community customs. Officialization of Creole in Haiti, to which I shall refer again, has been blocked by the continuation of the French-speaking Duvalierist political and economic apparatus designed unashamedly to prevent mass participation, plus an ambivalent ideology about the utility of Creole, to say nothing about the absence of teaching materials and pedagogical expertise.

In cooperation with these other policies, language choices of the state or of groups within the society serve three broad political goals: to maintain the state or societal status quo, to reform either one or the other, or to transform the state and/or the society. It is impossible to affect the identity of the state without affecting the identity of the society, but it seems that a change in one is bound, sooner or later, to affect the other.

Before proceeding to investigate how language choice helps reach these three broad political goals, I must note that forces external to the state and society influence policy making. Other states and external societal groups may have some influence over the choices; in some cases they help make policy for populations in a foreign country, while the local state institution plays little or no role. This is most likely to occur in the Caribbean and African countries, whose economies, cultures, and political systems are more easily penetrated by outsiders than elsewhere. These countries are also most dependent on outside assistance for their own survival, which gives foreign powers and institutions a considerable influence over policy making in all domains. The foreign actors, such as Unesco, the Ford Foundation, governments such as those of France or the United States, missionaries, and linguists, are pursuing their interests and ideologies through the promotion of a language policy, and this fact may eventually put them into conflict with other foreign actors or with groups in the target society. The resulting clash of interests affects internal group relations and state-to-state relations far beyond narrow questions of what is the language of education or of government business. It is an important subject, dealt with only in passing here. My focus is more on domestic choices to maintain the status quo, to reform, or to transform.

Language Policies to Maintain the Status Quo

State elites, often allied with societal elites belonging to certain ethnic groups or economic groups, can try to ensure that state language policy will strengthen and maintain the state as it is. Maintaining the status quo means resisting change in qualifications for state employment and voting, keeping the symbols of state and societal identities intact, guarding patterns of external relations, and preserving extant distribution of wealth. Language policies of the Haitian government and several countries in Africa seem to guarantee a status quo that limits access to desirable values to a small elite group; these policies are coordinated brilliantly with other political, educational, and economic programs, such as not building schools in certain areas and resisting land reforms.

Carol Myers Scotton has coined the term "elite closure" to describe such policies. In a paper to be published within the year she explains that elites guard their positions by two methods: unofficially keeping their variety of language as different as possible from what the masses speak and write, and supporting "official language policies as well as unofficial usage allocations which designate a linguistic variety known largely only by the elite as necessary for participation in situations which yield power" (Scotton n.d.).

One strategy is purely societal without state intervention, while the second strategy requires official action. In the first of Scotton's cases, elites encourage the notion, already shared by the masses, that the colonial language, which only the elites in the now-independent states have mastered, is the appropriate, and even the only, means of communication in important domains. In India the passage of four decades since independence has not decreased the prestige of English. It is obvious to all urban dwellers from the Hindi north to the Dravidian south that the best-paying jobs in the most important private and most powerful public sectors go to those with good English-language skills. As a result, observers report a flourishing of new, private, hastily organized English-medium schools, to which lower-middle-class families send their children in emulation of middle-class families, who have long patronized English-medium schools. My own observations in English discussions at the university level in India is that young men and women who have studied through English-medium schools are more self-confident and aggressive in class discussions and in general comportment with foreigners like me, while those who studied English as a subject in, for example, a Tamil-medium school are easily intimidated by their classmates, even though they are fluent in English. The tension between the two groups is almost palpable, and anecdotal evidence supports the hypothesis that such tension and problems carry over into the work place.

An enthusiastic supporter of Tamil in southern India, who insisted his only child attend a Tamil-medium school, found, much to his chagrin, as he told me, that she was at a serious disadvantage when she later attended a secretarial institute. Secretaries working for large companies would be expected to conduct all written work in English, not Tamil, and the young woman had to work very hard to close what she and her family perceived as a serious deficiency in her education. Because she would never speak with a certain high-prestige pronunciation, the family feared she would always be at a disadvantage.

Most African state policies support private-sector notions about the alleged superiority of English, French, or Portuguese, which became official during the recent colonial period. In these largely multilingual societies, state elites argue that choosing one of the national languages as official would put members of groups speaking other languages at a serious disadvantage, which is true. They consistently claim (disingenuously, in my view), that the colonial language is somehow "neutral" because it is no one's mother tongue in the country and because, they claim, everyone has the same difficulty in learning it. Clearly, this assertion is not true, since middle-class parents are able to speak the language already, and they facilitate their children's access to the middle class by introducing them to the language through conversations at home and through the media even before they go to school. After school, they can show their assignments to parents for help and encouragement. Moreover, schools were opened by Europeans in certain regions, such as the coast, where their penetration of Africa began or in select areas where missionaries decided for one reason or another to establish posts. The ethnic groups living in those areas had a head start.

Furthermore, in many societies parents must pay something for the education of their children, even if it is only the cost of school uniforms or books. Payment in very poor societies limits attendance no matter how small the amount of money. Thus, no language is "neutral."

The most candid statement of elite interest in blocking the way to mass mobility by a restrictive language policy comes from Haiti, where middle-class parents from the urban areas complained, after the temporary semi-officialization of Creole as a language of instruction in schools, that their children would have to compete for jobs with peasant children. Valdman correctly wrote that "the extension of Creole into any new . . . activity represents the loss of privilege for the bilingual elite since the simple fact of its fluency in French no longer ensures it will have the exclusive control of this activity" (cited in Weinstein and Segal 1984, 70). The only surprising aspect of my Haitian example is that the parents did not seek to hide their class interests.

Economic policies work in tandem with language policies to ensure the security of the Haitian urban elites. For example, prices paid to peasant producers of exported agricultural products, such as coffee, have been set by a small coterie of Port-au-Prince traders who enjoy privileged information about world market forces. There is restricted competition, and thus the exporters and speculating middlemen have enjoyed financial success at the expense of producers ignorant of world prices and restricted to a few buyers of their products. The systematic political terror under the Duvalier regime prevented producers from shopping around for higher prices or from forming large cooperatives.

At the international level, the French state uses francophonie to help ensure its power in world politics. Francophonie is part of a global strategy that includes an independent nuclear policy and an economic and political program designed to assert French freedom of action in the age of the superpowers. The main linguistic purpose of the more than one hundred government and private organizations promoting the French language around the world is to maintain it as the official or co-official tongue in Africa, Quebec, Haiti, Lebanon, and other countries where English has become popular because of American investments, trade, or cultural imports, or where there are demands to use local mother tongues such as Wolof in Senegal, Arabic in Lebanon and the Maghreb, and, of course, Creole in Haiti. Facilitating translation of science books into French obviates the need to learn English; university exchange programs and organizations of French-using legislators, lawyers, physicians, and others give support to the maintenance of French's official status. State elites in Africa, whose positions depend in part on the language policy, are sure of outside French support for their often-fragile political positions, while the French state is able to claim in the United Nations, the European Economic Community (EEC), and elsewhere that it speaks for a large population outside its European frontiers. Its power in world politics is augmented, and the use of French facilitates trade among states where it is official.

Within France, language policy is "purist," and its target is French society, which has found in certain facets of American culture and language much that it admires and copies. As a result of the success of American popular culture after World War II, including music and films, and as a result of American innovations in space technology, mass media, and science, many English words have entered into the daily spoken and written usage of society's elites. Although the absolute quantity of the words is not large, state elites are worried about society's identity. French state elites fear that loss of what they call cultural independence will affect political and economic independence.

In reaction to these concerns, the government has created several agencies over the last thirty years to remove English words from official usage and to discourage private enterprises from using English in their publicity and contracts with employees. Agencies work to invent new words or to revive archaic words in order to replace English. Laws provide penalties for use of English in written form in certain situations.

Another perceived threat to the present identity of French society, in the view of state elites, is the assertion of regional identities in France. One slogan of the French Revolution and the Jacobin, or centralizing, ideology was "One Nation, One Language." Some of the threats to the new republic originated in different regions where languages other than the original "French," that is, the *langue d'oïl*, were spoken. They included *langue d'oc* in the south, Flemish in the north, and Alsatian in the east.

James Jacob has traced the history of policy with respect to languages other than French since 1951. In that year, the legislature passed the Deixonne Law, which permitted the very-limited study in public schools of a few regional languages such as Basque, Breton, Catalan, Occitan, and later Corsican (Jacob n.d.). Socialists promised future changes in France's cultural centralization beginning in 1981 with the election of François Mitterrand to the presidency. A new pluralism stood high on their proclaimed agenda, although their opponents warned about possible secession movements. In 1985, the president created the Conseil National des Langues de France in response to a great interest shown in schools for the regional languages which the Deixonne Law introduced. Another goal may have been to co-opt leaders of effervescent and sometimes violent regional movements in Corsica and elsewhere. These ethnic movements found inspiration in Marxist ideology, and some leaders began to question the structure of French society. Opponents of pluralism and defenders of the status quo quickly reacted by preventing the council from obtaining what might be called significant funding and by insisting that individual French citizens could use any language they chose in their private, personal relations, but that the state could not promote languages other than French (Jacob n.d.).

Paralleling and supporting these language policies have been the educational, economic, military, and political initiatives of successive governments. General de Gaulle distanced his country from the NATO alliance out of fear of losing French defense initiative. He tried for years to keep the British out of the EEC in order to preserve French predominance in that important regional organization and because he feared indirect American influence. As soon as Britain entered, one of the first complaints was that English would eclipse French as a language of deliberations and documentation, but it has not. The French state allied its former colonies with the EEC to ensure continued trade and investment advantages for both the Africans and the French. Instead of being merely defensive, the French state has also expanded activities in African countries where a significant elite knows the French language. Zaire, Angola, former Spanish Guinea, former Portuguese Guinea, and others have been drawn toward the French orbit at first by cultural policies, including language policy. The former Spanish colony eventually joined the franc zone, and the study of French has reportedly increased. Scholarships permitted students and future elites to receive their higher and technical education in France or in another French-speaking country. They would eventually become part of an international network of French-speaking politicians, bureaucrats, savants, and business people.

The great prestige enjoyed by the French language and culture assisted French policy. Without the idea that French is superior to local languages, that it is "neutral" with respect to access to wealth, power, and prestige, and that it is an effective instrument for the acquisition of knowledge, the policy would not have succeeded. Nor would it have succeeded without dynamic French economic-aid programs, political advice to insecure state elites, and military policies.

Language Policy to Reform the State and Society

The political goals of some language policies are to alter the state and society without changing their fundamental structures, ideologies, and overall identities. The Belgian state has, for example, slowly evolved from an officially unilingual, politically unitary kingdom in 1830 toward what Aunger calls "permissive bilingualism" in 1873, to "obligatory bilingualism" in 1921, to "official bilingualism" in 1962 (Aunger 1987, 23-24). In the first phase, only French was the language of government business; in the second, Flemish could be used in court proceedings; in the third, government officials in Flanders had to know Flemish to keep their jobs; and in the present phase, French and Dutch are equally valid for laws and courts. (By Dutch I mean a standardized language, which is very close to Netherlands Dutch.) In addition, the two language communities are proportionately represented in the civil service, and the government uses both in communication with the society.

This evolution took place as a result of a *prise de conscience* among the Flemish people of their identity and their ability to organize and to put pressure on politicians as the democratization of the voting franchise took place. Democratization ensured a loud voice for the Flemish because they are the majority. As language legislation changed, the structure of the state evolved toward a federal system. In 1962 language boundaries were drawn, and officially unilingual regions were the result. Eight years later the state recognized German as official, too, and set up four government or community councils: the French region, the Dutch region, the German region, and the bilingual region. Each region has a certain amount of control over cultural matters and economic planning (Aunger 1987, 25). Thus, the Belgian state has changed, but it has been preserved along with the monarchy and the economic system.

The changes have affected the society in important ways. The Flemish emerged from their low status into a self-confident, culturally productive majority. They formed groups to defend their interests, and some coalesced into political parties that adopted universalistic ideologies beyond the narrow concerns of language. In other words, they stepped outside their somewhat parochial concerns to plan for broad reforms within Belgium. During the last three decades, the Flemish share of high-ranking positions in all realms of Belgian society has increased dramatically. They now occupy very important positions in the civil service and military, which means a strengthening of the elites. Both state and society have changed, in part because of language policy.

The post-Franco Spanish state and society have been reformed in similar ways. The constitution of 1978 "explicitly states a multi-lingual language policy," a sharp divergence from the Franco insistence on only Castilian. The effect is to provide for the officialization of languages in addition to — not in place of — Castilian in the various regions (Cobarrubias and Lasa 1987, 146). Beginning in 1978, many regions became autonomous communities. The most important are the Basque country, Catalonia, and Galicia. Each of these three communities now has its own government and language policy. The powers of the respective governments, more limited to cultural matters, are less than those of the Belgian regions, I believe. The central government retains more power than does the Belgian government.

Castilian is still official everywhere in Spain, but the reform has facilitated and encouraged further development of the respective languages, which are now the media of instruction in some of the schools. This means there must be a modernization of the lexicon. Assertion of regional identities has doubtless affected a sense of self-worth and respect. In 1987, the Basque government sponsored a World Congress to demonstrate and promote its language and culture, and also to show the world another side of the Basques, since most publicity about them in recent years has come from the terrorist actions of the Euzkadi ta Askatasuna (ETA). Franquist centralizers do not accept even symbolic decentralization, and rumblings in the Spanish military have threatened the reforms. They continue with the outside encouragement of the other European powers, which welcomed Spain into the EEC. Language reforms have clearly worked to support a general democratization of Spain under its constitutional monarch.

An example of language policy to reform the society can be found closer to home in the bilingual programs in the United States. The purpose of federal legislation concerning bilingual education seems to me to be completely reformist. It is worth repeating that the motive force for the legislation was the concern that Mexican Americans and others were being excluded from full participation in American society, and that the principles of democracy dictated that actions should be taken to remove barriers to participation in existing political structures. Growing out of the reformist civil rights movement, the language movement succeeded by 1968 in winning approval and federal assistance for bilingual education programs. The creation of the Office of Bilingual Education within the existing Department of Education, and congressional establishment of a National Advisory Council on Bilingual Education show how reformist, rather than radical, it was. In the famous Supreme Court case *Lau v. Nichols*, judges ruled in 1974 that "because the Civil Rights Act of 1964 had forbidden discrimination or the exclusion of anyone from a federally assisted program on the basis of 'race, color or national origin'" and because the children's inability to speak English was "related to their national origin" (even though they were born in America), the city of San Francisco would have to take some action to remedy this situation (Weinstein 1983, 112). This judgment was also reformist. As long as the thrust of bilingual education was on transitional forms beginning with the mother tongue and then moving on to English, the language policy was reformist. Efforts to use public funds to maintain and develop further the languages and cultural heritages of Mexican Americans and others in the name of societal pluralism seem to me to be motivated by transformationist goals. Because, as other contributors to this book show, non-English speakers want to learn English and are making efforts to do so, both mandatory bilingual education programs and the explicit officialization of English are unnecessary. Market forces seem to be resolving a communication problem, and gratuitous government intervention may only heighten ethnic consciousness and provide fuel for certain elites trying to build local constituencies.

Parallel to the language movement in the United States has been the organization of Spanish-speaking Americans into various interest groups, the creation of a Hispanic Caucus in the Congress, and the effort to create a political party. Continuing questions about bilingual education, bilingual signs, and counterefforts to declare English official mean that this issue is far from being resolved. The rhetoric on both sides has sharpened with accusations of racism from one side and accusations of particularism and secessionist tendencies from the other side. In the meanwhile, there is plenty of evidence that people who do not speak English want to speak and write it.

We are too close to U.S. language policy to judge its long-term effects. A look back at language policy in nineteenth-century Japan shows how reformist a policy can be. Florian Coulmas has written an interesting piece about language policy working together with political and economic reform and creating what is known as the Meiji Reformation. The year 1868 marked the beginning of an internal restructuring of the Japanese state and society along with an opening to the outside world that altogether preserved the basic values of the Japanese culture.

Language played a key role in the Meiji Reformation, partly because intellectuals and others wished to read Western books. The books had to be translated, which meant "completely alien notions and relationships had to be expressed in Japanese; but . . . before this could be done, the Japanese language had to be made fit to incorporate these novel notions and relationships" (Coulmas n.d.). Individual translators played the key role, according to Coulmas, in supplying new words and in "narrowing the gap between spoken and written language" (Coulmas forthcoming, 10–11), without discarding the distinctive Japanese writing system. Centralization of power around a modernizing emperor, the expansion of trade with other countries, and acceptance and further experimentation with new technologies were steps, along with language policy, in Japan's path to world-power status.

Regionally based language policy can work to alter political, economic, and administrative relationships in a federal system. Policy making in states or provinces of federal political systems can reform the particular state or the larger state, while affecting the society. In Quebec, language policy reformed state and society; in West Bengal, India, it is probably now beginning to reform the state.

Although Quebec seems, in the view of many, to be an example of radical change or transformation, it fits better into my reformist category. The rhetoric of one of the political parties proposed independence in order to assure the French identity of the state and society, to guarantee state control over the economy, and to open access of a new urban middle class to greater wealth and prestige. Its actions, once it had power, were reformist. The provincial government, controlled by the Parti Québecois (PQ) from 1976, submitted the first timid stages of political change to a referendum, which it lost. Through Bill 101 in 1977, which reaffirmed the 1974 Bill 22 passed by the previous Liberal government, the PQ made French official. The immediate effect was to raise the prestige of French and force new immigrants' children into the French-speaking community through the school system. The longer-term effect was to ensure jobs for the educated urban bourgeoisie interested in working in executive positions in private enterprise and in the state bureaucracy. It is true that companies moved from Montreal to Toronto to avoid Francization, but no radical restructuring of the economy took place.

The law provided that the public sector must use French in oral and written communication including contracts, signs, names, and communication with private bodies. Professional corporations such as the Medical Association must ensure that their services are available in French. French was strengthened as the medium of instruction for most students while access to English-medium schools was severely restricted. The legislation protected and promoted French in the workplace and on public advertising and signs. Institutions created by the law watched over the Francization process in private firms (Daoust n.d.).

Denise Daoust of the Office de la Langue Française has traced the process of Francization, which has been quite successful in private firms. Usage of standardized French by government and private firms has also improved because of the activities of the Quebec Bank of Terminology, which provides assistance to all persons searching for an acceptable French term as a replacement for an English term. Daoust found that "since 1971 the percentage of Francophone workers who say they work exclusively in French, or nearly, has risen slowly but steadily from 66 percent to 71 percent in 1987, a gain of about 5 percent. More dramatically, the number of English speakers working in French has jumped by 10 percent.

This tendency is also reflected in a large drop in the number of Anglophones working only in English and in a large increase (19 percent) in the number using both languages" (Daoust n.d.). Vaillancourt, another Quebec scholar, has shown the slow but steady growth in Francophone ownership of enterprises in Quebec from 47.1 percent in 1961 to 54.9 percent in 1978 (Vaillancourt 1988, 24). At the level of individual incomes, Vaillancourt found that "English speaking men, whether monolingual or bilingual, earned because of their language abilities a salary or wage higher than French monolinguals" (Vaillancourt 1988, 26). But ten years later the Anglophones were earning less than monolingual Francophones. Most interesting is the increase in Francophones in executive positions in private enterprise, from 64.9 percent in 1971 to 75.8 percent in 1981 (Vaillancourt 1988, 26).

Daoust and Vaillancourt found that the pressure that led to the state policies came from the society, as it did in Belgium. State elites adopted language policies that helped change the identity of Quebec society and state into that of a French-speaking province. They altered patterns of access to existing institutions without transforming them. The institutions were probably strengthened by the language policies.

A reform of the society took place because of the added prestige of French alongside English, and the advent of the urban, modernizing, secularizing middle classes to power. They took political control from rural-based Catholic-inspired middle classes who spoke French but who accepted Anglophone control of the cities and industries. With the relative disappearance of the independence movement, the Quebec state and Francophone elites in the society continue to shape and defend laws and language regulations designed to safeguard French against continuing Anglophone challenges, which are likely to continue to the end of this century.

West Bengal state elites are at an earlier stage in their efforts to reform the Indian federal system. Chaklader (n.d.) has pointed to certain anomalies in the Indian federal constitution with regard to relations between central and state governments and has shown how language policy is designed in part to resolve the problem by reforming the political structures. One problem, for example, is that state courts use the official state language such as Bengali in West Bengal and Tamil in Tamil Nadu, but the Supreme Court of

India can only use the official languages of the Union — Hindi or English. The question arose since India has a unified court system. "How can the Supreme Court receive and preserve its supervisory power if its language is different from the language of the lower courts?" (Chaklader n.d.). Furthermore, language policy and planning at the state level is seen by many Indians as one way to protect state rights against the ever-present threat of encroachment by the central, or Union, government. Lastly, in West Bengal, as in other states, the popularity of English conflicts with the desire of educationists and nationalists to emphasize Bengali as a medium of education and creativity.

The advent of the Left Front government in 1977 signaled the beginning of the implementation of a pro-Bengali policy. This policy included stepped-up use of Bengali in internal state documents and in state circulars issued to the public, the purchase of Bengali typewriters for the state, and answering communications from the public in Bengali if the original letters were written in Bengali. In the dozen years since the beginning of this new push for Bengali, the state and nongovernmental groups within the society, composed of writers and journalists, have acted to modernize the corpus of the language and to insist on its prestige. The anarchy of the court system, the perceived threat of central government dominance, and the popularity of English have provided the impetus.

Accelerated use of Bengali in new domains forced policymakers to attempt to modernize the lexicon the way Japanese writers modernized their lexicon. A key issue has been script reform, due to the need to use typewriters and word processors. Compound letters or mixtures of letters could not be put on a keyboard because there are so many of them, according to Chaklader. Writers and newspapers have taken the initiative by eliminating most compound letters.

Because state governments in India have more control over education systems than does the central government, the West Bengal government has initiated its own language policy for schools. In 1949, the All-India University Education Committee recommended a three-language formula for the country's schools: a regional language, Hindi, and English; but the states seem to have opted, for the most part, two languages: a regional language and English.

Tamil Nadu was most explicitly opposed to Hindi as a second or even third compulsory language, and West Bengal relegated Hindi to a third language to be taught for only two years, and even then not compulsorily. The students may choose a language other than Hindi. In other words, Hindi is not compulsory even though it is supposed to be the sole eventual national link language. With respect to English, the government has decided children are not to study it before their sixth year in school. These actions assert the key place for Bengali.

Similar localization of language policy has been going on in other states of India. This factor, plus the rise of regional parties appealing to ethnic sentiments and state or regional loyalties and the growing perception of corruption and other wrongdoing in the central government, are together a challenge to the contemporary federal system. Employment opportunities are also increasingly closed to people from outside the respective states. Chaklader estimates that in West Bengal "more than 95 percent teachers of different categories are recruited from the Bengali community. Similar is the case with respect to employment in state services. Since fluency in the official language of the state is the prerequisite for employment in administrative services, preference is given only to those whose mother tongue is the official language of the state" (Chaklader 1989, 32). Bengali is increasingly used in the courts, while the central government is calling for increased use of Hindi.

West Bengal and other states are making financial demands alongside language demands. The state governments want financial autonomy, for example. The conclusion of a series of political, economic, and linguistic steps is growing pressure to reform the Indian federal system to recognize more autonomy in the states with respect to culture, economics, and politics. Reform is the goal. Secession, which would transform the state, is not an issue among Bengalis and Tamils.

Language Policies to Transform State and Society

I have already mentioned language policy in Haiti, whose state elites are desperately defending themselves against efforts to transform the state. Beginning in 1985, an adult literacy program under the aegis of the Roman Catholic Church added a few drops of water to the seeds of a radical transformation of the Haitian state under the nose of the then dictator. The motto of Misyon Alfa was *"Se goute sèl pou louvri je,"* or "Taste salt to open your eyes." In Haitain culture, salt represents liberty: zombies free themselves from their masters or mistresses by consuming a little salt. Haitians thought of themselves as zombies under their two Duvalier Presidents for Life.

The literacy program had a very short life. It was terminated after the Duvalier flight into exile by the church itself. The reasons have to do with the contents of the literacy instruction. Allegedly, the instructors, inspired by liberation theology, were integrating subtle challenges to all authority, including the authority of church hierarchy. The bishops, as I was told during a research visit in 1988, perceived the revolutionary and violent potential in the lessons and believed that using Creole would permit the message of class conflict to reach a wide audience. The 1987 constitution made Creole co-official with French, but the military suspended the constitution in mid 1988. The 1989 restoration of the constitution has not promoted Creole because of growing chaos in the country.

Despite these twin failures, Creole is now much more widely used in high-status exchanges and in the media. Instead of using French, the military rulers of post-Duvalier Haiti speak in Creole, for example. During a lecture I gave at a prestigious institute of administration in December 1988, one of the most elegantly attired and articulate students asked me a question in Creole. Since he knew perfectly well that I did not understand Creole, he was making an ideological statement that had nothing to do with the content of his question. The chair of the meeting told me later that a few years ago anyone speaking Creole at a formal lecture or meeting would have been driven out of the hall by the laughter. Political and other developments in the next few years will involve important decisions about Creole.

The perspective offered by the passage of several decades permits us to say that elsewhere, notably in Israel and in Turkey, language policy has successfully transformed states and societies. Jacob Landau of the Hebrew University of Jerusalem has written about both cases from the perspective of 1989. At the end of the nineteenth century, Eliezer Ben-Yehuda, writer and lexicographer, coined new terms for his eventual seventeen-volume historical dictionary; he created a nongovernmental Hebrew Language Committee that the State of Israel transformed into the Academy for the Hebrew Language, a government body, in 1949, or a year after independence. Ben-Yehuda also promoted "Hebrew as the language of instruction in all Jewish schools in Palestine" (Landau n.d.). He and his growing group of colleagues also promoted a well-defined pronunciation, that of the eastern Jewish communities living in Arab lands. The purpose was to provide another symbol of the State for purposes of identity and legitimacy; to help unify the Jews arriving from Europe, the Americas, India, North Africa, South Africa, and finally Ethiopia; and to help integrate Hebrew-speaking Jews into the Arabic speaking countries of the Middle East. Younger generations of Israelis have absorbed Arabic expressions in informal ways into colloquial Hebrew, and the planning agency searching for ways to Hebracize looks first in biblical Hebrew and then in Arabic, Aramaic, Canaanite, and Egyptian literature (Landau n.d.). The only goal that the planners have not reached was to help integrate Israel into the Middle East in a political sense, but the failure only shows how other nonlinguistic factors must support language policies in order for the goals to be attained.

Today, as is well known, Hebrew is the language of government in both its written and oral forms; it is the language of instruction up to and including all higher degrees in the universities; and it is the language of private-sector activities of the most prestigious kind. In order to enter the university, students are also supposed to know English as a second language, but perhaps due to their pride in Hebrew and a sense of its importance to Israeli society, many Jewish students do not learn English very well. At the societal level, therefore, Hebrew serves to unite, and without it people have a difficult time participating in the institutions of the country, both state and private. The government has set up *ulpanim*, or courses for immigrants and others, so that they will have access to government and jobs through Hebrew competency. For them, Hebrew represents the new state, the new Jewish person free from the ghetto and the possibilities of a new culture and literature linked with twenty-eight hundred years of extant writing.

Unlike Hebrew, Turkish was already used in everyday intercourse in the nineteenth century, but the disparity between spoken and written forms impeded mass literacy and probably identification with the state. Before World War I, there was, in fact, no Turkish state, but even before the collapse of the Ottoman Empire some literary elites from the society endeavored to inspire the state to make some language choices. Out of the disorder following the war, which destroyed Ottoman control of Arab territories, a new state elite headed by Atatürk created a new state and society.

Language policy played an important role in shaping a brand-new Turkish identity. The spoken language of Istanbul served as the standard; the Roman alphabet replaced the Arabic-based script; and new words replaced Arab and Persian terms. This action paralleled the writing of a constitution, stabilization of frontiers, and the establishment of a secular republican state. Policymakers gave the Turkish people new symbols for unity and pride, while the state, like the Israeli state, took its legitimacy from the symbols of Turkish nationalism, including language, which was consciously shaped into a symbol. Successfully freeing Turkey from the threat of complete dismemberment and outside control added legitimacy to the new state. Parallel purification efforts by writers helped legitimize institutions and gave the Turks a sense of their special identity separate from other Muslims, such as Arabs, but linked with the Turkic peoples to the east. Citing official Turkish sources, Landau wrote that "only 35–40 percent of the terms used in 'formal language' before 1932 . . . were Turkish, increasing to 75–80 percent by 1983" (Landau n.d.).

The issues in the three countries of the Maghreb were similar, but the outcome has been different. Emerging from French colonial rule, Moroccan, Algerian, and Tunisian leaders wished to legitimize the newly independent states in the eyes of their society and to ensure the modernization of the political and economic systems. Algerian and Tunisian leaders, in particular, were secularists who believed in the benefits of mass education and science as well as an opening to the outside world. To reach these goals they tried to develop their secular universities, import technology, and expand trade relations; and they welcomed assistance in developing natural resources. At the same time, they responded to the nationalist message articulated during their struggle for independence which, in the case of Algeria, was an eight-year war. Gilbert Grandguillaume has written about language policy, or Arabization, by which the three states replaced French with Arabic as the national and official language.

Replacing French by Arabic to legitimize the new modernizing state became a greater problem than originally anticipated because "French has acquired a certain kind of legitimacy during the colonial period without people fully realizing it" (Grandguillaume n.d.). Even the most committed nationalists recognized French as the instrument of modernization, and they had their nagging doubts about Arabic, particularly in its classical, or Koranic, form. Yet, it was this form that linked the new states with the rest of the Arab world and to the traditions of Islam that served to legitimize the new state.

State elites thought they could provide a symbol of legitimacy and an instrument of modernization by transforming the official language into a variety called "Modern Arabic" or "Median Arabic," which is "intermediate between the Koranic variety and the spoken language" (Grandguillaume n.d.). This language, like its counterpart in Egypt, would be modern particularly in terminology and in its "lighter syntax." It would be accessible to the masses but tied to the traditions of Islam and Arab identity. It would help legitimize the new states in their effort to capture and hold mass loyalty. It would also facilitate access to power, wealth, and prestige.

Policymakers faced a serious dilemma, however: how to avoid undermining modernization in which French would, for a few years, play its role while gradually introducing a sense of national authenticity through a modernized Arabic. Grandguillaume found that "no government had ever made a clear choice between the options," but that they fluctuated between an emphasis on French and an emphasis on Arabic (Grandguillaume n.d.). Algeria's first postindependence literacy program was in French, not in Arabic, for example. For years, the graduates of Arabic-medium educational programs up to and including the university level were relegated to work in less-important government ministries than graduates of French-medium programs. Arabic-medium graduates regularly demonstrated for better positions and more respect in Algeria. Pressures from these graduates, the ideology of the independence struggle, and the exigencies of Islam as a legitimizer of the state forced policymakers to provide for an increasing role for Modern Arabic more quickly, probably, than they wished.

According to Grandguillaume, the advantages and problems with this variety of language are that although the basic form is that of Koranic Arabic, "in its essence it is a language with a double reference to French — semantics and function" (Grandguillaume n.d.). This was the result of translation and of its use in modern domains of state and industry. For state modernizers it was the perfect solution, but for a growing group of Islamic fundamentalists it was a fraud.

Arabization through state choice of Modern Arabic met with resistance and faced attack from some societal elites because of the failure of other state policies, notably economic policies designed to develop resources and infrastructure, and finally to improve the quality of life. Declines in oil and other mineral prices, corruption, nepotism in granting jobs and services, population growth, and inefficiencies of various kinds condemned many development projects. Once stagnation and decline began to affect the masses of people, religious leaders close to them and inspired by events in Iran began to label state policies as immoral, anti-Islamic, and generally detrimental to the society. They called for an assertion of Islamic values to solve all problems — an assertion that would, of course, give power and prestige to the elite of clerics and Muslim scholars.

Fundamentalists did not ignore the Arabization policy of the state, but, rather, they rejected it with the slogan "Arabization is not Islamization," which was enough to condemn state language policy in the eyes of millions of believers (Grandguillaume n.d.). As a result of this frontal assault, states have been struggling to earn legitimacy and to maintain order by adopting some Islamic measures or promising to weed out corruption. Recent riots in Algeria, whose state had a high degree of legitimacy after the liberation war, frightened political leaders sufficiently to make them promise important political and economic changes. With the removal of President Habib Bourguiba in Tunisia, state elites hope for a more secure future. None of the states has resolved its language problem any better than its political problems, however.

Other African states to the west and east have felt less pressure to use language to transform the postindependence state, because few elites integrated language or a specific language into nationalist rhetoric. Ghanaian, Nigerian, Mozambican, and Kenyan leaders feared their African languages could not play the role of medium of government business and education because these languages were not so developed as the European languages or Arabic, and they sensed a danger to fragile societal unity if one or two of the many spoken languages were chosen as symbols and instruments for the new states and societies.

Tanzania was one of the exceptions, but at independence it already enjoyed the luxury of a widely spoken lingua franca, Swahili. Bernd Heine has shown that officialization of Swahili has helped transform the postcolonial state according to a certain image of African authenticity and has facilitated processes of democratization.

Most states of tropical Africa follow what Heine calls an "exoglossic" language policy, which is to say that they prefer to use an external European language in official domains of government and education. A few states, such as Tanzania and Somalia, follow what he calls an "endoglossic" policy, which means officialization of an African language (Heine 1989, 3–4). Each policy involves more than language in a narrow sense; it leads to a cutting of other ties: "An active endoglossic policy, most of all, serves the goal of sociocultural independence from the outside world, especially independence from Western culture and ideology" (Heine n.d.).

In support of its language policy Tanzania has, for example, proclaimed its adherence to principles of nonalignment, even though its poverty constrained its freedom of action in world politics. In contrast, Kenya, with a lesser commitment to the promotion of African languages and a free-market economy, signed a military cooperation agreement with the United States in 1980. Through its international policies and its language policy, Kenya has earned the reputation of a free-market state linked with the West and, in the view of some observers, not so independent as Tanzania.

Internally, Tanzania has made an ideological commitment to equality while the Kenyan state has emphasized individual accomplishment by "rewarding those with higher skills which meant inter alia English" (Heine n.d.). The results, according to those who compare the two countries, are that there is less disparity in Tanzania between rich and poor, between high-ranking civil servants and low-ranking civil servants, between political leaders and their constituents. These differences do not necessarily mean that one country has achieved successful material development, however. Due in part to nationalization, oil price rises, and state inefficiency, Tanzania's economy has suffered, but social cohesion is probably greater, as is legitimacy, in Tanzania.

The Republic of Guinea initiated an endoglossic policy during the rule of Sékou Touré, which lasted from the country's break with France in 1958 to the president's death in 1984. Language policy; cutting ties with the franc monetary zone, and creating a national currency; innovations in the education system in the name of authenticity; nationalization of banks, property, and some industries; style of dress; and other policies were supposed to be part of an effort to assert an authentic African identity for the state and to transform patterns of participation within the society. After Touré's death, the new military government quickly reversed course in all areas. They performed a volte-face in language policy by reestablishing French as the only official language of government and education almost overnight. Accusations of corruption, ethnic favoritism, and an extreme personalization of power blemished and undermined the endoglossic policy. In this case, a policy that promoted African languages was seen by many as part of decay, not development.

My last example of transformation comes from Uzbekistan, one of the constituent republics of the Soviet Union. William Fierman has explained that there was no Uzbekistan prior to the Revolution of 1917. Soviet policymakers created this state, and they shaped the Uzbek people out of neighboring Turkic peoples, in part through language policy.

For the first two decades after the Revolution, the planners in Moscow wished to build a new sense of identity among this people and to facilitate participation in good positions in the state rather than to colonize the area with literate Russian speakers from elsewhere in the Soviet Union. Thus, they modernized the agricultural economy, attacked Islam as part of a secularizing process, and tried to weaken regional identities other than Uzbeki. They fought ideas of pan-Turkism and pan-Islam, while promoting the idea of a special, clearly defined Uzbek identity. Needless to say, they also wished to legitimize the new state, the Soviet Union, to improve production, and to promote eventual literacy in Russian.

Language policy was an important pillar of transformation policy. In 1927, the Congress of the Uzbekistan Communist Party "demanded use of Uzbek language in all government offices" (Fierman 1989, 14), forcing even Russians to begin to study the language. In the meanwhile, writers and planners worked on Uzbek to provide a standard for education and government and to modernize the lexicon. As in Turkey, planners here discarded the Arabic script in favor of the Roman alphabet and then, as Russification pressures grew, in favor of the Cyrillic script. Arabic words were purged from the language in favor of Turkish words, and then of Russian words. Contemporary assertions of regional and ethnic identities in the U.S.S.R. may lead to further transformation. Language policy is already part of important political movements in Estonia and Armenia.

These transformation policies are the most dramatic examples of the intimate link between language choices and political change. The connection is also present and important in efforts to maintain the status quo and to reform society and state. In many countries, of course, language decisions have little to do with the most important problems, such as democratization in Argentina or Chile or corruption and fluctuating commodity prices in Mexico and Egypt. Elsewhere, an examination of the language choices of the state sheds light on the interplay between state elites' and societal elites' struggles and alliances to affect the identity of the state and society and to affect patterns of participation. For this reason, the study of language policy should go beyond the linguistic and communicative goals to the final political goals.

References

Aunger, Edmund A. 1987. "Belgium: Building the Bilingual State." In *Indigenous Minority Groups Multinational Democracies*, edited by John Jenkins, 13–49. Waterloo, Ont.: Wilfrid Laurier University.
Chaklader, Snehamoy. N.d. "Language Policy and Reforming India's Federal Structure: The Case of West Bengal." Forthcoming in Weinstein n.d.
Cobarrubias, Juan, and Carmen Garmendia Lasa. 1987. "Language Policy and Language Planning Efforts in Spain." In *Proceedings of the*

International Colloquium on Language Planning, edited by Larne La-forge, 143–92. Quebec: Les Presses de l'Université Laval.

Coulmas, Florian. N.d. "Language Adaptation in Meiji Japan." Forthcoming in Weinstein n.d.

Daoust, Denise. N.d. "A Decade of Language Planning in Quebec: A Sociopolitical Overview." Forthcoming in Weinstein n.d.

Fierman, William. N.d. "Language and Political Development in Uzbekistan from the Revolution until 1953." Forthcoming in Weinstein n.d.

Grandguillaume, Gilbert. N.d. "Language and Legitimacy in the Maghreb." Forthcoming in Weinstein n.d.

Heine, Bernd. N.d. "Language Policy in Africa." Forthcoming in Weinstein n.d.

Jacob, James. N.d. "Language Planning and Political Development in France." Forthcoming in Weinstein n.d.

Landau, Jacob. N.d. "Language Policy and Political Development in Israel and Turkey." Forthcoming in Weinstein n.d.

Nordlinger, Eric A. 1987. "Taking the State Seriously." In *Understanding Political Development*, edited by Myron Weiner and Samuel P. Huntington, 353–90. Boston: Little Brown.

Scotton, Carol Myers. N.d. "Elite Closure as Boundary Maintenance: The Case of Africa." Forthcoming in Weinstein n.d.

Vaillancourt, Françoise. 1988. "Le statut économique du Français et des Francophones au Québec." *Interface* (Montréal) 9(5) (Sept.–Oct.):23–27.

Weinstein, Brian. 1983. *The Civic Tongue: Political Consequences of Language Choices*. New York: Longman.

Weinstein, Brian, ed. N.d. *Language Policy and Political Development*. Norwood, N.J.: Ablex. Forthcoming.

Weinstein, Brian, and Aaron Segal. 1984. *Haiti: Political Failures and Cultural Successes*. New York: Praeger.

8

The Ideology of the Application of Linguistic Knowledge

Glendon F. Drake

This discussion is about the relationship of applied linguistics to ideology. To begin, a personal example may be useful: In the late 1960s I was involved with the sociolinguistic movement in its effort to investigate the validity of black English. In the fervent atmosphere of that decade I wrote, in reference to what seemed to me some doubtful applications of linguistic knowledge to the teaching of black students, that: "Thus do the linguists and the teacher place themselves in support of the corporate state" (Drake 1973, 222). Now I knew that I didn't live in a corporate state. What, then, was this ideologically loaded, nondescriptive term doing in the supposedly "scholarly" analysis? Conventional analysis might say that I was trying to inflame and mislead the unreflective, but I knew that my audience knew what sort of state they lived in. In effect, I was in this case, as are all applied linguists, in a relationship that is analogous to the relationship of a psychiatrist with his patient. In this relationship the psychiatrist plays the dual role of participant and observer. As "participant-observer" (cf. Percy 1961, 39–40) the psychiatrist must note not only the patient's behavior but his own behavior as well. For the psychiatrist will crucially affect the situation by eliciting responses from the patient and by motivating the patient's further behavior. In this light, my use of the loaded term "corporate state" was not simple propaganda, but an effort to seize on a metaphor to convey as well; for my

189

purpose was to influence the situation that I was observing. This is the source of the dilemma that most applied linguists face, for we are necessarily in "participant-observer" relationships with our "clients." As linguists we are good at understanding conceptualizing our observer role; but as applied linguists, I submit, many of us do not understand our participant role on the same level. We get ourselves caught up in the web of "Mannheim's Paradox."

The development of the sociology of language or sociolinguistics has been due to three factors: (1) a search for a sounder empirical base for linguistic theory, (2) the conviction that social factors play a larger role in the evolution and operation of language than most linguists had been willing to admit, and (3) the feeling that linguistic knowledge should be applied. It is this last factor that leads to the concern of this paper. Sociolinguistics has seen healthy prospects in the rapidly developing relationship with applied linguistics (for example, Fishman 1972a). I agree that the prospects may be healthy, but I submit that the blessing of this union are mixed. Dysfunction, as well as social advance, may follow the application of linguistic knowledge to social and educational problems.

The danger is involved with what in the sociology of knowledge is called "Mannheim's Paradox." This paradox arises from the inevitable social element in the pursuit and perception of truth and knowledge. Karl Mannheim pointed out that sociopolitical thought "is always bound up with the existing life situation of the thinker" (1954, 3). Thus, the scientific observer observes from his location in history and social structure. Because of this location, his observations and inferences are bound up and colored by his own ideological thrust. Despite scientific rigor, the separation of scientific fact from ideological beliefs is difficult and probably impossible. Staring too long and hard at this paradox could lead the social scientists to despair and apathy or, as it did Mannheim, to extreme relativism. However, failure to confront the paradox at all leads the social scientist into shallow orthodoxy at best, and sociopolitical mischief — including tragic mischief — at worst.

Sociolinguists are more prone to confront the paradox than other linguists because we generally seek an application of our knowledge in areas of great ideological loading and motivation: ethnic inclusion or exclusion, minority/majority rights, class differences, economic and educational opportunity, social mobility, etcetera. Because we attempt to apply our knowledge, we tend to become participants as well as observers. Consequently, we often find ourselves on a "side" of an issue — usually the side of the angels, in our view, or against the naive or the oppressor or even the evil. Usually our knowledge is for use in some presumed social good such as the educational success, economic opportunity, and human rights of a minority group such as blacks or Hispanics. As educated citizens with well-developed moral sentiments, we can hardly stand aloof from the humanitarian dimensions of the causes our discipline exposes us to. However, as social scientists we need to detach ourselves from the ideological themes and discern the "facts" and "truths," and here we find ourselves frustrated by the paradox.

To suppose that we can be objective observers and pay no heed to our own ideological involvement in the data with which we work is simply to reject the substance of the sociology of knowledge. Yet, some investigators appear to virtually celebrate Mannheim's Paradox. Here, for example, is a sociolinguist writing in the 1970s: "Never before in this country has a linguist had a greater opportunity to do social engineering. . . . Many of us who are involved with the linguistics of bilingualism have been, and will continue to be, called upon to represent the linguistically and socially repressed minorities" (Keller 1976, 1). At first glance, this statement seems straightforward. To represent a repressed minority is, indeed, a high calling and to perform social engineering a suitable and rewarding activity for the knowledgeable social scientist and concerned citizen. At the same time, this is a person whose role as a social scientist is to critically examine evidence about bilingualism gained from careful, objective observation, to skeptically test his hypotheses, and to draw valid inferences based upon the evidence — all this within the stated content of his ideological advocacy. This is a difficult dilemma indeed.

Examples of the operation of the paradox in this history of sociolinguistics are not difficult to find, but I do not propose a pathological examination here. Examples of severe pathology do not represent the normal state of the field. Better examples of the paradox are those found mixed in substantial contributions by accomplished social scientists. For the sake of illustration, I will refer briefly to a couple.

Consider the case of the work on the history of black English by J. L. Dillard (1972). Shortly after the publication of *Black English*, I complained mildly about some scholarly aspects of the book to a highly accomplished, pioneer student of black English. His response, I think, is of interest to us here: he brushed off my concerns about the nature of the evidence and the structure of the argument as insignificant in the face of the social good accomplished by the book. He said, "That single book has more social good than all my work put together." Clearly, "social good" was one of the important aims of the book. Dillard wished, together with many other sociolinguists, to establish the validity of black English as a language variety and thus, by affecting the generally unfavorable attitudes toward black English on the part of most of the educated, intelligent public, to enhance the status, educational success, and general well-being of the 80 percent of black Americans who habitually use the black English variety. Dillard, with the publication of *Black English*, went one step further than other scholars and attempted to reach out to the intelligent, educated general public.

It seems to me that in showing the structure and function of black English, Dillard has created some social good. But I think also that Mannheim's Paradox has operated to complicate the issue. Dillard's main thrust in *Black English* is to establish the validity of the creole origin of black English, thus providing the variety with a respectable history and, in a measure, setting it off from other varieties of English, to which it had been related historically by earlier scholars. Early on in the book, Dillard shows that he is interested in historicity as well as history (cf. Carpenter 1974). He writes:

> Only the kind of historical explanation which scholars like Whinnom, Thompson, Steward and Volkhoff (i.e. the Creolist explanation) would possibly provide a basis for linguistic dignity for the Negro. The idea is so new — and terms like pidgin are subject to such general misunderstanding — that even black leaders are sometimes resentful of what may seem like a less favorable presentation of Negro language history but one which, upon close examination, turns out to be the only one consistent with black self-respect. (Dillard 1972, 10–11)

Elsewhere in the same chapter in which this passage appeared, Dillard calls for "healthy skepticism" around linguistic issues. At the same time, it is clear that his own "chisel of skepticism [is] driven by the hammer of social passion," to quote Polanyl (1958, 4). Dillard places himself in the dilemma of advocating the same activity he is investigating, namely historicity. Historicity is an apparent sociolinguistic imperative in which every community of speakers feels the need to establish a respectable history of its variety in order to lend it authenticity and vitality (Fishman 1972b, 20).

Moreover, because of the nature of his study, Dillard has a vexing problem with evidence, in that actual speech data of black speakers of an earlier period is not available. He must rely mostly on literary "eye" dialect and upon anecdotal evidence. The tone with which he defends the nature of his evidence displays little skepticism but a great deal of his passionate commitment to his hypothesis. And the same can be said for his cavalier and even sarcastic treatment of contrary evidence and hypotheses.

This may be an appropriate place to state that ideology may serve a useful function, especially in areas in which we are likely to seek an application of our sociolinguistic skills. It is the fashion in recent years to attach a pejorative meaning to ideology, but there is no reason that this should necessarily be so. Ideologists may distort the nature of things, but they also call attention to problems and mobilize groups to action, which, of course, is one of Dillard's aims. It has been the political mobilization of such groups as blacks and Hispanics in the United States that has brought to attention the linguistic problems of minorities. Linguists, like Dillard, have only followed in the wake of these movements. These movements have facilitated the climate of opinion that allows for the application of our science. Science tends to be a handmaiden to ideology. That is the opportunity, the problem, and the paradox.

Moreover, there exists the distinct possibility that to be a participant as well as an observer leads to greater knowledge. Hymes on this point quotes Chairman Mao Tse-tung's remark: "If you want to know a certain thing or certain class of things directly, you must personally participate in the practical struggle to change reality, to change that thing or class of things, for only through personal participation can you uncover the essence of that thing or class of things and comprehend them" (Hymes 1974, 209).

Dillard's hypothesis is strong. In all likelihood, in my view, he is probably to some substantial degree right, although the nature of the evidence is such that we may never be able to reject or accept the creolist's hypothesis. In more recent years, however, Dillard's views have been given greater credibility by the work of such creolists as Derek Bickerton (1973, 75, 81). Clearly, Dillard's work is important in the development of the creolist hypothesis, which is a major contribution to modern linguistic studies.

However, one of the problems of the creolist theory as presented by Dillard is that the social good that Dillard seeks may not even depend upon his being right. He can be *wrong* and establish social good, and conversely, he can be right and create dysfunction. If he has succeeded in establishing in the minds of the community a sense of the vitality of black English, his evidence will probably be accepted as dogma, as items of belief rather than of observation, regardless of its scientific validity. In the long run, however, he will have simply established another ideology, with which future social scientists will clash. If he is right, social dysfunction may still follow.

The reason Dillard may be right and still create social dysfunction is that, once one is caught in the vortex of the paradox, where one will end is hard to predict. In Dillard's case, by joining in an ideological effort to establish historicity, he also inadvertently, I think, became an ideological advocate of the autonomy of black English vis-à-vis ordinary English. Here he parts company from other scholars and from the preponderance of evidence. Linguists who work with black English recognize that it is a separate system set off from the surrounding white dialects by a number of persistent and systematic differences. They also recognize, however, that despite the difference, and whatever its history, black English is closely related to the white dialects. In other words, the autonomy that exists is seen as the *ausbau* type rather than *abstand* type (Fishman 1972a, 19–20). Some language varieties are autonomous by virtue of sheer abstand, that is, real linguistic distance between one variety and another. On the other hand, language varieties between which there is little linguistic "distance," little difference phonologically, lexically, and grammatically, may be perceived attitudinally and psychologically by speakers to be quite different. These are what Kloss calls ausbau varieties ('extension' may be the nearest English rendering of *ausbau*), because they differ by dint of psychological effort (Kloss 1952, 1957). Rather than investigating this phenomenon, Dillard seeks to contribute to it.

In Dillard's book a notion of autonomy becomes concomitant with the notion of historicity, and it is here that one can see the dysfunction occur. For example, another popularization of linguistics, Peter Farb's *Word Play*, picks up the autonomy notion and carries it to a logical, but mistaken, conclusion. He writes: "The problems faced by the . . . black speaker are *the same* [emphasis added] as those faced by American-born children of immigrant parents who entered school knowing Spanish, Italian, Greek, Yiddish, Polish, Hungarian, or other foreign languages" (1974, 162). Farb does note that teachers are less sympathetic toward black English than toward the foreign tongues, but seems to imply that establishing the autonomy of black English would remedy this. In the same way, many other linguists have been led to argue that the black-English-speaking child in the schools is in an analogous situation with a foreign-language-speaking child. For example, W. A. Stewart, whose work forms much of the basis for Dillard's book, has urged this position with respect to teaching black speakers to read materials written in black English (Stewart 1972). The extreme of the autonomy notion has been in the proposals put forward by some linguists that black English speakers be made eligible for federal funds for the teaching of non-English speakers.

Thus Dillard's well-intentioned effort to create social good leads to some seriously dysfunctional consequences. The concept of latent function is well known to sociologists, and is manifested in the case of Dillard's *Black English*. Latent function occurs when

> a pattern of behavior shaped by a certain set of forces turns out, by a plausible . . . coincidence, to serve ends but tenuously related to those forces. A group of primitives sets out, in all honesty, to pray for rain and ends by strengthening its social solidarity . . . an ideologist sets out to air his grievances and finds himself contributing, through the diversionary power of his illusions, to the continued viability of the very system that grieves him. (Geertz 1964, 56)

Dillard sets out to establish the humanity of a minority group by giving a respectability to its language variety and ends by providing the larger community with yet another basis for setting that minority apart by treating its language as something apart.

In the case of Basil Bernstein (1975), his clear advocacy of a certain middle-class ideology, combined with his unreflective use of the Sapir-Whorf notion of linguistic determinism, led him to present his material in such a manner as to lead to its repeated misunderstanding and misuse by other social scientists intent upon social and educational engineering. In particular, Bernstein's construct of "restricted" and "elaborated codes" formed from his earlier notions of "public" and "formal" language aroused much passion of an ideological kind, as well as a dismissive kind. In Bernstein's case, it appears that his considerable contributions to the sociology of language have survived these misunderstandings. Both the misunderstanding and salvation of Bernstein can be traced in a recent sympathetic and understanding book by Paul Atkinson (1985). Nevertheless, for a time his scientific credibility was in danger of being destroyed by the consequences of his well-intended social passions.

Indeed, it is interesting to note how often the Sapir-Whorf notion is utilized for ideological purposes rather than viewed as a social/psychological/linguistic hypothesis. In truth, the hypothesis exists almost entirely in applied circumstances (Swenson 1977, 81). As a theory, it resists testing and formalizing and there is little evidence of any conclusive sort of its viability. For example, the linguistic relativity notion was central to the development of the women's liberation movement in the United States. Within this movement, there was and is a great concern with changing linguistic habits, such as the generic use of *his*, in order to change perceptual behavior patterns. This is virtually a given of the movement. The movement takes the statement of the Sapir-Whorf hypothesis in the place of evidence for a casual connection between language and the treatment of women. The almost inevitable application of the Sapir-Whorf hypothesis to the linguistic aspects of various ideologies is a good example of how sociolinguistic scientific notions can be turned to serve ideology. I suspect that the relativity notion is so attractive for this purpose because there is so little empirical evidence to complicate its application.

Surely, the most important and significant application of linguistic knowledge has been as one of the engines of the bilingual education movement in the United States. Here, too, in my opinion, sociolinguists have fallen victim to Mannheim's Paradox.

Many, including myself, have written much about other difficulties with the so-called bilingual education movement: definitional confusion, ideological conflict, technical difficulties, failure to inform public opinion, and an ahistorical stance (Drake 1984; for a full definitive treatment, see Edwards 1985). In my opinion, the underlying reason for these difficulties can be seen in the operation of Mannheim's Paradox.

Linguists believe that bilingualism psychologically, that is to say, in the individual, is under most circumstances a desirable phenomenon. The Saint Lambert Experiment (Lambert and Tucker 1972), and other similar experiments that have followed in its wake, have tried to demonstrate that bilingualism does provide intellectual, cognitive, and attitudinal advantages to the individual over monolingualism. As linguists, we celebrate linguistic dexterity, we understand diglossia, bidialectalism linguistic registers, and other commonplace linguistic behaviors in the society that go unnoticed or, if noticed, are disturbing to the linguistically naive, but intelligent observer. We know about and are fascinated by linguistic drift and linguistic maintenance, and the shift that occurs over generational or multigenerational time. Most otherwise-informed citizens live in the linguistic present emotionally and intellectually; they are time-bound and place-bound in their visceral response to language. Indeed, most people are threatened by the linguistic differences and changes that delight us as linguists. This is not to disparage the linguistic layperson. We as linguists, as the bilingual hassle has demonstrated, are just as blind to aspects of human behavior in our own ways.

The operation of Mannheim's Paradox has caused many of us engaged in the study of language and society to convert our knowledge to social passion in our zeal to apply our specialized understanding and sensitivity in a humane and useful way. In our zeal, we have ignored or bristled at other specialized knowledge and sensitivity that tends to blunt our passion.

Let me provide an illustration. It is common to read in the sociolinguistic literature that we must choose either the assimilationist's or the pluralist's side as a policy base for bilingual education (Kjolseth 1973; Rubin 1977). The problem is that neither position in its pure form is acceptable or has been found to be acceptable historically. The assimilationist in seeking the elimination of ethnic boundaries — and language is seen as a boundary-maintenance device — teaches rejection and contempt for things that resist rejection and deserve respect. The assimilationist trades affection and loyalty for autonomy and mastery, achieves the pursuit of individual success at the cost of identity, and assumes that an individual needs only the opportunity to prove his worth. This leads to alienation and self-hatred on the part of those who fail to prove their worth in the assimilationist's terms (Abrahams 1972; Higham 1975).

Pluralism, on the other hand, insists on a rigidity of boundaries and a commitment to the group that American society simply will not permit. Pluralism limits the autonomous, the adventurous, and the ambitious. It breeds suspicion, narrow-mindedness, and prejudice against the outside world — a deadly environment in which to educate. An individual is at the mercy of the group. Thus, in our zeal for spreading the benefits of linguistic diversity, many of us have defined the conflict and picked a side that assures we will lose even if we win.

John Edwards's discussion of this issue in chapter 4 of his book *Language, Society and Identity* (1985) sheds light and common sense in saying that pluralism and assimilation should not be thought of as polar opposites. He suggests that we must find a way for "group continuity *and* mainstream participation." (1985, 165). In this assertion I believe Edwards signals that he understands the way American culture works.

To move beyond Edwards, the ethnic markers American culture mostly tolerates are those on the periphery of the ethnic group: food, rituals, clothing, dances; not language, kinship, family structure, or other culturally controlled markers that would, over the long run, hinder mainstream participation or cause conflict. This process can be cruel to some members of some generations, and change usually takes three generations to occur.

A hippie friend of mine, who became famous writing books about his flower-child generation, told me once at the twilight of that movement that his subculture was doomed when Sears started selling tie-dyed shirts. This was co-optation surely, but there was co-optation in the other direction as well: American culture became a bit more open, tolerant, hippized, "green." This, too, was signaled by Sears selling the tie-dyed shirts. Slow mutual co-optation is one sure device by which American culture accommodates changes and maintains stability and continuity. Clearly, Edwards's solution to the pluralism/assimilation conflict accords with this understanding.

The culture has worked in this way with respect to bilingual education. There are elementary schools in some cities in the United States where Anglo children go to school mostly in Spanish. Moreover, middle-class parents in these cities are lined up impatiently to enroll their children. At the same time, the assumption is that the Anglo children as well as the Spanish-speaking children in the schools will use English as their first language. Recent literature (such as Edwards 1985) would strongly suggest that cultural pluralism as a basis for bilingual education has been rejected. At the same time, there is an awareness in the wider culture of the vitality of ethnic culture and of the pains and problems of assimilation.

Some vexing problems remain, however. One pragmatic issue manifests itself if one browses the library stacks where bilingual education texts and materials are shelved. The shelves sag — dare I say groan — under the weight of materials that either assume extreme pluralism as the instructional goal or communicate the common confusion in the definition of bilingual education. How many teachers have been trained by government-funded programs that assume pluralism as guiding principles, or where the definitional confusion buzzes and booms? Has cultural pluralism as a goal, although rejected by the society, been institutionalized by well-meaning teachers, administrators, and applied linguists in the throes of Mannheim's Paradox? Or have the values of the larger society overridden the intentions of linguistic engineers intent on constructing cultural pluralism? Has the Edwardian model of "middle ground" prevailed? I don't know the answers to these questions, but they deserve investigation.

This issue leads to the most serious question emerging from the bilingual education debate, a question that just won't go away no matter how much it offends linguists: cultural relativism. Most advocates of pluralistic bilingual education are at least vexed and at most outraged by the fact that the public opinion of most non-linguist, non-anthropologist elites, as well as of the mass of Americans, insists that serious conflict would occur if ethnic language and, by extension, other deep cultural beliefs were permitted to abide. Many linguists, on the other hand, envision a stimulating (romantic?) diversity in the same prospect. In the extreme case, these linguists look forward to an expansion of cultural pluralism until it results in many coexisting separate cultures.

The popular suspicion of pluralism is so often attacked in scholarship that I would like to suggest, for the sake of balance if nothing else, that intelligent, well-educated observers are constantly presented with evidence that their fear of the consequences of unfettered pluralism is reasonable. Let us move beyond the usual discussions of conflict in Canada, Belgium, or India to a contemporary issue that reasonably calls into question the efficacy of cultural pluralism.

Consider the intense interest and grisly events in the spring of 1989 around the Salman Rushdie affair, following the publication of his novel *The Satanic Verses*. What has this religious/literary controversy to do with the issue of bilingual education? Commentators in the United States and in Europe have been quick enough to see the connection.

For example, consider Nathan Gardels, the editor of *New Perspectives Quarterly* (1989). He asserts that the book is really a novel "about the metamorphosis of the contemporary world brought about by migration and communication." It is "about the conflicts and spiritual dislocation of fragmented individuals in a fragmented world wrestling with its plural identities." He sees the same conflicts of the schoolrooms in Los Angeles, his home, written larger on the global scale in the novel. He sees the reflection of "the kind of frictions that transpire daily in . . . cities like Los Angeles which have no identity other than plurality. We are a little bit Seoul, Saigon, Taipei, Hong Kong, Mexico City, Managua, San Salvador, Tokyo, even Teheran."

Gardels quotes Rushdie: "What I am saying in *Satanic Verses* is that we have got to come to terms with our plural identities. We are increasingly becoming a world of migrants, made up of bits and fragments from here, there. We are here. And we have not left anywhere where we have been." What Gardels develops is the argument for the dark side of the faith in cultural pluralism.

Gardels goes on to point out the irony that the Ayatolla Khomeini's death sentence of Rushdie "mimics the very theme of *The Satanic Verses*." That is, Rushdie's life can be endangered only in the kind of integrated globe that his novel describes. Milan Kundea (as paraphrased by Gardels) has said that "the novel is able to exist in the West because it requires ambiguity and relativity, not a unique truth that must be conformed to." In the world of the Boeing-747 and the fax machine, the sacred values of the West — skepticism, relativity, pluralism, tolerance — clash with the absolutism of Khomeini's faith. In this, there are ironies within ironies.

Gardels asserts that Khomeini's death sentence is really against the idea of the novel, a cultural artifact of the West (though I doubt Rushdie finds solace in this).

These ironies lead other commentators, such as William Pfaff (1989), who lives in Paris, to review the qualms of many American intellectuals about what he calls the "multicultural ideal," the fear of the consequences of "countries with big immigrant minorities radically different from the host population in religious or political-cultural convictions." He points out tellingly that Rushdie's problems began in *Britain*, not Iran. One in seven of the population of Bradford, a city in Yorkshire, is of South Asian origin. Bradford Muslims publicly burned the novel to create the consequent notoriety that led to Khomeini's deadly pronouncement.

Pfaff reviews the American and French devices for assimilation, to which both countries are committed. He believes that Britain has taken a different course and adopted the goal of a "multicultural society." He acknowledges the pain that the French and American assimilation policy causes immigrant groups, and he recognizes its dark side in the possibility of "cultural chauvinism," or even something close to racism. But he concludes with this point:

> The fact is that without a community of values and cultural assumptions there is no community at all. Do you believe that Rushdie . . . has the right to . . . publish whatever he has on his mind? Do you think that the freedom to do so is essential to the political community in which you wish to live? Or do you believe that God's truth, as you understand it, should be enforced against false ideas. . . .
>
> You can believe one or the other, but you can't believe both. A coherent political community cannot exist without a consensus of agreement on one or the other.

As Pfaff and Gardels dramatically show, the Rushdie affair is the pluralism dilemma writ larger. Personally, I am persuaded by my study of American intellectual and social history and by the preponderance of contemporary evidence that in this country assimilation on the part of immigrants and indigenous minority groups is secure. However, the reluctance of many applied linguists to tolerate and seriously confront the sobering concerns of other observers, such as Gardels and Pfaff, is due to Mannheim's Paradox and remains a serious problem.

For the social world can change as a result of transportation and communication technology. This factor has to be taken into account. More important, a policy thrust cannot succeed if it ignores the strength of the concern raised by conflicts so dramatically illustrated by the Rushdie affair. Ultimate success will depend on a serious, rather than a dismissive, confrontation that encourages dialogue and mutual understanding. The parties on each side must find a way around Mannheim's Paradox.

But this is not to say that sociolinguists run amuck "in an orgy of autistic fantasy" (Geertz 1964, 72). There are a number of checks on Mannheim's Paradox. In the first place, a vital tradition of social science operates to provide its practitioners with rigorous procedures for minimizing its effects. It may be that sociolinguists need more formal training in those procedures and in social theory in general. It's possible that our genesis as a rather marginal discipline has provided us with this training in a rather hit-and-miss way. A strong base in empirical data for our studies, as, for example, exhibited by the work of Labov, to name but one, is one of the surest checks. In many communities a system of competing ideologies itself prevents much mischief. There are also those fortunate cases where ideology and science do not clash but run in a congruent path. In the language-planning area, the establishment of Hebrew as the language of the State of Israel is one of those cases.

A science without ideology is impossible, but ideology without science can be disastrous. (Of course, the last part of this statement is an ideological position, namely the position that drives certain Western nations, such as the one in which I live, to seek to rationalize all functions. Thus, the paradox asserts itself here; it follows social scientists around as original sin follows the Calvinist.) Ideology and science are different but related activities (Geertz 1964, 72). In this relationship is one way to confront Mannheim's Paradox without giving in to apathy or despair. Nor do we need to leave the scope of sociolinguistics to find help. Fishman, in a reference to the problem I raise in this paper, has written:

> I am . . . frequently reminded of the obvious dreadful misuse of the applied sociology of language by totalitarian regimes, not only yesterday, but today. Thus, my conviction that knowledge must and will be used [that] is increasingly tempered by concerns with philosophy, aesthetic and religious pursuits quite far from the sociology of language per se. (1972a, 362)

These are wise words, but I submit that we can temper our knowledge with the tools of our sociolinguistic trade and have no need to leave the sociology of language per se.

My notion is that the study of ideology and of the sociology of knowledge are clearly and primarily *linguistic studies*, and that ideology operates as an "ordered system of symbols" reflecting and influencing social reality. Sociology of knowledge is in effect "the sociology of meaning" (Geertz 1964, 59). In order to avoid apathy or extreme relativism in the face of Mannheim's Paradox, we must assume some degree of a nonrelative reality base for perception. Yet we must account for the great divergence of the varying perceptions of reality and for the wide divergence of belief systems among social groups and subgroups. *If the divergences are taken to be in the symbolic systems, a study of the operation of those symbolic systems is at once a sociological study because it is a study of social action and a linguistic study because it involves a language in a fundamental way. Consequently, such a study is centrally a sociolinguistic study.* Such a study would not only enhance the scope of our discipline, but it would protect its validity, as well, by making us more keenly aware of the symbolic operation of ideology. This could only make us better social scientists and perhaps help prevent our becoming so often involved in socially well-intentioned but scientifically doubtful projects, such as so many of us were, for example, in the compensatory education movement of the 1960s.

Some linguists, especially sociolinguists, are so apt to be vexed and confounded by ideology, that it is surprising that members of the discipline have not been more active in admitting the study of the operation of cultural symbols into the scope of linguistics. One finds such linguistic studies, where they exist, in the work of literary critics, such as Kenneth Burke (1941); philosophers, such as C. S. Pierce, and Charles Morris (1946); or even in the commentary of a literary artist such as Walker Percy (1961). But the poachers have been taking out game little noticed by us. Morris's concern, for example, for the role of language in the distinctions and relationships among belief, truth, and logic is central to the relationship of language and society, tonic for one dispirited by Mannheim's Paradox, and central to the understanding of human behavior. By following his and other examples, linguists could enrich the scope of their discipline and at the same time strengthen and sharpen its methodology—especially as regards the paradox—and thus do well by doing good.

I believe there have been earlier calls for this. For example, virtually every linguistics student is quickly presented with a famous paragraph from Sapir's 1929 paper (1958) "The Status of Linguistics as a Science." It reads: "Human beings do not live in the objective world alone, nor alone in the world of social activity as ordinarily understood, but are very much at the mercy of the particular language which has become the medium of expression for their society" (1958, 162). This, of course, is taken as one of the statements of linguistic determinism with which Sapir's name (along with Whorf's) is generally attached. As such, it has assumed such a symbolic loading as a ritual statement of linguistic relativity that we have ignored its context and failed to perceive the wider message in the passage. Sapir goes on to say: "It is an illusion to think that we can understand the significant outline of a culture through sheer observation and without the guide of linguistic symbolism which makes the outline significant and intelligible to society." Later he adds: "Language is a guide to social reality." Here, Sapir was discussing the value of linguistics to social science. I perceive that he was calling for a sociolinguistics of the sort that I am urging here. More recent calls have included Geertz (1964), which has already been cited. Hymes's call for a study of "social meaning" also, I think, belongs in the same category (1974, 80–81, 206–9).

Moreover, such a study could have consequences far beyond the examples seen so far in this paper. It would add a new social system to the institutional repertoire in sociolinguistics. For ideology can be viewed as a cultural system (Geertz 1964, 72), as a system of social action expressed in symbols. The novelist Walker Percy has written: "The embarrassing fact is that there does not exist today a natural empirical science of symbolic behavior as such" (Percy 1961, 41). As a result of some subsequent events, this statement does not have the same bite now as it did in 1961 when it was written. We have, for example, the continued struggle of semiotics as a discipline — still somewhat swampy ground. The growing interest in pragmatics and discourse analysis gives hope. Percy's statement is, however, still pertinent. Sociolinguists, above all, could profit from the maturing of such a science. Sociolinguists, above all, have the vision, tools, training, and *need* to establish such a science.

References

Abrahams, Roger D. 1972. "Stereotyping and Beyond." In *Language and Cultural Diversity in American Education*, edited by Roger D. Abrahams and Rudolph C. Troike, 19–29. Englewood Cliffs, N.J.: Prentice Hall.

Atkinson, Paul. 1985. *Language Structure and Reproduction: An Introduction to the Sociology of Basil Bernstein*. London: Methuen.

Bernstein, Basil. 1975. *Class, Codes and Culture*. New York: Schocken Books.

Bickerton, Derek. 1973. "On the Nature of a Creole Continuum." *Language* 49:640–49.

_____. 1975. *The Dynamics of a Creole System*. Cambridge: Cambridge University Press.

_____. 1981. *Roots of Language*. Ann Arbor: Kaloma Press.

Burke, Kenneth. 1941. *The Philosophy of Literary Form: Studies in Symbolic Action*. Baton Rouge: Louisiana State University Press.

Carpenter, Martha R. 1974. "History versus Historicity in the Matter of Black English Vernacular." Unpublished paper.

Coser, Lewis A. 1968. "Sociology of Knowledge." In *International Encyclopedia of the Social Sciences*, edited by David L. Sills, 428–34. New York: MacMillan and Free Press.

Dillard, J. L. 1972. *Black English*. New York: Random House.

Drake, Glendon F. 1973. "Black English and the American Value System." *Kansas Journal of Sociology* 9(2) (Fall):217–27.

_____. 1979. "Ethnicity, Values, and Language Policy in the United States." *Language and Ethnic Relations*, edited by H. Giles and B. St. Jacques. New York: Pergamon Press.

_____. 1984. "Problems of Language Planning in the United States." In

Linguistic Minorities, Policies and Pluralism, edited by J. Edwards. London: Academic Press.

Edwards, John. 1985. *Language, Society and Identity*. London: Basil Blackwell.

Farb, Peter. 1974. *Word Play: What Happens When People Talk*. N.Y.: Alfred A. Knopf.

Fishman, Joshua A. 1972a. *Language in Socioculture Change*. Stanford, Calif.: Stanford University Press.

_____. 1972b. *The Sociology of Language*. Rowley, Mass.: Newbury House.

Gardels, Nathan. 1989. "Misfits in the Urban Collage." *Los Angeles Times*, 4 Mar., pt. 11, 8.

Geertz, Glifford. 1964. "Ideology as a Cultural System." In *Ideology and Discontent*, edited by David E. Apter, 45–76. Glencoe, Ill.: The Free Press.

Higham, John. 1975. *Send These to Me*. N.Y.: Atheneum.

Hymes, Dell. 1974. *Foundations in Sociolinguistics*. Philadelphia, Penn.: University of Pennsylvania Press.

Keller, Gary D. 1976. "Constructing Valid Goals for Bilingual Education: The Role of the Applied Linguist and the Bilingual Educator." In *Bilingualism in the Bicentennial and Beyond*, edited by G. Keller, R. Teschner, and S. Viera, 17–35. New York: Bilingual Press.

Kjolseth, Rolf. 1973. "Assimilation or Pluralism." In *Bilingualism in the Southwest*, edited by Paul Turner, 3–27. Tucson, Arizona: University of Arizona Press.

Kloss, Heinz. 1952. *Die Entwicklung Nueer Germanischer Kulturspra-chen*. Munich: Pohl.

_____. 1957. "'Abstand' Languages and 'Ausbau' Languages." *Anthropological Linguistics* 9:29–41.

Lambert, Wallace E., and Richard G. Tucker. 1972. *The Bilingual Education of Children: The Saint Lambert Experiment*. New York: Newbury House.

Mannheim, Karl. 1954. *Ideology and Utopia*. New York: Harcourt.

Morris, Charles. 1946. *Signs of Language and Behavior*. New York: Braziller.

Percy, Walker. 1961. "The Symbolic Structure of Interpersonal Process." *Psychiatry* 24(1) (February):39–52.

Pfaff, William. 1989. "Rethinking the Multicultural Ideal." *The Los Angeles Times*, 4 Mar., pt. 22, 3.

Polanyi, Michael. 1958. *The Logic of Liberty*. Chicago: University of Chicago.

Rubin, Joan. 1977. "Bilingual Education and Language Planning." In *Frontiers of Bilingual Education*, edited by Bernard Spolsky and Robert L. Cooper, 282–94. Rowley, Mass.: Newbury House.

Sapir, Edward. 1958 (1929). "The Status of Linguistics As a Science." In

Selected Writings of Edward Sapir, edited by David Mandelbaum, 160–66. Berkeley: University of California Press.

Stewart, William. 1972. "On the Use of Negro Dialect in the Teaching of Reading." In *Language and Cultural Diversity in American Education*, edited by R. Abrahams and R. Troike, 262–73. Englewood Cliffs, N.J.: Prentice-Hall.

Swenson, Douglas V. 1977. *The Sapir-Whorf Hypothesis: An Update.* Unpublished M.A. thesis, San Diego State University.

9

Empirical Explorations of Two Popular Assumptions: Inter-Polity Perspective on the Relationships between Linguistic Heterogeneity, Civil Strife, and Per Capita Gross National Product

Joshua A. Fishman

Among the major charges against linguistic heterogeneity that are encountered in the popular press in political discussions are the claims that it leads to or exacerbates civil strife, on the one hand, and that it lowers national productivity, on the other hand, in both cases because linguistic heterogeneity — and, by extension, bilingual education too, as an undertaking that fosters or promotes linguistic heterogeneity — presumably counteracts rationality, civility, optimal communication, and the smooth operations of society, government, and industry alike. These are charges to which some of my own recent research pertains,[1] and it may prove instructive to compare popular thinking and sociolinguistic scholarship in this connection.

Each of the foregoing charges can be translated into a formal inter-polity hypothesis, namely:

1. The greater the degree of linguistic heterogeneity in a country ("degree of linguistic heterogeneity" being operationalized as

the proportion of the population claiming as its own the major mother tongue of any given country; the smaller that proportion, the greater the degree of linguistic heterogeneity, and, correspondingly, the larger that proportion, the smaller the degree of linguistic heterogeneity), the greater the frequency and severity of civil strife in that country.
2. Similarly, the greater the degree of linguistic heterogeneity in a country, the lower the per capita gross national product in that country.

How Can This Problem Be Studied Empirically?

Until quite recently, it would have been virtually impossible to do conclusive, worldwide, empirical research on hypotheses such as the above because of the large number of countries (that is, polities) and the large number of additional variables that need to be examined in order to rigorously test these hypotheses. There are approximately 170 polities in the world today, and if these were simply to be compared two at a time, in order to determine whether the linguistically more homogeneous one differs significantly (with respect to severity or frequency of civil strife and/or with respect to per capita gross national product) from the linguistically less heterogeneous one, over twenty-five thousand individual comparisons would have to be made. Obviously, it would be both inordinately difficult to undertake and then to make sense out of so many comparisons.

Actually, however, the methodological problem indicated above for two variables and 170 countries is compounded many times over, if we realize that in order to test our hypotheses we also need to simultaneously consider many, many other variables that are descriptive of the countries of the world *in addition to* the two that we are focusing upon. What we really want to know is whether linguistically more heterogeneous and less heterogeneous polities differ in connection with civil strife and per capita gross national product *over and above* (independently of) the differences between such countries due to any and all other factors to which civil strife and per capita gross national product may be indirectly related.

Civil strife, for example, should be considered, too, when we are looking into the relationship between degree of linguistic heterogeneity and per capita gross national product. This is necessary so that we can tell whether any relationship encountered between the degree of linguistic heterogeneity and per capita gross national product, whatever that may be, is masked by or even due to the relationship between civil strife and per capita gross national product. And the same is also true, of course, with respect to the degree of religious heterogeneity, the degree of racial heterogeneity, the proportion of the annual budget allocated to military expenses, and so on, and so on. *Only if we can also consider all other possibly contributing variables can we tell whether linguistic heterogeneity per se really makes an independent (that is, a nonredundant) contribution to per capita gross national product.* However, there are an almost endless number of such "other possibly contributing variables" (indeed, political scientists have perfected about 230 different dimensions [238 to be exact], all in all, for describing countries), and all of these need to be utilized simultaneously, together with linguistic heterogeneity, when attempting to account for inter-polity differences in civil strife or in per capita gross national product.

Thus, our task is to compare all countries simultaneously on all variables simultaneously if we really want to find out whether the degree of linguistic heterogeneity is *a truly independent (necessary, nonredundant) correlate* of either civil strife or per capita gross national product. The price of bananas and the number of gloves sold on a particular day may correlate substantially. However, only if we include all other variables that might also possibly influence the cost of bananas on a particular day (for example, average daily temperature in the banana groves, daily transportation costs between the groves and the markets, labor costs in the groves and in the markets, et cetera, et cetera) can we safely avoid coming to the specious conclusion that the number of gloves sold is really genuinely (that is, independently) related to the cost of bananas. Does this sound like an impossibly tall order: to analyze hundreds of countries and hundreds of variables simultaneously? Do we have the necessary data to do that, and do we have the necessary methods to do that?

The Data and Methods Utilized in This Study

Fortunately, the variety and even the quality of the data we need has been provided by the cross-polity data banks that American political scientists, both in government and in academia, have prepared and repeatedly revised and expanded during the past quarter century. These data banks provide sifted, corrected, and continually updated data on all the countries of the world in conjunction with over 230 different economic, political, social, cultural, historical, geographic, and demographic variables. This data is not perfect, but it is the best available today anywhere in the world, and, since quite a bit of American economic, political, and military planning and policy is based on this data, it must at least be reasonably good on the whole, and it may even be quite a bit better than that.

The analytic methods to do what needs to be done have been provided by statisticians and computer specialists who have relatively recently perfected approaches (primarily cumulative multiple correlation and factor analysis) that make it relatively easy, on the one hand, to examine huge amounts of multivariate data and, on the other hand, to parsimoniously zero in on the relatively few variables in any large data set that are really the only independent (and, therefore, the only crucial) variables in explaining or in accounting for the variation in any given criterion variable. My co-workers and I are, I believe, the first to put both the exhaustive data sets and the new statistical analytic methods to joint use in relating inter-polity variation in linguistic heterogeneity to cross-polity variation in civil strife and in per capita gross national product.

Perhaps an apology is in order for this brief detour into methodological issues, which, no matter how brief it may be to the specialist, inevitably seems overly long and insufficiently understandable to the nonspecialist. My concern is basically related to the usual scholarly preoccupation that findings, interpretations, and conclusions rest upon foundations that are as firm as possible. It is also related to an attempt to get away from a contrasted approach, which may be referred to as "the favorite country approach." Journalists, politicians, and academics alike, we are all good at arguing from "preferred cases:" cases that predictably provide *negative* answers to the questions we have initially posed about linguistic heterogeneity's possibly harmful consequences by examining them only in connection with Switzerland (where linguistic heterogeneity results in neither heightened civil strife nor in lowered per capita gross national product); or cases that answer these same questions in the *positive* by referring only to India, without even pausing to consider the many other dimensions (besides linguistic heterogeneity) on which Switzerland and India differ substantially and in ways that are directly related to civil strife and/or per capita gross national product. It is to escape from this more usual approach of arguing from "preferred (and biased) cases" that I have gone out of my way to study *all* available variables and *all* documentable countries simultaneously in order to clarify the true (that is, the independent) relationship between linguistic heterogeneity, civil strife, and per capita gross national product.[2]

Examining Civil Strife

Political scientists have kept records on four different indicators of civil strife in all of the countries of the world: (1) magnitude and frequency of conspiracy against the established government, (2) magnitude and frequency of internal warfare due to revolution, sedition, or secession, (3) magnitude and frequency of internal turmoil (riots, strikes, protests), and (4) a composite average of the above three.[3] The last is the only measure of civil strife that will be discussed in this paper, although essentially identical results obtain from analyses of the contribution of linguistic heterogeneity to civil strife as measured by each of the other measures of civil strife as well.[4]

A cumulative multiple correlation analysis that begins by aiming over 230 variables at the composite civil strife measure (our criterion or dependent variable at this point) reveals that the differences in composite-magnitude and frequency of civil strife across all of the countries of the world are both highly predictable and parsimoniously predictable. Out of about 230 possible predictors of this criterion, only a certain thirteen make truly independent contributions that, taken together, yield the optimal multiple correlation of .82 (see table 9.1 with respect to variable 1). Particularly noteworthy for our purposes is the fact that *linguistic heterogeneity is not a member of this optimal subset of predictors*. Of course, linguistic heterogeneity does have a certain correlation (.21) with civil strife and, therefore, if we were to disregard, for a moment, its redundancy with other variables it would, at most, explain only 4 percent (or .21²) of the total variance in civil strife.

TABLE 9.1
Linguistic Heterogeneity, Civil Strife, and
P.C. Gross National Product

CRITERION	MAXIMUM CR OBTAINED	MOST POWERFUL PREDICTORS	r WITH LH	LH IN OPT. SUB.?	FACT. STRUCT. OF OPT. SUB.
1. Civil Strife	.82 $(CR^2 = 68\%)$	• Short- and long-term deprivation • Absence of central coercive power • Presence of organized lawless groups	.21 $(r^2 = 4\%)$	No	I, II, III
2. p.c. GNP	.90 $(CR^2 = 81\%)$	• Government modernization • p.c. newspaper circulation • Multiparty parliamentary government	-.32 $(r^2 = 10\%)$	No	I, II, III
3. LH	.88 $(CR^2 = 78\%)$	• Christianity or Islam dominant religion • Religious and racial homogeneity • Western or early westernized	–	–	I, IV, V

Note: The correlation between Civil Strife and p.c. GNP = $-.28$ ($r^2 = 82\%$).

However, when linguistic heterogeneity is confronted with all other possible predictors of civil strife, it is eclipsed entirely, and it becomes clear that it itself explains nothing at all in connection with civil strife that is not explained better (that is, less redundantly or more independently) by other variables. What are the variables that displace linguistic heterogeneity from any consideration as an independent predictor of civil strife? They are variables such as (1) short-term deprivation, (2) persistent deprivation, (3) the absence of coercive potential by the government, and (4) the presence of organized outlaw groups that exert pressure for their own particular benefit. Just a few variables such as these immediately come to the fore to form the relatively small optimal subset of thirteen indispensable predictors that, when taken together, account for 68 percent (or $.82^2$) of the worldwide inter-polity variance in composite civil strife.

A cumulative multiple correlation of .82 is quite an impressive accomplishment, but, of course, this still leaves about 32 percent of the variance in civil strife to be accounted for by variables not yet utilized (that is, by variables not yet in the total data set of about 230 variables) or by better measures of the variables that *have* been utilized in this data set. In either case, it is relatively certain that linguistic heterogeneity will not be among them, because we have already utilized it in two different measurement modes[5] and the results have been identical: linguistic heterogeneity simply does not appear in the optimal subset of independent variables needed for the maximal and most parsimonious prediction of civil strife. We may have the conviction that in one country or another linguistic heterogeneity *does* make an important contribution to the explanation of civil strife, and perhaps that is indeed so. Civil strife in each country is overdetermined by its own historical circumstances, but in the world as a whole, across all countries and across all historical circumstances, once deprivation, central coercive potential, and the presence of organized anomic groups are taken into consideration, it is entirely unwarranted to posit linguistic heterogeneity itself as a co-cause of civil strife. Whatever minor and redundant importance it may have is entirely attributable to its redundancy with the stronger independent predictors that do wind up in the optimal subset of predictors of civil strife.

Examining Per Capita Gross National Product

Turning now to our second criterion variable, we proceed to ask whether worldwide inter-polity variance in linguistic heterogeneity makes an independent contribution to the explanation or prediction of worldwide inter-polity variance in per capita gross national product.[6] Once again it becomes evident that the worldwide inter-polity variance in our second criterion variable is highly predictable on the basis of a relatively small subset of optimal predictors. Out of our original pool of 238 available variables, only a certain ten are needed in order to yield a cumulative prediction of .90 and, once again, linguistic heterogeneity is not a member of this optimal subset (see table 9.1 with respect to variable 2). Linguistic heterogeneity naturally has its own correlation with per capita gross national product, a correlation of −.32, which, at best (that is, were it to be nonredundant) would indicate that linguistic heterogeneity could explain only 10 percent (or .32²) of the worldwide inter-polity variation in per capita gross national product. However, linguistic heterogeneity is far from being a nonredundant predictor of per capita gross national product. When linguistic heterogeneity is confronted with all other possible predictors of per capita gross national product it is eclipsed entirely, indicating that in itself it really explains nothing at all about per capita gross national product.

The cross-polity variables that do wind up in the optimal subset of predictors of worldwide inter-polity variation in per capita gross national product are primarily (1) governmental modernization, (2) per capita newspaper circulation, (3) presence of a multiparty and parliamentary-republican government, and (4) industrial rather than agricultural concentration of the work force. All in all, these cumulatively account for 81 percent (or .90²) of the total worldwide inter-polity variation in per capita gross national product, leaving 19 percent still to be accounted for either by additional variables, above and beyond the 238 already conceptualized, operationalized, and defined to date, or, alternatively, by the same variables measured more reliably and more validly. Even then it seems unlikely that linguistic heterogeneity would wind up in the optimal subset of predictors of per capita gross national product, because it is probably not sufficiently independent of the optimal subset of predictors, nor sufficiently powerful in comparison to them, to do so. There are simply much more immediate and much more independent predictors of cross-polity variation in per capita gross national product for us to be able to posit linguistic heterogeneity as a serious copredictor, over and above what is contributed to governmental modernization, parliamentary democracy, popular literacy, and large-scale industrialization.[7]

Examining Linguistic Heterogeneity as a Criterion Variable

We have twice looked at linguistic heterogeneity as an independent (or nonredundant) predictor variable and have found it to be a distinctly weak one.[8] We can now try to arrive at a clearer understanding of what inter-polity variation in linguistic heterogeneity *is* related to by viewing it itself as a criterion variable and then asking what other variables in our data set tend to predict inter-polity variation in linguistic heterogeneity. Once again, we obtain a relatively small and parsimonious optimal subset of predictors that, when taken together via cumulative multiple correlation procedures, yield a correlation of .88 (see table 9.1 with respect to variable 3). The most powerful variables in the optimal subset, a subset that accounts for 78 percent (or .88²) of the worldwide cross-polity variance in linguistic heterogeneity, are (1) Christianity or Islam as the dominant religion of a polity, (2) degree of religious and racial homogeneity, (3) whether a polity is historically a former Spanish colony, and (4) whether a polity is Western or early-Westernized rather than late-Westernized under colonial auspices.

Several comments are in order about the above optimal subset of predictors. First of all, they are all *negatively* correlated to the criterion of linguistic heterogeneity; that is, they all tend to make for linguistic homogeneity rather than for heterogeneity. Second, we should note that neither civil strife nor per capita gross national product are in this subset, further confirming what we have reported in the two prior analyses, immediately above. Finally, it should be noted that if deprivation is the major underlying dimension of civil strife, and if modernization is the major underlying dimension of per capita gross national product, then homogenization, whether religious. demographic, or political-developmental, seems to be the major underlying (negative) predictor of linguistic heterogeneity. Obviously, at a deeper conceptual level, there *are* weak relationships between the three *criteria* that we have been predicting (civil strife, per capita gross national product, and linguistic homogeneity) as well as between their respective *optimal subsets of predictors*. This can be gleaned from the fact that civil strife and per capita gross national product correlate $-.28$ with each other, somewhere in between the correlation of linguistic heterogeneity with civil strife (.21) and the correlation of linguistic heterogeneity with per capita gross national product ($-.32$). Nevertheless, these links are weak, and no one criterion is among the best predictors of the other two. This means that each can be best predicted without the other, because each is influenced by the other not only weakly but indirectly, that is, via the influence of more primary and less redundant predictors.

The inescapable implication of these findings would be that

lingua francas and bilingualism enable many polities to attain higher per capita gross national product and to avoid civil strife regardless of their degree of linguistic heterogeneity. It also implies that polities that are low in per capita gross national product and high in civil strife are, on the whole, characterizable as such regardless of their degree of linguistic heterogeneity, some of them being linguistically very homogeneous indeed. There may actually be very few, if any, countries that are communicationally penalized due to linguistic heterogeneity per se because folk bilingualism on a regional basis, elitist bilingualism on a nationwide basis, and the spread of national (and international) languages everywhere facilitate interactive processes. Furthermore, education, urbanization, commerce and industry, the mass media, and travel or migration all inevitably lead either to the erosion of minority languages (such erosion continuing to be particularly rapid and widespread in the United States)[9] or to the establishment of widespread and stable minority bilingualism along sociofunctional lines (referred to as *diglossia*), wherein each language is normatively accepted in minority society with minimally redundant functions of its own.[10]

Another Approach

That our three criteria are weakly (and redundantly) related but fundamentally separate is demonstrable by yet another approach known as "factor analysis." The optimal subset of variables for cumulatively predicting civil strife contains thirteen variables. The optimal subset of variables for cumulatively predicting per capita gross national product contains ten variables. The optimal subset of variables for cumulatively predicting linguistic heterogeneity (when the latter is measured as a continuous variable) also contains ten variables. These three subsets of optimal predictors are totally nonredundant; that is, there is no predictor that is optimal for more than one criterion. This itself is a powerful indicator of the major extent to which these three criteria are separate and distinct from each other.

However, thirty-three predictors are too many to keep in mind simultaneously and, therefore, difficult to understand or to discuss meaningfully. Factor analysis is a statistical method that enables us to derive from any large set of measures the smallest number of maximally different "dimensions" (that is, *factors*) to which the large set can be mathematically reduced. If we apply this technique to our original universe of 238 variables, we discover that it can be quite successfully reduced to about 20 factors, the first five of which alone account for more than half of the total variance in the original universe. Obviously, this means that there is quite a bit of redundancy in the original matrix, and that many of the original predictors correlate highly with each other and may even be different ways of measuring the same thing. If we now examine our three optimal subsets of predictors relative to this underlying factor structure in the data universe from which they were selected (via the cumulative multiple prediction method that we discussed quite early in this paper), the following picture emerges (see table 9.1): the optimal subset of predictors in connection with civil strife are primarily associated with factors I, II, and III. This is also the case in connection with the optimal subset of predictors in connection with per capita gross national product. However, when we turn to the optimal subset of predictors of our third criterion, linguistic heterogeneity, we find that these are primarily associated with factors I, IV, and V. It must be stressed that these factors are orthogonal, that is, unrelated to ("maximally different" from) each other. What the three optimal subsets of predictors have in common is factor I, the well-known "common factor" that "varimax orthogonal" factor analysis is expected to yield. Thereafter, the factor structure of the optimal predictors of linguistic heterogeneity differs greatly from the factor structure of the optimal predictors of either civil strife or per capita gross national product, and the total variance accounted for by the differences in factor structure is much greater than the total variance accounted for by their similarities.[11]

Why Is There Even a Weak Correlation Between Our Three Criteria?

Why do even weak relationships obtain between the three criteria we have been studying? Another type of statistical analysis, known as "path analysis," might possibly help clarify this question somewhat, but rather than burden this presentation by yet a third statistical technique,[12] let us permit ourself the instant gratification of a brief speculative interlude. All of the variables that political scientists have perfected for the study of inter-polity differences and similarities may be thought of as dealing with positive and negative "resources" vis-à-vis polity functioning. Most of these resources, by design, are *current resources*, and no historical dimension is supplied in connection with them. However, over centuries, those polities whose resources were relatively greater or more accessible generally attained modernization, unification, and democratization more quickly. In the past, the processes of modernization, unification, and democratization probably did undercut linguistic heterogeneity. However, by the end of the twentieth century, the period to which the bulk of our data pertains, we are dealing with the end results of the above, hypothetical, trends. Now, in an age of social, economic, demographic, and even cultural planning by rich countries as well as by poor ones, by stable countries as well as by unstable ones, the relationships that may once have existed, particularly along a long-term historical dimension, are now exceedingly attenuated and indirect at best.

Polities that value, accept, and cultivate linguistic heterogeneity have learned to do so while simultaneously fostering per capita gross national product and counteracting civil strife. There has been less politicized ethnolinguistic factionalism in the half century since the end of the Second World War, notwithstanding the large numbers of Third World polities that have come into existence since then, than in the half century preceding it. The underdeveloped, nondemocratic, multiethnic empires and colonies (where ethnolinguistic animosity was often stirred up by colonial masters seeking to divide the indigenous population) that may have given ethnolinguistic diversity a bad name ("Balkanization") in former times are hardly the proper model to use nowadays in order to understand the relationships between the criteria we have been studying. The weak relationships between these criteria are both resultants of past circumstances, and indications that those circumstances do not now commonly obtain in the world at large.

Might There Be Some Positive Consequences of Linguistic Heterogeneity?

Thus far, we have done no more than discredit the necessarily negative consequences that are commonly attributed to linguistic heterogeneity. However, the absence of negative consequences is not at all the same thing as the presence of positive consequences. The verifiability of any positive consequences of linguistic heterogeneity, if, indeed, there are any, is a question for future research to pursue. It may be that the pursuit of such consequences will be an equally thankless one, since in that connection, too, linguistic heterogeneity may be an exceedingly weak independent (that is, nonredundant) inter-polity dimension. Perhaps what is involved, insofar as any possible positive consequences of linguistic heterogeneity are concerned, is not so much the *degree* of such heterogeneity as the type of policy adopted vis-à-vis linguistic heterogeneity. A serious problem in connection with the exploration of whatever positive correlates there may be of linguistic heterogeneity is the sad fact that political and other social scientists have not yet exhaustively studied the countries of the world with respect to those very dimensions that seem to me to present the best prospects of yielding such findings. Taking these two considerations together, (1) positive policies (or positive language-status planning) with respect to linguistic heterogeneity and (2) possibly positive consequences of linguistic heterogeneity, I would opt to investigate linguistic heterogeneity and such variables as (1) proportion of the minority-language population that has acquired the majority or dominant language (examining oralcy and literacy separately), (2) proportion of the minority-language population that has completed secondary education and received higher education, (3) proportions of the minority-language population that is employed and that is living above the poverty line, (4) some measure of positiveness of intergroup relations, and (5) some measure of degree of bilingualism and biliteracy in the dominant-language population.

These possibly positive consequences of a more positive (culturally pluralistic) policy toward linguistic heterogeneity are no more than hunches derived from the social science literature. Their exploration will require a combination of expanded inter-polity data, statistical sophistication, and sociolinguistic expertise. Their exploration will get us away from constant "damage control" with respect to linguistic heterogeneity, where we are always concerned with either containing or disproving the alleged negative consequences of linguistic heterogeneity, and into the domain of "positive bilingualism," that is, into the domain philosophically advanced by J. G. Herder, B. L. Whorf, and H. Kallen.[13]

Another lead that deserves to be investigated, which flows directly from the above discussion, is the possibility that, if the policy toward linguistic heterogeneity is nonaccepting, negative, or punitive, then the converse of the above tentative hypotheses might be confirmed, as might some of the other negative consequences of linguistic heterogeneity that have long been suspected. It would be more than I dare hope for to believe that such further research (of either kind) might overcome the emotional and nonrational climate in which issues of linguistic heterogeneity have long been discussed. Emotional issues do not respond easily to empirical evidence. Nevertheless, having devoted much of my life to the empirical study of emotional sociolinguistic issues, I continue to believe that the possibly positive and the possibly negative correlates of linguistic heterogeneity have been too little studied contextually, and that those who are not afraid of being "confused by the facts" and not too impatient to pursue the facts wherever they may lead, have a great deal of work ahead of them before light can begin to counterbalance heat in this sensitive area.[14]

Notes

1. This paper summarizes four previous studies, all of which I conducted together with Frank R. Solano, and one of which also benefited from the collaboration of Grant D. McConnell.
2. Prior to my own most recent research, almost all worldwide interpolity studies of linguistic heterogeneity concentrated on only a very few variables at a time (see, for example, Pool 1969; McRae 1983, 5–33 and particularly 24–25). My own early contribution to research on the inter-polity correlates of linguistic heterogeneity *did* examine all variables available at that time, but it did so, by and large, one variable at a time rather than via statistical approaches that permitted all variables to be examined simultaneously and contrastively with each other (see Fishman 1966). The analytic approaches that I have adopted in the present round of studies (cumulative multiple correlation and factor analysis) seek to accomplish the same analyses, ceteris paribus, that would be undertaken if countries were matched on all variables and then compared only on two remaining variables: linguistic heterogeneity and the particular criterion variable under study (civil strife or per capita gross national product). The latter methodology, so commonly expected by the intelligent layman, usually cannot be followed in the social sciences because of sampling limitations, on the one hand (for example, in our studies the number of countries

is finite and cannot be increased for research purposes) and, on the other hand, the very large number of other variables that need to be controlled. Even more directly tackled by our adopted methodologies is the problem of indirect causes, cumulative multiple correlation analysis actually being the method of choice if such concerns are to be set aside.

3. For full details as to the separate as well as the composite worldwide inter-polity measurement of civil strife, see Feierabend and Feierabend 1972).

4. This section briefly summarizes Fishman and Solano 1989a. The correlation between linguistic heterogeneity and civil strife reported in the present paper is that which obtains when the former is measured as a continuous variable. A lower correlation obtains (.12) when linguistic heterogeneity is measured as a dichotomous variable. For $N=200$, a correlation of .18 is significant at the .01 level and a correlation of .14 is significant at the .05 level.

5. Two measures of linguistic heterogeneity were employed, a dichotomous measure and a continuous measure. The dichotomous measure characterized each polity as either having or not having at least 15 percent of its population claiming a mother tongue other than the dominant mother tongue of the country. The continuous measure characterized each polity by the exact proportion of its population claiming a mother tongue other than the dominant mother tongue of that country. The identical nature of findings utilizing these two different measures of linguistic heterogeneity is reported in Fishman, Solano, and McConnell 1990.

6. This section briefly summarizes Fishman and Solano 1989b. The correlation between linguistic heterogeneity and per capita gross national product reported in the present paper is that which obtains when the former is measured as a continuous variable. A lower correlation obtains (.25) when linguistic heterogeneity is measured as a dichotomous variable. For $N=200$, a correlation of .18 is significant at the .01 level and a correlation of .14 is significant at the .05 level.

7. Popular literacy may be as much a cause as a consequence of per capita gross national product, as far as cumulative multiple correlation analysis is concerned, but linguistic heterogeneity is apparently neither the one nor the other in a strong or nonredundant fashion.

8. This section briefly summarizes Fishman and Solano 1989c.

9. International perspective on language spread more generally and on recent language shift in particular may be gained from Dow 1987–88; Fishman et al. 1985, particularly chapter 6, "Mother-Tongue Claiming in the United States since 1960: Trends and Correlates"; and Veltman 1983.

10. A history of the diglossia concept and the huge literature devoted to it, as well as a review of its current status and suggestions for the modification of this concept, are all available in Britto 1986.

11. For the substantive specification and resultant naming of these factors, see the discussions in Fishman and Solano 1989a, 1989b, and 1989c.
12. A path analysis study of our data is currently underway and will be reported separately in the near future.
13. For a discussion of "positive bilingualism" and a review of Herder's, Whorf's, and Kallen's theoretical contributions to that topic, see Fishman 1978.
14. I am greatly indebted to my colleagues and friends Ofelia Garcia, Ricardo Otheguy, and S. R. Sridhar for their comments and queries, which helped me revise an earlier draft of this paper.

References

Britto, Francis. 1986. *Diglossia: A Study of the Theory with Application to Tamil*. Washington, D.C.: Georgetown University Press.

Dow, James R., ed. 1987–88. "New Perspectives on Language Maintenance and Language Shift." *International Journal of the Sociology of Language*, nos. 68 and 69 (entire issues).

Feierabend, I. K., and R. L. Feierabend, eds. 1972. *Anger, Violence, and Politics: Theories and Research*. Englewood Cliffs, N.J.: Prentice Hall.

Fishman, Joshua A. 1966. "Some Contrasts between Linguistically Homogeneous and Linguistically Heterogeneous Polities." *Sociological Inquiry* 6:146–58. Reprinted, in *Language Problems of Developing Nations*, edited by Joshua A. Fishman, Charles A. Ferguson, and Jyotirindra Das Gupta, 53–68. New York: Wiley. 1968.

Fishman, Joshua A. 1978. "Positive Pluralism: Some Overlooked Rationales and Forefathers." In *International Dimensions in Bilingual Education*, edited by James E. Alatis, 42–52 (Same as *Georgetown University Round Table on Language and Linguistics*.) Washington, D.C.: Georgetown University Press. Reprinted in Fishman et al. 1985, 445–55.

Fishman, Joshua A., and Frank R. Solano. 1989a. "Cross-Polity Perspective on the Importance of Linguistic Heterogeneity as a Contributory Factor in Civil Strife." *Canadian Review of Studies in Nationalism*. Forthcoming.

Fishman, Joshua A., and Frank R. Solano. 1989b. "Cross-Polity Linguistic Homogeneity and Per Capita Gross National Product: An Empirical Explanation." *Language Problems and Language Planning*. Forthcoming.

Fishman, Joshua A., and Frank R. Solano. 1989c. "Societal Factors Predictive of Linguistic Homogeneity/Heterogeneity at the Inter-Polity Level." *Cultural Dynamics*. Forthcoming.

Fishman, Joshua A., Frank R. Solano, and Grant D. McConnell. 1990.

"A Methodological Check on Three Cross-Polity Studies of Linguistic Homogeneity/Heterogeneity." In *In the Interest of Language: Contexts for Learning and Using Language*, edited by Mary McGroarty and Christian Faltis. Berlin: Mouton de Gruyter. Forthcoming.

Fishman, Joshua A., M. Gertner, E. Lowy, and W. Milán. 1985. *The Rise and Fall of the Ethnic Revival*. Berlin: Mouton de Gruyter.

McRae, Kenneth D. 1983. *Conflict and Compromise in Multilingual Societies*. Waterloo, Ont.: Wilfred Laurier University Press.

Pool, Jonathan. 1969. "National Development and Language Diversity." *La Monda Lingvo-Problem* 1:140–56. Reprinted, slightly revised, in *Advances in the Sociology of Language*, edited by Joshua A. Fishman, 213–30. The Hague: Mouton. 1972.

Veltman, Calvin. 1983. *Language Shift in the United States*. Berlin: Mouton de Gruyter.

10

The Federal Role and Responsibility in Bilingual Education

Carol Pendas Whitten

Overview

The federal government has now been officially involved in the effort to help the non-English-speaking student learn English for twenty-one years. In this time, the well-intentioned and clear purpose of the original federal legislation has been obscured by debates over secondary issues, such as the mandating of a certain method of English instruction or the civil rights concerns of the non-English-speaking student. In a speech to the American Federation of Teachers on 5 July 1983, President Reagan said, "Bilingual programs should serve as a bridge to full participation in the American mainstream. They should never segregate non-English-speaking students in a way that will make it harder, not easier, for them to succeed in life."

No other educational issue stirs American passions more than bilingual education. The nation's newspapers are filled with editorials and "Letters to the Editor" discussing bilingual education and the learning of English. This debate over bilingual education burns hot in the United States. It is fueled by the fact that many Americans misunderstand the federal role, not only in bilingual education, but also in all American education.

In fact, the federal role in American education is a supporting one. The Department of Education does not build schools, does not run schools, does not decide what children are taught. That the federal role is limited is also clear from statistics on the financing of education. For example, in 1986 state and local governments spent approximately $159 billion on elementary and secondary education. The federal government contributed approximately $10.5 billion, which is 7 percent of the total. Therefore, typically 93 percent of all money spent on American education comes from state and local governments. Many Americans do not realize that the main role in the education of our nation's young lies with the states, and that, in actual practice, the responsibility lies primarily with our sixteen thousand local school boards. For two hundred years, people at the local level have set the course for our nation's educational system.

It is not surprising, then, that the federal government has no desire to dictate methodology to states and local educational agencies. In fact, the Constitution of the United States does not give the federal government the right to do so. In 1970, Congress spelled out this prohibition, stating, "No provision of any applicable program shall be construed to authorize any department, or agency, or employee of the United States to exercise any direction, supervision, or control over the curriculum, program of instruction, administration, or personnel of any educational institution, school, or school system." Furthermore, when the Department of Education was established in May 1980, Congress reiterated its position, specifically restraining the department from developing a curriculum for our nation's schools.

However, Congress gave in to pressure from special interest groups when it departed from this historically established tradition and inserted in the 1974 Bilingual Education Act the requirement that local education agencies follow one and only one method of instruction — transitional bilingual education. This created more confusion on the proper role of the federal government in education. The real issue to be debated is who should decide the method of education to be used — local schools and parents, or the federal government.

What all of us in the field of bilingual education must face is that we have no sure, hard solutions to the teaching of our children. Education is not biology, not math, not engineering. From a research point of view, education is a social science; from a practitioner's point of view, it is an art. We must, therefore, avoid looking for the one answer, the one solution.

For example, the Fairfax County school system in northern Virginia is a very successful school system that has recognized this need for diverse solutions. It now provides special instruction to thirty-eight hundred limited-English-speaking students who speak seventy-five different languages. Over the years, Fairfax has designed and developed a serious, nationally recognized program that has met with great success. And yet, in 1985 Fairfax County did not and could not receive any federal Title VII funds from the Office of Bilingual Education.

As a World Bank review of selected international bilingual education case studies concluded, "There is not one answer to the question of what language to use for instruction, but several answers, depending on the characteristics of the child, of the parents, and the local community, and of the wider community" (Dutcher 1981, 25). And Iris Rotberg observed that "a number of other variables affecting student achievement are difficult to control for in comparisons of different program models. Students' socioeconomic status, the length of time they have lived in this country, their general language skills, and their proficiency in various subjects clearly interact with the effects of alternate instructional models" (1982, 157). Christine Rossell and J. M. Ross also concluded that "the research, however, does not support transitional bilingual education as a superior instructional technique for increasing the English language achievement of limited-English-proficient children" (1986, 413).

The question of methodology was further explored by education historian Diane Ravitch:

If the research is in fact inconclusive, then there is no justification for mandating the use of bilingual education or any other single pedagogy. The bilingual method may or may not be the best way to learn English. Language instruction programs that are generally regarded as outstanding, such as those provided for Foreign Service Officers or by the nationally aclaimed center at Middlebury College, are immersion programs, in which students embark on a systematic program of intensive language learning without depending on their native tongue. Immersion programs may not be appropriate for all children, but then neither is any single pedagogical method. The method to be used should be determined by the school authorities and the professional staff, based on their resources and competence. (1985, 271)

Clearly, federal reform in bilingual education should always focus on this one goal: returning to local schools their historically established right to develop educational programs that fit their local conditions regardless of methodology used. Our Hispanic, our native American, our Chinese, our Vietnamese, and our Eastern European youth need intensive, effective instruction that will provide them with the English skills necessary to succeed both in school and the workplace.

Legislative History of Federal Bilingual Policy

In 1968, when the first Bilingual Education Act was enacted, Congress was especially concerned with the problems of Hispanic schoolchildren living in the Southwest. These children, who were often being punished in schools for speaking Spanish, the only language they knew, were performing very poorly in schools and were dropping out at a high rate. Frequently, no effort was being made to provide them with the special English-language instruction they needed to participate fully in the classroom. The original intent of Congress in enacting bilingual education legislation was clear from the beginning: to encourage local school districts to develop "new and imaginative . . . forward-looking" school programs for the special educational needs of these children, "who are educationally disadvantaged because of their inability to speak English."

In the 1967 Senate Committee Report on pending bilingual education amendments, the committee wrote:

Because of the need for extensive research, pilot projects and demonstrations, the proposed legislation does not intend to prescribe the type of programs or projects that are needed. Such matters are left to the discretion and judgment of the local school districts, to encourage both varied approaches to the problems and also special solutions for a particular problem for a given school.

Congress wanted very much to play a role in bringing non-English-speaking children into the educational mainstream, but

Congress did not want to interfere in local schools' affairs by dictating a method or approach to the teaching of English.

That the local school districts had a responsibility to these non-English-speaking students was confirmed by the Supreme Court in its 1974 *Lau v. Nichols* decision. The court concluded that the San Francisco School System was not providing equal educational opportunity to its non-English-speaking Chinese students. However, like Congress in 1968, the Court refrained from mandating a specific approach to the teaching of this special school population. The *Lau* decision simply stated: "Teaching English to students of Chinese ancestry is one choice. Giving instruction to this group in Chinese is another. There may be others."

Despite the flexibility built into the original 1968 legislation, and despite the Supreme Court's affirmation of the rights of local schools to determine the best approach to teaching their limited-English-speaking students, the federal government moved in the opposite direction in 1975. In that year, the U.S. Department of Education Office for Civil Rights (OCR) published the "Lau Remedies," which allowed for a limited set of options for elementary and intermediate schools by mandating programs that relied heavily on native-language instruction. This approach, mandated by the Office for Civil Rights, came to be known as transitional bilingual education. Although the Lau Remedies were never formally enacted into law, since 1975 the Office for Civil Rights has negotiated compliance agreements with over five hundred local school districts based on these remedies. Consequently, school districts have been very reluctant to make adjustments in their teaching methods over the years, fearing that they would lose their federal funds if they were found to be in violation of OCR's Lau Remedies.

Local schools lost their right to develop instructional programs not only through these civil rights mandates, but also through the Bilingual Education Act of 1974. When Congress reauthorized the act in 1974, it curbed local control of program design and prescribed transitional bilingual education to all school districts seeking federal funds. As a result, school districts that used any other methodology were rendered ineligible to apply for federal funds to develop their bilingual programs. Ironically, just as the federal government began mandating this curriculum, which was designed for the teaching of homogeneous groups, the demographic make-up of America's immigrants began to change dramatically. In the 1970s, the United States opened its doors to tens of thousands of immigrants from Southeast Asia, China, the Philippines, East and West Africa, the Middle East, and Eastern Europe. And the trend that began in the 1970s continues into the present decade. Since 1980, almost half of all legal immigrants to the United States have come from Asia, and another 12 percent have come from Europe. School districts face classes that include speakers of Farsi, Arabic, Cantonese, Rumanian, and dozens of other languages in addition to Spanish and Chinese.

The Los Feliz Elementary School in Los Angeles is a classic example of a school affected by this new trend. A number of years ago, Los Feliz was a school with a significant number of Mexican-American minority students. In an ideal world, with enough bilingual certified teachers, bilingual programs could be geared to this homogeneous group of Spanish speakers. But suddenly, in the 1980s, everything changed. The school began to receive students who immigrated to the United States from all over the world, students who spoke Armenian, Cantonese, Vietnamese, Korean, and ten or twelve other languages. Presently, more than 70 percent of the student body at Los Feliz are classified as language-minority, and both federal and California state bilingual laws require that the school teach all these children using a native-language approach. Moreover, California state law requires instruction in native culture and heritage. School officials are struggling to serve these students, to meet educational mandates, and to maintain academic standards. Ironically, some of these students speak languages that are rare or new to the school district. Therefore, even if the district tried to teach in the home languages, it would be impossible to find qualified professionals. No school can properly serve *all* its students' needs while adhering to right native-language instruction requirements. We all know that. Unfortunately, advocates of a strict transitional bilingual approach have not yet fully recognized how much the conditions have changed since 1974.

Due to this situation, it was not surprising that Secretary of Education William Bennett's first goal in 1985 was bilingual education reform was to return to local schools the right to determine the best method of teaching their limited-English-speaking students.

After seventeen years of mandated bilingual instruction, it is clear that school districts face many hardships in meeting these strict requirements. Furthermore, it is clear that the people Congress sought to help have not been helped. For example, Hispanics still constitute only 3 percent of all U.S. college enrollment, even though Hispanics constitute 7 percent of the nation's population. The Scholastic Aptitude Test (SAT) scores of Hispanics remain unacceptably below the national average. Making the situation even worse is the fact that these scores only reflect the achievement of half of all Hispanic students, since more than half of all Hispanic high school students in the United States drop out before graduation. Of these dropouts, 40 percent never reach the tenth grade. In many urban areas, the situation is desperate: in Chicago, 70 percent of all Hispanic students drop out; in New York City, the reported figure is an alarming 80 percent.

Realizing full well that America's non-English-speaking students who drop out of school face unemployment, illiteracy, and poverty, Secretary Bennett called for a major reform of the federal role in bilingual education to ensure that at least those students in federal programs would have the skills necessary to succeed. This reform was an effort to return to local communities the right to determine the best method of teaching their non-English-speaking children. Three specific steps were taken.

First, regulations were issued in 1986 that represented a very important first step in bringing about reforms of the federal role in bilingual education. There were three main objectives of these regulations.

1. School districts were informed that they had broad discretion under the statute to determine the extent of native-language instruction that was required in a transitional bilingual education project. The preamble to the proposed regulations explained that bilingual education legislation provides for instruction in the child's native language only "to the extent necessary to allow a child to achieve competence in the English language" and "in all courses or subjects of study, which will allow a child to meet grade-promotion and graduation standards." As a result of this clarification, local educational agencies, rather than the federal government, could decide the amount of native-language instruction to be used, as well as the manner and duration of its use.

2. Recognizing that parental involvement is crucial to children's success in school, the regulations emphasized the statutory requirement that parents become involved in their children's bilingual education programs. The regulations called for extensive parental participation on the two advisory councils that the law required for each school district. One of these advisory councils assists the district in preparing applications for federal funds; the other provides consultation to the district for the duration of the federal grant. School districts were also required to notify parents of the program's instructional goals and of the progress that their children were making, as well as of the fact that parents have the opportunity to decline enrollment of their children in programs assisted under the act.

3. School districts were required to demonstrate that they were building local capacity to finance bilingual education programs. Each school district was required to develop a plan for managing and financing its bilingual education program for a time when federal funds would no longer be available. This requirement ensured that only truly necessary programs would be developed, since a school district would not use its own limited resources to fund an unnecessary program.

Secretary Bennett's second step, in addition to making regulatory changes, was to seek legislative amendments to the current Bilingual Education Act. The secretary asked Congress to remove the 4-percent limit on financing for alternative programs that do not use the native language to teach English. Lifting this ceiling would enable the Department of Education to serve any school district that needed help to educate limited-English-proficient students without requiring any single, mandated methodology in our nation's schools. The need for a variety of methods is great. For example, in 1985 approximately one-quarter of all applications for bilingual funds were from school districts that were applying for the 4 percent of the money that was available under the special alternatives program, reserved for programs that did not use transitional bilingual education.

Third, in keeping with the goal of restoring flexibility to bilingual education, the Department of Education notified those school districts that had negotiated Lau-compliance agreements with the Office for Civil Rights that the department intended to permit reconsideration of those agreements. School districts with Lau plans were advised that they had considerable discretion in choosing an educational program that met the needs of their non-English-speaking students, as long as affirmative steps were taken to provide for the effective participation of these students in the schools' educational programs.

With these legislative, administrative, and regulatory reforms, the Department of Education recognized the major role that the local community plays in bilingual education. It recognized that the sixteen thousand independent school districts must decide how best to teach their limited-English-speaking students, must develop the infrastructure necessary for these programs to continue, and must involve parents fully in the development of bilingual education programs.

The department received widespread support for these reforms both in newspaper editorials and in personal letters from the American public. The support came for one very good reason, expressed best by an editorial headline in the *Washington Post* of 27 September 1985: "Secretary Bennett Makes Sense!" The editors of the *Post* went on to say that "[c]hildren with language difficulties must be given special help, and the cultures of their native lands deserve respect and understanding. But we need not apologize, as Secretary Bennett points out, for offering assistance in a form that brings children more quickly into American language and culture and strengthens their ability to participate more fully in national life."

The *New York Times* of 27 September 1985 editorialized, "Mr. Bennett proposes returning to the principle of maximum local flexibility. He will ask Congress to remove the 4 percent cap. He's right: the Federal Government should not limit funds to only one pedagogical method. It should be concerned with the ultimate goal, helping children become proficient in English as quickly as possible."

The editors of the *Washington Post* and the *New York Times* did not in any way want federal support for language-minority students reduced or eliminated. Favorable editorials also appeared in the *Chicago Tribune* and the *Houston Chronicle*. As mirrors of their communities, these newspapers recognized that the federal government should simply increase flexibility in its program, and thereby reestablish the original focus of the program: helping children to learn English and to enter the educational mainstream as quickly as possible. These reforms were also supported by the National Association of State Boards of Education, the National Association of State Legislators, the National Association of Secondary School Principals, and the American Legion.

On 29 April 1988, a new bilingual education law, P.L. 100-127, was signed by President Reagan. The new law did not call for total flexibility; rather, it is another compromise. It is, however, a significant improvement over the previous law. At the bill-signing ceremony, the president said, "The bill recognizes a fundamental truth, that the primary responsibility for educating lies with the local communities and the states, not the federal government." However, one of the federal government's responsibilities is to develop the capacity of local school districts to teach their non-English-speaking students, and towards this end the 1988 Bilingual Education Act authorized $200 million for 1989.

Broadly, this legislation allows funding for four types of programs.

Part A funds instructional grants to school districts to develop their capacity to teach non-English-speaking students. Although 70 percent of Part A funds are now reserved for transitional bilingual education programs, which must use the home language, the secretary of education can now reserve up to 25 percent of Part A funds for special alternative programs that may use English-based instruction. In the previous legislation, a maximum of 4 percent of funds could be used for special alternative programs.

Part B funds are for data collection, evaluation, and research.

Part C funds are for teacher training programs to develop teachers and school administrators to serve non-English speakers.

Part D funds are for assistance to administer federal funds.

Other significant new provisions of the law included a three-year limit on a student's participation in a transitional bilingual program or a special alternative program. Additional years in a program must be justified and reviewed on a case-by-case basis. The school must conduct a comprehensive evaluation of the student's performance and then decide if his performance is still hindered by a lack of proficiency in English. Only after this is determined will a student be enrolled in a fourth or fifth year of a bilingual program.

Furthermore, no student will be kept in a bilingual or special alternative program for more than five years. The limit on Part D grants, made to state agencies to process and identify all students, were raised from fifty thousand dollars to seventy-five thousand dollars. Also, pre-service and in-service training now had to meet state certification requirements, and the programs must fund at least five hundred graduate students each year (Cubillos 1988).

Obviously, the major reform in the law was the increase in funding of English-based programs from a 4-percent maximum to a 25-percent maximum. It is also important to note that the regulations introduced in 1985 permitted English as a Second Language programs that use only a minimum of the native language to be funded under the transitional bilingual education program rules. The 1988 Bilingual Education Act is a major improvement in federal bilingual policy because it acknowledges that "regardless of the method of instruction, programs which serve the limited-English-proficient students have the equally important goals of developing academic achievement and English proficiency."

The Problems of the Non-English Speaker

Despite a twenty-year federal involvement with language-minority students, today's Hispanic children still perform below national educational norms. Today's non-English speaker will be the young adult of the 1990s and the twenty-first century. Without proficiency in English and a formal education, how will these students hold jobs and support families?

Furthermore, the United States no longer stands alone as the leader of international business and industry. Our next generation will have to be educationally competitive; otherwise, business, jobs, and opportunities will be lost to other countries. Our children will live in a world that is very complex and demanding, a world whose complexities will be understood only by well-educated adults. All our children will need to read well, write well, and think well. They will also need a knowledge of foreign languages and cultures.

However, it is estimated that forty million Americans are functionally illiterate. And in the Hispanic community 56 percent of all adults may be functionally illiterate. The National Assessment for

Progress in Education (NAPE) administered under contract to the Department of Education, found that 80 percent of all Hispanic high school students can't read well enough to go to college. It also found that seventeen-year-old Hispanics are reading at the level of thirteen-year-old Anglos. When we discuss education and literacy, the Hispanic community is especially important, because Hispanics constitute the youngest and fastest growing population in the United States. In a few years, Hispanics will constitute a majority in the schools of many American cities. Since Hispanics are the most highly urbanized population in the United States today, with 86 percent living in metropolitan areas, a description of our urban schools is, to a large degree, a description of Hispanic schools with large populations of non-English-speaking students.

More than any other group, Hispanics suffer from a lack of the language skills and formal education essential to success in our competitive society. Presently, 28 percent of all Hispanics live below the official poverty line, and 38 percent of all Hispanic youths under age eighteen live in poverty. Unemployment among Hispanics is 40 to 50 percent higher than the national rate. Millions of Hispanics are also underemployed, working intermittently or working part-time while needing full-time jobs (National Commission on Secondary Education for Hispanics 1984, 19–27).

In a 1983 paper, McManus, Gould, and Welch concluded that "differences associated with English-language skills explain virtually all of the Hispanic wage differentials usually attributed to ethnicity, national origin, and time in the United States" (pp. 121–22). The Twentieth Century Fund and the Council on Economic Development both conducted studies that also concluded that proficiency in English is the most important skill that the non-English-speaking student must master.

Since the most important task for Hispanic students is to learn English, some school districts need the flexibility to use English-based teaching methods. Some Hispanic students live in communities where English is rarely spoken. These children use Spanish at home, read Spanish newspapers, listen to Spanish radio, and watch Spanish TV. In these areas, more than anywhere else, one finds that parents want their children to learn English and recognize that only the school can provide their children with exposure to English.

Hispanic youths should be studying English and Spanish and should be getting ready to move into jobs, offices, and the decision-making structure of American financial institutions. The truth is that our Hispanic youth are needed in America today. Our country needs their language skills, needs their fine moral character, needs their good attitude toward work. Our country needs their participation. In order for our nation to remain economically, socially, and morally strong, we need our Hispanic youth.

As Secretary of Education William Bennett, in a speech given to the Association for a Better New York on 26 September 1985, has said, "there ought to be no confusion or embarrassment over our goal. The rise in ethnic consciousness, the resurgence of cultural pride in recent decades is a healthy thing; the traditions we bring with us, that our forefathers brought with them to this land, are too worthwhile to be discarded. But a sense of cultural pride cannot come at the price of proficiency in English, our common language."

References

Cubillos, E., ed. 1988. "The Bilingual Education Act: 1988." Vol. 7. Washington, D.C.: Comsis Corporation.

Dutcher, Nadine. 1981. "The Use of First and Second Languages in Primary Education: Selected Case Studies." Washington, D.C.: The World Bank.

McManus, W., W. Gould, and F. Welch. 1983. "Earnings of Hispanic Men: The Role of English Language Proficiency." *Journal of Labor Economics* 1(2):121–22.

National Commission on Secondary Education for Hispanics. 1984. *Making Something Happen*. Washington, D.C.: Hispanic Policy Development Project.

Ravitch, Diane. 1985. *The Schools We Deserve: Reflections on the Educational Crises of Our Time*. New York: Basic Books, Inc.

Rossell, Christine, and J. M. Ross. 1986. "The Social Science Evidence on Bilingual Education." *Journal of Law and Education*. Fall.

Rotberg, Iris. 1982. "Some Legal and Research Considerations in Establishing Federal Policy in Bilingual Education." *Harvard Educational Review* 52(2):157.

11

A Practicing Teacher's Views on Bilingual Education: The Need for Reform

Sally Peterson

Bilingual education has been presented as the program that would help our limited-English-proficient (LEP) students develop literacy in English, thereby achieving academic success, while they retained pride in their culture and heritage. But it has not succeeded, and it must be reformed.

With the enactment of the Bilingual Education Act of 1968 and the Supreme Court's *Lau* decision in 1974, this country embarked on a program that was academically deficient at its birth. The *Lau* decision did not mandate transitional bilingual education (TBE), but TBE was set up, not just as the preferred, but as the only acceptable method of education for LEP students after little academic input. For over twenty years, we classroom teachers have forged ahead within the constraints of TBE programs. These programs have been presented as sound educational theory, but they have proven to be seriously flawed in classroom application.

The Los Angeles Unified School District (LAUSD) mandated educational policy for LEP students in 1976, and again in 1978 with its LAUSD Lau Plan. These plans created a permanent TBE bureaucracy that has mandated and controlled the education of LEP students. California's TBE program has been mandated by the California Bilingual Education Improvement and Reform Act of 1980 (Assembly Bill 507), by Assembly Bill 37, and by California Education Code 52100.

California and Los Angeles have been influential nationwide in bilingual education, and their programs have frequently been taken as models for other states' and cities' bilingual education programs. California has the largest LEP population in the nation, nearly 600 thousand students. Los Angeles alone has 160 thousand LEP students in eighty-seven different language groups. In the LAUSD, 59 percent of the students are Hispanic, 16 percent are non-Hispanic whites, 17 percent are black, and 8 percent are Asian and other. In Los Angeles, TBE is mandated for all Hispanic LEP students, but almost all students from other language groups are taught in programs that focus on English-language development.

The Experience of Glenwood Elementary School

For the past twenty-five years, I have taught at Glenwood Elementary School, in Sun Valley, a small Southern California city that is located in the San Fernando Valley. Glenwood Elementary is part of the LAUSD. The student population of Glenwood has shifted from 85 percent white to 85 percent Hispanic during these twenty-five years. Now most of our students are the children of blue-collar workers, many uneducated and many illegal aliens, who work in the light industry that surrounds the school.

Throughout all of this period, the faculty at Glenwood Elementary has been small and heterogeneous, with little turnover. A large majority of teachers have been deeply involved in the school and the community. Glenwood had a strong principal, Mrs. Lois Krenz, for thirty years. She made a practice of knowing all of the one thousand students of the school, as well as their families. She took a personal interest in each child and in their personal development. This total cohesiveness of faculty, parents, and the principal was important for the community, and it was especially important when the ethnic composition of the school changed. When students entered Glenwood with little or no English, they were welcomed as children who could and would achieve regardless of their language or their ethnicity. This feeling of warmth and caring provided a nurturing that was vital to each student. It allowed students to put aside their fears and their preconceived notions about their ability to learn. Students were cherished for the languages they brought to us, and they were encouraged to achieve to their greatest potential.

During this transitional period, some teachers at Glenwood acquired bilingual credentials. Many others learned new techniques to teach LEP students in college courses and in district in-service classes. To develop a better awareness and understanding of our Hispanic students, the staff at Glenwood volunteered to be the pilot class in a new course on culture and methodology that was being developed by the California State Department of Education. We added an English as a Second Language (ESL) pullout program. Our Hispanic bilingual teacher, Mrs. Terry McArthur, was particularly successful in giving valuable extra attention and one-to-one instruction to her students. She felt very strongly that her students should learn English quickly, and they did.

The students who came to Glenwood speaking Spanish were never completely isolated by their language. Many of their classmates spoke Spanish as well as English, and Glenwood encouraged bilingual students to communicate with newcomers in their own languages. But as many other language groups came to Glenwood, it became impossible to provide teachers who were skilled in the home language of each minority group. Thus, we continually expanded our ESL classes and our use of sheltered English techniques. We praised those who brought other languages to us for having their language skills, while at the same time we helped them to develop fluency in English. As our LEP students continued to develop English fluency, both the students and their teachers gained a sense of pride in accomplishment.

Glenwood also worked to involve parents in their children's education. Many parents did not participate in school activities because they were unable to speak English or because they were aliens whose immigration status in the United States was illegal. This remained a problem for many years. With the advent of the amnesty program for illegal immigrants and with years of adult English classes offered by Glenwood, we are now experiencing a resurgence of parental involvement. Parents now realize that, regardless of whether they speak English, Spanish, or another language, they are welcomed at their children's school and are necessary to their children's education. Their struggles to learn English are encouraged by our staff, and we all feel a shared joy in their success.

Transitional bilingual education classes were begun at Glenwood in 1979. Mrs. June Frankenberg, a bilingual fifth-grade teacher, became our first TBE teacher. I was asked to participate in the bilingual program in 1981, and I was assigned to a standard TBE-model class, with a very capable Spanish-bilingual aide. Two-thirds of my students were LEP or non-English-proficient (NEP) and one third were fluent-English-proficient (FEP) students.

In Los Angeles, the school district set up strict guidelines for LEP students: "Students identified as having primary language proficiency shall receive instruction as follows: a) Basic skills instruction in the primary language. b) A structured English-language program to develop their English-Language skills" (Los Angeles Unified School District 1982, 8). In layman's terms, this means native-language instruction that includes twenty minutes of ESL per day, as required by law. This approach had been mandated on both the state and federal levels as the logical choice of instruction for the LEP student.

The entire staff was anxious to see how this new program would work. We had all been exposed to the methodology that mandated TBE, and the "transfer of learning" theory made a great deal of sense to me and to all of us on the Glenwood staff. It seemed that students who learned their primary languages until they were fluent and literate should acquire English as a second language more effectively.

Along with most educators, most politicians and community leaders accepted this view at the time. But it was evident from the start that many of the techniques that had been developed by the theorists in charge of the bilingual program did not function well in a classroom setting. The program that was promised to be a two- to three-year transitional program was seriously flawed. In reality, it became a long-term, monolingual, Spanish-language development program.

I struggled to make the TBE program work, as did my colleagues working in bilingual classes. However, we finally had to admit our concerns about the implementation of TBE and the validity of its theory. We all echoed a common concern: *it doesn't work!*

However, because of the political pressure that has been exerted to support TBE, few bilingual educators, politicians, or community leaders have been willing to criticize these programs. The education and policy establishment has turned a deaf ear to the experience of rank-and-file teachers. Never before in the history of education has a program that has been such a failure received so many accolades.

As teachers, we know that no single approach will work for all children. This educational premise is accepted in all areas of learning, with the exception of bilingual education. In this area, TBE has continued to be mandated by law for most LEP students, regardless of its results.

By perpetuating the misguided notion that TBE is a success, the Los Angeles Unified School District has caused more damage to LEP students than has any other single group in this country. The bureaucracy of the bilingual education program has been impossible to penetrate. The program is as seriously flawed as the research behind it, but the LAUSD has rejected any attempts to reform the program. This very powerful school district has rejected the challenging role of leading in the reform of the education of LEP students.

It was promised that TBE would lower the drop-out rate of LEP students. But today, "students with non-English language backgrounds drop out at roughly twice the rate of those with English language backgrounds (Olsen 1988, 90). Non-English-speaking children continue to be isolated in schools. They are denied a chance to compete on an equal basis in an English-speaking society. And teachers are forced by a TBE waiver system to leave their local schools.

Abuses of the Transitional Bilingual Education Program

In this section of my paper, I shall give an overview of the problems that Los Angeles educators are experiencing. Please keep in mind that these abuses are not isolated instances, but that they are widespread throughout this 702-square-mile school district.

Home-Language Surveys and Parent Permission Forms

The law setting up the bilingual plan stated that parents had the right to decide whether to place their children in a bilingual program. Many bilingual educators oppose this parental choice, arguing that we don't allow parental choice over other elements of the curriculum. That is true, but the bilingual program determines the language in which children will be taught, and that choice is very much the parents' right. Curriculum and content are in the academic domain, but the opportunity to learn English supplants all other considerations.

In practice, however, parental choice is often evaded in bilingual programs. Let me describe a typical scenario. The parent who brings a child to a school is given a home-language survey. This survey inquires about the languages spoken in the home and so forth. If the parent says that any person in the home speaks any language other than English, the child is targeted as a possible LEP student. The child may in fact be fluent in English, but he is now en route to becoming a statistic.

Next, the parent is given the bilingual program permission form. This is printed both in English and in the primary language of the student or parent. After reading the description of TBE on this permission slip, few parents would oppose enrolling their children in the program. The description states, in glowing terms, that the child will be taught core subjects in his or her native language but that, as his or her ability increases, instruction in English will also increase. Instruction in both the native language and English will continue until the child is proficient in the native language, at which time the child will receive all instruction in English. Most parents agree to this plan readily.

But this description of the TBE program is shamefully misleading. In reality, most students will be locked into their native languages, and little emphasis at all will be placed on English-language development.

The alternative to a TBE program is an Individual Learning Plan (ILP), which allows the child's teacher to use any or all of the available educational techniques to focus on English-language development. But the LAUSD intervenes when too many parents at any given school site sign their children out of the TBE program and select ILPs. The LAUSD regional office sends bilingual education staff members to the local school site and calls in targeted parents who have selected ILPs. These parents are lectured on the benefits of TBE and told that it is the best method for their children. They may be shown an illustrative film. This film depicts a happy, well-dressed child who is learning in his native language and a sad, downtrodden, miserable child who is learning in English. The film continually repeats that learning in English is harmful.

In many cases, parents will sign their children into TBE after this session. However, parents who continue to insist upon ILPs will often be the target of repeated phone calls from LAUSD bilingual program officials. This kind of harassment and duress is an insult to parents, but there is even more to the school district's manipulation of the parental consent process.

At some schools, bilingual coordinators aggressively pursue the placement of children in TBE. I have seen bilingual permission forms that have mistakenly been signed by parents in both the "yes" and "no" columns. When these forms eventually reach the classroom teachers, the "no's" have been scratched out and the "yes's" have been left in place. It is also not uncommon for ILP permission forms to "disappear" and for parents to be required to come to the school to sign additional forms.

The school district's procedure for signing permission forms has also changed. In the past, it was a simple matter for a parent to sign a child out of TBE. The parent could request the form from the classroom teacher or the school office, sign it at home, and send it to the school. At schools where too many parents have signed their children out of TBE, however, this procedure was changed, first to require parents to obtain the permission form from the office of the bilingual coordinator. Then it was changed to require parents to make an appointment to see the bilingual coordinator to obtain the form. As a matter of practice, the bilingual coordinator is not readily available to parents who wish to sign their children out of the program. Parents who drop in to get a form are always turned away and told to set up an appointment, regardless of whether the bilingual coordinator was available at that time.

I have personally witnessed the pressure put on parents at their meetings with bilingual coordinators. I have attended parental meetings at which school personnel describe wonderful successes of TBE that are not actually occurring and at which those who are critical of TBE are forbidden to speak one word.

Parents of FEP students are treated similarly. They are given parental permission forms to sign their children into the bilingual program as Spanish as a Second Language (SSL) students. The latest parental permission slip for FEP students offers only the TBE option. When parents are given it at registration time, they will most likely sign it as a matter of routine. Many parents want their children to learn a second language, and agree to place them in the program. In reality, the SSL program is a disgrace. Most SSL students rarely learn to do more than to count from one to ten and to name the colors in Spanish. FEP students are useful as language role models in bilingual classrooms; the bilingual classes are not useful to them. They spend most of their day simply listening to lessons in a language that they do not understand.

At Glenwood, all of our classrooms are now bilingual. Thirty-three of these classrooms are targeted as TBE models. If parents do not want their children in the TBE program, they are told that the children will remain in a bilingual classroom but will participate in the English-only portion of the program. Most of the student's instructional time is wasted; he or she will hear more Spanish than English during the allotted instructional period.

Program Placement

There are five questions on the Home-Language Survey regarding the languages used in the home. If any of these questions shows a language other than English, even if it only indicates that someone in the household speaks another language, the child is automatically assumed to need a Basic Inventory of Native Language (BINL) to determine whether he or she is as proficient in that language as in English.

In the BINL, the child must describe a series of pictures to the tester, both in English and in his or her native language. The examiner is required to write down the child's words, phrases, and thoughts. The test may give inaccurate results in any number of ways. If the child rambles without making sense, but still produces enough verbiage, he or she can be labeled as FEP. If the child is frightened by the surroundings in the new school, by the unfamiliar people, by the new test, he or she may not respond sufficiently, may not produce the required word count, and may be labeled as limited-English-proficient or non-English-proficient, even if he or she has a much higher level of language ability. A child who speaks only English, but who is hampered by the testing situation, will be placed in a Spanish bilingual classroom as a LEP student, and given instruction in all core subjects in Spanish.

In June 1988, when one of these pictures was shown at a Los Angeles Board of Education meeting to the president of the board, Mrs. Roberta Weintraub, she described it as a picture of a boy sitting on a rock. Since the picture was supposed to depict the child sitting on the back of a water buffalo, Mrs. Weintraub gave an incorrect description, though with enough verbiage to escape actually being classified as LEP herself. All of the board members found this situation to be very amusing, but it graphically demonstrates the shortcomings of the BINL testing instrument and the fallacy of using it to determine linguistic ability.

The pictures used in the BINL test are very bad. They do little to stimulate children and to elicit from them the language that they need to pass the test. Even the Los Angeles Board of Education has agreed that this testing instrument must be replaced, yet we are still testing children with these same pictures. When a teacher used another set of pictures, and proved a higher percentage of children to be fluent in English, the teacher was ordered to stop using the new set and to use the designated pictures instead.

Testing and Exit Criteria

Once a child has been placed in the bilingual program, he or she is often unable to meet the unrealistic exit criteria. Students who are unable to meet predetermined reading levels in Spanish may languish in a bilingual classroom for years. Many of those who are able to make the transition to English classes find themselves so far behind their peers in vocabulary and English skills that they never catch up.

The new LAUSD Bilingual Master Plan raises the exit criteria, thus making it even more difficult for children to exit from the program. These inflated exit criteria negate the whole premise of a short two- or three-year native-language instruction period. The children are effectively locked into native-language or transitional classes. One in six school children in California is an immigrant, and this percentage is growing. Locked into TBE classes, these children are being denied their right to develop fluency in English.

Waiver System

In California, when the TBE model was set up, there were not a sufficient number of certified bilingual education teachers to implement the plan. To bypass this problem, the California Bilingual Education Act mandated a waiver program. Any teacher working in the bilingual program had to sign a waiver that allowed him or her seven years to study the targeted culture and language, and bilingual methodology and to pass tests to qualify for a bilingual credential.

An entire business enterprise grew up around fulfilling the waiver requirement: college classes, review courses, textbooks, courses of instruction, and tests. Many teachers found that the classes and review courses that they took in methodology taught only one methodological approach for all students, and that the courses they took in culture were in actuality an indoctrination in a radical Chicano political agenda.

The tests were a burgeoning business in themselves. The University of Southern California (USC) required a $65.00 testing fee for each section of the test, and the failure rate was phenomenal. In 1986, for example, four thousand teachers took tests at USC, and only 252 teachers received a Certificate of Competency. One explanation for this high failure rate may be that passing the tests required conformity to the radical Chicano political agenda promoted in the classes and review courses. The content of the courses and tests was so far removed from true Hispanic culture and methodology that Mexican teachers have been unable to pass tests in Hispanic culture.

The waiver system has become a form of blackmail by which teachers may be transferred against their wishes. School stability and faculty rapport have been sacrificed to the waiver program. By 1984, many teachers, I among them, began to take a stand against the waiver program and to refuse to sign the waivers. The threat of displacement hangs over us constantly. Regardless of our actual teaching skills or of our record of success, we are considered inadequate by the promoters of the waiver program.

The New LAUSD Bilingual Master Plan

LAUSD has tried many varied approaches to education. On many occasions, when it became obvious that a new theory or a new trend that had been experimented with was unsuccessful, that approach was changed or dropped. This kind of experimentation is part of the continuous challenge of teaching. Bilingual education is yet another educational theory and program that classroom teachers soon realized was not working. When the California Bilingual Bill was sunsetted in June of 1987, classroom teachers who sought bilingual reform were eager to give our input to the new master plan being developed by LAUSD. I was selected as one member of the 140-person LAUSD Task Force.

Unfortunately, I was one of the few, if not the only, member who felt that other educational options should be explored. Most people on the panel had been hand-picked for their loyalty to the TBE program. I was continually told that my views were welcomed, and that the LAUSD Task Force would allow for a diversity of views. In reality, however, the entire series of meetings held by the LAUSD Task Force had been designed to lead to one preordained conclusion.

The new LAUSD bilingual education plan completely ignores the failures of the past fifteen years. It sets up a program that is even more rigid and dogmatic. This program will certainly lead to continued academic failure. The criteria for exiting from TBE programs have been raised. TBE programs have been expanded to include prekindergarten through the twelfth grade. TBE classes are mandated wherever there are ten LEP students. Elementary school ESL pullout classes have been completely eliminated, and prekindergarten teachers have been mandated to use Spanish for 80 percent of the school day.

The new LAUSD plan initiates a $5,000 annual bonus stipend for bilingual teachers. Historically, California teachers have had one salary schedule. This two-tiered system divisively pits the skills of one teacher against another. The new plan eliminates the waiver system, but introduces in its place a Language Development Specialist credential (LDS) that monolingual English-speaking teachers must acquire in order to remain eligible to teach LEP students. While the plan allows for some pairing of monolingual with bilingual teachers, it is obvious that monolingual English-speaking teachers are considered to be inadequate. Teachers from foreign countries, on the other hand, need not pass the California Basic Essential Skills Test (C-BEST). And those who have expertise in a targeted language may be hired to teach even if they have no college degree or fluency in English.

The Formation of the Learning
English Advocates Drive (LEAD)

During the past few years, many classroom teachers have been contacting state and local officials, the school district leadership, the school board, and our own union, the United Teachers of Los Angeles (UTLA), to create an awareness of the problems in the TBE program. In most cases, teachers' concerns have been dismissed, and the teachers have been told that they themselves were the problem. Academic circles have been closed to us. In private, teachers, politicians, and community leaders have encouraged us to continue the struggle for reform. But few are willing to take a stand publicly.

At one culture class, I recall expressing my concern that children were being locked into their native languages and that most of those who were able to exit the TBE program never caught up with their English-speaking peers. The response was that I was lazy and didn't implement the program correctly.

When a group of concerned teachers and parents made a presentation to the Los Angeles School District Board of Education in May 1988, the board president attacked us verbally, accusing us of being racist and antiminority, and said that the board was ashamed of us. When Mrs. Krenz, the former principal of Glenwood Elementary School, rose to protest this outrageous treatment, she was silenced. The board's audio tape of the meeting deleted this verbal attack.

LEAD, the Learning English Advocates Drive, is a grass-roots teachers' organization that was formed in March 1987 at Glenwood Elementary School. It seeks to reform, not eliminate, bilingual education and to expose the failure of TBE. We oppose TBE because "the educational theory and principles upon which bilingual education are based are not sound if the primary goal of this instruction is as effectively and efficiently as possible to develop in each child fluency in English (Rossier 1987, 8).

It is not LEAD's goal to impose an all-English education upon all students. As educators know, no single approach works for all students. We simply want to explore alternatives to TBE. It is because we are proud of the heritages, cultures, and languages that our students bring to our schools that we oppose the segregation of students based on their languages.

I shall discuss below the major reasons that we have been unable to achieve reform of bilingual education.

Labels and Intimidation Tactics

Unfortunately for our students, anyone who has tried to reform bilingual education has been subjected to name-calling and intimidation. Initially, it was shocking that the educational establishment would reject those who tried to call attention to students' needs and who wished to improve a program in order to help LEP students. But the establishment has effectively stopped all constructive criticism from taking place by the use of name-calling.

The bilingual education lobby has been very successful in creating a myth that anyone who did not favor TBE was antiminority or racist. This use of stereotypical labels has effectively masked the reality. The public perception of bilingual education is that it is great because its aims are great: to help non-English-speaking students learn English and to help fluent English speakers learn a second language. This perception, coupled with media attention that focuses on the need for special help for LEP students, has created the myth that TBE has been successful for all LEP students. The reality is that TBE does not encourage bilingualism. Instead, it perpetuates monolingualism and does not enable English speakers to learn a second language formally.

LAUSD and its personnel have used a variety of tactics in addition to name-calling to prevent speakers with classroom experience from revealing the problems and flaws in TBE. Life for the average grade-school teacher can be made very unpleasant through threats of public censure, grade displacement, school displacement, and disfavor from a principal. Teachers are frequently subjected to the whims of their immediate supervisors, and are not empowered or able to defend themselves. Usually, the only defense a teacher has is his or her union or professional association. A teacher who opposes a policy favored by both his supervisor and his union is very much alone. My personal experience can serve as an example. I have taught the third grade for twenty-four years, but I was reassigned to teach kindergarten two months after I helped found LEAD.

In this unhealthy climate, the majority of LEAD's members ask to remain anonymous. They call us, express their fears, and ask for reassurance that we will never reveal their names.

The Waiver System and the LDS Credential

The very unpopular waiver system was finally eliminated. But, as I wrote above, under the new master plan the waiver system has been replaced by the requirement that teachers in the program obtain a Language Development Specialist credential or a Bilingual Cross-Cultural credential (BCC). A certain amount of pairing of monolingual with bilingual staff members is allowed. However, displacement is still a possibility, and administrators are encouraged to place bilingual staff members at the primary level.

Most good teachers tend to specialize in one grade level or subject. They become unofficial advisors to other teachers who enter that grade level or subject. Admittedly, a California teaching credential allows teachers to teach various grade levels, but we are now experiencing grade-level changes in which teachers are moved around as if they were interchangeable pieces of furniture rather than valued and skilled employees.

As one example, I know of a teacher who was displaced from her school for not obtaining a bilingual credential. She was asked to return to the school to train her replacement, who spoke no English, who had never taught before, and who had been given an emergency credential. When she refused, she was assigned to another bilingual classroom at a school miles away from her home.

Most teachers in the LAUSD have been teaching ESL as a part of their classroom responsibility. Many have taken review classes to keep themselves current with the latest strategies for teaching ESL effectively. Under the new master plan, teachers must have Language Development Specialist credentials to be qualified as ESL teachers. Essentially, the waiver system has been replaced by the LDS credential.

Teacher Unions

One of the most frustrating aspects of this struggle has been the lack of support or the opposition of the various teacher unions. The official policy of the UTLA is to support TBE. The president of the union, Mr. Wayne Johnson, spoke with the staff of Glenwood Elementary and suggested that if we wanted to poll the membership on this issue that we gather signatures and submit them to him. This was done, but the poll was never published.

We presented a motion favoring English-language development, which was passed at the Valley-East UTLA meeting. The UTLA Chicano Bilingual Education Committee, which is controlled by a small group of very vocal activists, is responsible for setting UTLA's policy on education for LEP students. This committee greeted the motion with an angry, emotional, and racial attack, and rejected it outright.

We gathered the necessary signatures to bring the motion to a referendum of the entire membership of UTLA. Our opponents also qualified to place a referendum on the same ballot. In an August 1987 vote, 78 percent of UTLA's members supported our referendum. The second referendum was defeated. But the final status of this referendum is still in doubt, as no one in the leadership of UTLA will support the position of the membership and publicly advocate this shift in policy.

LEAD has also approached the National Education Association (NEA) and the American Federation of Teachers (AFT) and their state associates, the California Teachers Association (CTA) and the California Federation of Teachers (CFT). At this time, NEA and CTA have retained their strongly pro-TBE positions. But the membership of the AFT, at the national convention held in San Francisco in July 1988, rejected a motion to reaffirm support for TBE. It voted for a compromise motion that stated, "WHEREAS, transitional bilingual education is one method of teaching limited-English-proficient children, but other methods such as English as a Second Language and Sheltered English have also proven to be successful alternatives for many such children" (American Federation of Teachers 1988, 7). This was a major victory for the San Francisco LEAD members who had lobbied for four days during the convention. We found that many state delegations had been totally misled by the bilingual lobby, and thought that bilingual education focused on English development. Naively, we thought that this policy shift would receive national attention, but AFT has made no public policy statement on it to this date.

Political Reality

In California, bilingual education has unfortunately become a political issue that divides the political parties. The Assembly and the Senate have continually tossed the issue back and forth. Many Democratic politicians have equated bilingual education with liberalism and treated it as a benefit program for minority populations. Republican politicians, led by Frank Hill, an assemblyman from Whittier, have advocated flexibility and revisions in local plans.

This political division was displayed in the reconfirmation hearing on Mrs. Angie Papadakis as a member of the California State Board of Education. Mrs. Papadakis was one of the board's most devoted members, and she had a brilliant record throughout her tenure. Her reconfirmation should have been a mere formality. But she had taken a strong stand for parental rights and program flexibility in bilingual education, and for elimination of the waiver system. The California State Senate Education Committee subjected her to intensive questioning on her views on bilingual education. The hearings went on indefinitely, with several delays and postponements. When the committee voted, one member was conveniently out of the country and another member abstained, so that her reconfirmation died for lack of the necessary votes. She was told quite pointedly that she had been denied reconfirmation because of her opposition to the current bilingual plan.

On the federal level, by contrast, there has been significant progress in opening up and expanding programs for LEP children. Congress had previously allowed only 4 percent of federal funding for LEP students to be devoted to programs other than TBE. In the summer of 1988, it lifted this ceiling so that up to 25 percent of federal funding could be spent on alternative programs. This should encourage school districts to experiment with alternative approaches.

But the LAUSD has not taken advantage of this change to pursue varying options. Instead, it has reaffirmed its commitment to TBE as the sole theory to be implemented, and has rejected efforts to seek reform, and by doing so it has turned its back on the LEP child.

Research

When I became involved in this reform movement, I knew very little about most of the research projects. I had been taught the accepted theories and had been told that TBE was successful. When, because of my personal experiences and observations, I began to challenge the LAUSD over its bilingual plan, the struggle quickly shifted to the field of research. I have a great respect for those dedicated individuals who have worked so hard to generate valid research.

I am still not an expert in research, and I find most research projects to be intimidating at best. But, with the help of tutors such as Dr. Robert Rossier and Dr. Keith Baker, I have become knowledgeable about how research projects are used in bilingual education.

One example is typical. Congressman Augustus Hawkins (D-Calif.), chairman of the House Education and Labor Committee, commissioned a study by the Congressional Research Service to determine the effectiveness of TBE. The conclusion of that study was that "there is no consensus on a single successful instructional approach. . . . Well trained sensitive teachers who individualize their instructional approach . . . are successful in improving the academic achievement of LEP students" (Holland 1986, 38). Congressman Hawkins never publicized or utilized this report.

Instead, he sought a report from the General Accounting Office (GAO) on the same subject. This was to be an unbiased analysis of selected research. Yet Lily Wong Filmore, one of the panel members, helped to evaluate her own research project. After the report, which supported TBE, was released, two of the original panel members wrote letters of dissent. The Department of Education rejected the GAO report because of the bias of the panel members. Yet Congressman Hawkins promoted this report extensively, and gained widespread press coverage for this research "validation" to TBE.

This is but one example of the abuses that can occur when research data is manipulated and when advocates shop for favorable research findings. My own view on TBE is based on my experience as an ordinary, average classroom teacher. It has probably been best stated by Baker and de Kanter in their evaluation of volumes of research projects: "The conclusion is straightforward: there is no justification in terms of educational effectiveness for the proposed August 1980 regulations which would have mandated TBE as the sole instructional method for language-minority children. TBE has had mixed success. Although it has worked in some settings, it has proved ineffective in others and has had negative effects in some places. Furthermore, alternative instructional methods have been found to succeed — even to be superior to TBE — in some schools" (1983, 45–46).

As an educator, I espouse the simple but effective theory of linguistics that discusses language acquisition in terms of input and output. To teach a language, you must give extensive input of the target language in order to achieve an output. As Angie Papadakis wrote, "Ramon and his classmates will not learn English by being taught Spanish any more than they will learn the violin by playing the piano" (Papadakis 1986, 5). LAUSD mandates Spanish input and allows the public to believe that the output will be English.

Teacher Morale

TBE has done more to lower teachers' morale than any other program I know. From the onset of TBE, it was clear that the directors of the program thought that English-speaking teachers lacked the skills necessary to work with LEP students. Before this program, we were valued professionals who met the needs of LEP students with native-language support, ESL techniques, sheltered English, and cooperative learning. We experienced the joy in being able to help boys and girls of all nationalities succeed.

But since the onset of TBE, we have been told that we are

inadequate, if not also uncaring, teachers. We have seen our students in TBE programs fail to achieve their potential and be segregated by language groupings. We have seen the drop-out rate in Los Angeles rise to 40 percent. And we have seen that California's public schools, using the TBE approach, have been able to send only 3 percent of their Hispanic students to college.

A recently decided U.S. District Court case, *Teresa P. v. Berkeley Unified School District*, is significant. The suit contended both that the schools of Berkeley, California, did not provide enough instruction in native languages and that the students should not be taught by credentialed bilingual or ESL teachers. The attorneys for the Berkeley School District, Thomas Donovan and Celia Ruiz, were successful in disproving both of these allegations. The complainants sought to have TBE imposed as the sole method to be used for teaching LEP students in the schools of Berkeley, but Judge D. Lowell Jensen made the right, and commonsense, decision: "Good teachers are good teachers no matter what the educational challenge may be" (Jensen 1989, 21).

The ability to speak a language other than English should never be the sole determinant of whether a teacher is competent or should be accredited. As the case correctly determined, students with limited-English-proficiency can be taught well by teachers who do not have specialized bilingual education credentials, and these students need not be taught solely in their native languages.

As one rank-and-file classroom teacher, but also as the representative of many more of my colleagues, I ask for the freedom to use the teaching methods that are best suited for my students. I ask that we be allowed to give our LEP prekindergarten students the language skills that will enable them to start school on a par with their English-speaking peers. And I ask that we be allowed to concentrate on developing our students' English fluency and literacy, so that they may reach their maximum potential as successful citizens of this country.

References

American Federation of Teachers. 1988. *70th Convention of the American Federation of Teachers, AFL-CIO Committee Reports*. Human Rights and Community Relations.

Baker, Keith. 1984. "Ideological Bias in Bilingual Education." Mimeo.

Paper presented at the Annual Meeting of the American Educational Research Association, New Orleans, Louisiana, April 27.

Baker, Keith, and Adriana de Kanter. 1983. *An Answer from Research on Bilingual Education*. Washington, D.C.: U.S. Department of Education.

Baker, Keith, and Christine Rossell. 1987. "An Implementation Problem: Specifying the Target Group for Bilingual Education." *Educational Policy* 1(2):249–70.

General Accounting Office. 1987. "Bilingual Education: A New Look at the Research Evidence." Washington, D.C.: United States Government Printing Office. GAO/PEMD-87-12BR.

Holland, Rick. 1986. *Bilingual Education: Recent Evaluations of Local School District Programs and Related Research on Second-Language Learning*. Washington, D.C.: Congressional Research Service.

Jensen, D. Lowell. 1989. *In Re Teresa P. v. Berkeley Unified School District*.

Los Angeles Unified School District. Office of the Associate Superintendent. 1982. *Procedures for Implementing Requirements of the District Lau Plan and AB507 in Elementary Schools*. Instruction Bulletin no. 41. Los Angeles: Los Angeles Unified School District.

Olsen, Laurie, project director. 1988. *Crossing the Schoolhouse Border— Immigrant Students and the California Public Schools—A California Tomorrow Policy Research Report*. Los Angeles: California Tomorrow.

Papadakis, Angie. 1986. "Ramon Is Our Future, but What Is His?" *Los Angeles Times*, August 25, pt. 2, 5.

Rossier, Robert. 1987. *Analysis of Opinions of Legal Counsels on the Sunsetting of AB507*. Unpublished paper.

12

Reconsidering Bilingual Education: Toward a Consensus in the National Interest

Rudolph C. Troike

Few innovations in the history of American education have been surrounded by as much misunderstanding and acrimonious argument as the curricular approach known, often misleadingly, as "bilingual education." Of other curriculum movements in recent memory, perhaps only sex education ranks on a par with it for the passions it has aroused and the misconceptions it has spawned, both among adherents and opponents. The papers in this volume represent one of the first efforts to discuss some of the issues concerning the language-education needs of linguistic minorities in a balanced and dispassionate fashion. While not all the papers escape entirely from the hazard of implicit bias, nevertheless this is a good start toward a more intelligent search for a consensus on the most appropriate educational response to the needs of America's growing numbers of linguistic minorities. The present paper reconsiders some of the motivations and significant questions in the implementation of bilingual programs, offers suggestions toward a consensus that concentrates on the needs of the children involved, and moves beyond the often-obsessive focus on English to a perspective that engages the future national interest of this country.

Glendon Drake's exposition in his paper of Mannheim's Paradox provides an excellent vantage point from which to view all of the contributions to this volume, including the present one. Although Drake directs his discussion to linguistics, with which he is most familiar (and as a linguist, I must join in saying mea culpa),[1] the dictum that "thought is always bound up with the existing life situation of the thinker" (Mannheim), and therefore "the separation of scientific fact from ideological beliefs is difficult and probably impossible," applies to all of the papers herein. Thus, for example, dependence on statistical data to support a position antithetical to bilingual education reflects a positivistic ideological belief, common in psychology, in the supposedly objective scientific nature of quantification. We need to be aware that this view is being strongly challenged today by researchers emphasizing the need for qualitative understanding of specific life situations and circumstances. To indicate my own position in this regard, I must note that my background in anthropology biases me toward this new direction in scientific research, which questions the value of numbers except in appropriate complementary uses, such as survey research, when done in conjunction with qualitative inquiry. Here I should like to bring several relevant observations to bear, including some from my own personal experience, which may help in rethinking some of the issues in the education of linguistic-minority children.

The "time on task" or "length of exposure" argument in regard to language learning, which has an intuitive appeal and is often used as the basis for urging that non-English-speaking children should be immersed in an all-English curriculum, is seriously called into question by a variety of facts. First, it is important to acknowledge that far more than just language is involved in the educational equation for children from non-English-language backgrounds. This, which has come to be called the "language fallacy" as the basis for arguing for bilingual education, is now recognized even by most of its proponents. While language is clearly significant in many ways, it is not the sole determinant of educational achievement (Troike 1984). If it were, for example, we could not explain why, in tests such as the Scholastic Aptitude Test (SAT), the Comprehensive Test of Basic Skills (CTBS), and the Armed Services Vocational Aptitude Battery, both at the state and national levels, there is a consistent stratification among Anglos, Hispanics, and blacks, with the latter regularly placing below Hispanics, and Anglos placing at the top. Since most blacks are native English speakers and many Hispanics are not, how is it possible that Hispanics could score higher than blacks on tests conducted in English? The most evident answer for this distribution is provided by Ogbu's (1978) model of "caste-like minorities": the performance of these groups on the tests replicates their stratification in American society.

Indicative evidence questioning the primacy of language as a determining factor in educational achievement, and supporting the significance of other influencing factors such as status within the social system and native cultural values, comes from the research of Marie Clay in New Zealand. Clay (1970) compared the achievement of Maori children, who enter school largely monolingual in English, but who occupy a dominated role at the bottom of New Zealand society, and Samoans, who generally know no English on school entry but who come from an independent society that has maintained strong cultural pride. She found that by the third grade, the Maori students ranked ahead of the Samoans in knowledge of English, but the Samoans were ahead of the Maoris in overall academic achievement. Thus, knowledge of English is not an adequate predictor of school achievement when other social and cultural factors intervene.

Again, federal policy in the United States over a number of decades, which was directed toward the replacement of American Indian languages with English, together with other social and economic pressures, has largely succeeded in dooming most of these languages to early extinction. If knowledge of English were really the most significant determinant of school achievement, we should expect that American Indian children who have lost their ancestral language would now be doing much better academically than those who have not, but the tragic record of American Indian education amply attests that this is not the case. Indeed, Irene Serna has demonstrated in a recent University of New Mexico dissertation (1988) that Navajo children's knowledge of Navajo was a better predictor of school achievement, as measured in English, than was their knowledge of English. And Chesarek (1981) found that third-grade Crow-speaking children who had no exposure to English prior to entering school surpassed in school achievement children who had heard only English at home.

Several other examples contradicting the "quantity of exposure to English" argument for predicting English acquisition or school achievement may be pointed out. In one rather striking case, Edelsky and Hudelson (1979) found that several Anglo children participating in a bilingual classroom in Arizona showed no increase in knowledge of Spanish after an exposure of several hours a day over an entire academic year. The subordinate social position of Spanish evidently made it feasible for the children to willfully resist learning the language despite the extensive amount of exposure. On the other hand, research evidence from both Illinois and California (González 1986) has shown that immigrant children from Mexico who began school in the United States had lower achievement than did students who attended school in Mexico for two years prior to emigrating, when measured on a standardized achievement test (CTBS) in the sixth grade. In other words, children with two years' less exposure to English show better achievement when measured in English after four years. The U.S. Government Accounting Office (GAO) (1976), in a generally quite critical study of bilingual programs, found that school achievement correlated positively with the amount of native language use; that is, the less English was used, the higher students' academic achievement was as measured in English.

Such seemingly counterintuitive results clearly call for an explanation. Several factors are probably at work. First is the affective consideration that the children who began their schooling in Mexico did not find any stigma placed on them because of their language, nor was their ability in Spanish regarded as a disadvantage (while on this side of the border it is discounted as of no value, and they are considered handicapped). A second probable factor is that they were able to acquire academic knowledge and skills through their native language, which gave them the head start that Walberg alludes to, and they were able to transfer this to advantage into English in the U.S. school context. The children who began school here, on the other hand, were confronted with the message that English is the only language that really matters, and that their language was of no value in the larger sphere and unworthy of further development. Even in schools with so-called bilingual education programs, extending for the most part only through the third grade, the same message would be clearly conveyed, since their language would be tolerated only for the first few years, and transition into English would be promoted as the overriding goal.

Since the children in the González study were carefully matched for family background to remove socioeconomic effects, it is clear that two years of prior schooling in Mexico (entirely in Spanish) provides a definite advantage for ultimate achievement in English in U.S. schools. (It should also give us pause to recognize that all U.S. Nobel Prize winners of Chinese ancestry received their basic education in Chinese before coming to this country.)

One further factor working in favor of the children who received prior education in Mexico is that the level of reading required in Mexican textbooks is much higher than that at comparable grade levels in the United States. This factor was very evident some years ago when the first successful bilingual education program was developed for Cuban refugee students in Miami. The former director of that program, Dr. Rosa Inclán, has told me that the academic level of the materials used in the Spanish component of the program was so much higher than that used by mainstream students in English that it became necessary to "dumb down" the Spanish materials to the English levels to avoid the embarrassment of having the Cuban students outperform their American peers. (Parenthetically, I should like to suggest that if we are really concerned about the future of this country, we should put our emotional energies into demanding that the educational standards here should be at least what they are in Mexico, even if we do not feel capable of matching such countries as China, Korea, or Japan, as newspaper editorials excusing low American achievement scores would seem to indicate.) My own personal experience in learning Spanish in school, and subsequently doing graduate study in Mexico, argues against the importance of the quantity of exposure to a language as a necessary condition for reaching the ability to learn through that language. I studied Spanish the "old-fashioned" way, by conjugating verbs and translating sentences, for five years in junior high school and high school, and one year in college, during which time it was never spoken in class. (It is embarrassing, in retrospect, to recall that half of the class members were native Spanish speakers who regularly made Cs and Ds, while Anglos who could barely put a sentence together made As and Bs.) The only time we were ever required to use the language was at the end of the fifth year when we read prepared five-minute speeches. After having no contact with the language for six years, I had the opportunity to attend the National School of Anthropology and History in Mexico City, where graduate courses were conducted entirely in Spanish, and was naturally apprehensive as to whether I could follow lectures. Much to my own surprise and relief, I found when I attended my first class (on the history of the Aztecs taught by the internationally known scholar Wigberto Jiménez Moreno), that I was able to take notes at about the same rate as if the lecture had been given in English.

In reflecting subsequently on how this could have been possible, I have realized that it was largely because I already had what cognitive scientists call a schema in mind for the subject, having previously taken courses on the topic in English, and because at the level of formal professional discourse there is a great deal of common cognate vocabulary. Revealingly, although I was able to perform satisfactorily in seminars discussing archaeological and linguistic theory, I was never able to use the informal language involved in casual social interaction with my fellow students during class breaks. Thus, I was able to transfer the knowledge and skills I had acquired in my native language rather rapidly into Spanish, using a "top-down" cognitive strategy.[2] The rather limited three hours a week of grammar-translation of Spanish in school, though it might have seemed insufficient, in fact proved adequate for me to attain successful graduate academic achievement in the language, which is what really mattered (and which is what really matters for non-English language background students in our schools). My experience is certainly far from unique, and other examples can readily be found among the thousands of international students successfully doing graduate study in American universities today.

Another objection sometimes raised to bilingual education is the claim that it is nearly impossible to develop literacy in two languages. This argument is strongly contradicted by the experience of dual-language schools throughout the world. Throughout Latin America and many other countries of the world, such schools have tremendous prestige, and parents vie to have their children admitted. In many of these schools, there are two separate teaching staffs, one for the national curriculum and the other for the second language curriculum (often, though not exclusively, English), and there is little articulation between them. Usually one is taught in the morning and the other in the afternoon. The success of these schools provides living evidence of the possibility and viability of dual-language instruction. However, the fact that the success of these schools has been almost entirely ignored in the literature on U.S. bilingual education — both pro and con — is revealing of the parochial perspective that has been taken on public bilingual education in this country. In most countries, bilingualism is a highly prized ability among the elite, who are willing to pay for their children to acquire it. (The same is true in this country, as noted in the fact that a large percentage of the undergraduates at Georgetown University have been to private French-medium schools.) In the context of the American legacy of xenophobia, public bilingual education has been viewed almost entirely as compensatory rather than as enrichment, with all of the consequences that this entails.

The perceptual disassociation was strongly brought home to me by an experience in San Francisco, where I was visiting schools in company with a lawyer from the Office of Civil Rights shortly after the handing down of the Supreme Court's *Lau v. Nichols* decision. The lawyer, new to the topic, seriously asked why bilingual education should be provided for Chinese children in the San Francisco schools. Later in the day, he casually mentioned how much it was costing him to send his daughter to a private school which taught half of the curriculum in French. Only after it was pointed out to him did he recognize the parallelism.

It has been forgotten that the first impetus for bilingual education in the recent period came from the foreign language teaching profession. But when the President's Commission on Foreign Language Study during the Carter administration wished to consider bilingual education within their purview, the then commissioner of education Ernest Boyer refused, on the grounds (as expressed to me in the words of two of his aides) that it was a "can of worms." In other words, even from the very highest levels of the federal government, bilingual education has not been seriously regarded as an educational matter, but merely as a political sop to minorities. The continued emphasis in discussions of bilingual education solely in terms of the acquisition of English skills (which becomes the mandatory basis for exiting such programs in many places), rather than in terms of knowledge acquisition, further betrays the underlying compensatory bias held by most people, in which I would include even the majority of educators involved in bilingual education programs.

The sad truth of this is reflected in the generally suppressed fact that the majority of so-called bilingual education programs are largely or even entirely monolingual English programs. This shocking revelation has been documented in several studies (U.S. GAO 1976; O'Malley 1981), which have shown that the amount of native-language used in bilingual education classrooms generally ranges from 0–33 percent, hardly the picture of linguistic apartheid hysterically reported in *New York Times* editorials or depicted in the normally responsible columns of Albert Shanker. (O'Malley actually found that more English was used in bilingual programs than in the ESL programs he surveyed.) Thus it is particularly ironic to hear calls for greater flexibility in providing programs for limited-English-proficient children, when this flexibility and more has already been surreptitiously going on under the rubric of bilingual programs. Attacks on bilingual education are in most cases beating a straw man, since many—perhaps most—programs are primarily ESL programs (or less) in disguise.

When the oft-repeated question, "Does bilingual education work?" is raised (here it should be noted that no one ever asks "Does mathematics education work?" or "Does reading education work?"—even though there is ample comparative evidence that they do not), it must be clear that we really cannot answer this question without more specific qualitative information about what goes on in actual classrooms, since what goes on under the name of "bilingual education" more often than not is not genuinely bilingual. Quantitative studies that do not contain this sort of qualitative information are therefore meaningless, and no conclusions can be drawn from them.

Beyond this, the often-negative contexts under which bilingual education programs operate—all documented in various places—such as administrator antipathy, lack of teacher commitment, ghetto school environments, and program marginality, as well as the compensatory orientation that negates their potential enrichment possibilities, may further doom even conceptually good programs to ineffectiveness. Several years ago I asked the state director for bilingual education in Texas to name an exemplary program that I might visit, and he acknowledged that there were none that he could recommend. I am possibly the first person on record to state that "there are still too many bad programs in this country" (Troike 1978, 16). The same is probably true today. José Cárdenas has repeatedly said that bilingual education has hardly ever even been tried in this country. Thus I strongly agree with the position of thoughtful critics that we should not automatically take for granted the assumptions on which bilingual education is based, but should constantly be searching for the best ways to educate children, and avoid taking rigidly polarized ideological positions.

An important point that has been overlooked in much of the discussion of evaluations of bilingual programs is that most of the programs are of a transitional variety, with students limited to three years in the program. In the paper cited above, I reviewed evaluation results from two programs that extended through the sixth grade, one in Navajo and English from Rock Point, Arizona, and one in Spanish and English from Santa Fe, New Mexico. The important finding that emerged from both was that there was a cumulative effect of bilingual instruction, which did not begin to become strongly evident, particularly in the Rock Point case, until after the third grade, precisely the point at which most programs terminate. Comparison with students from similar backgrounds in an ESL program in nearby schools showed that at the end of the third grade, the ESL-educated children scored slightly higher. However, from the fourth grade onward, the scores of the children in the English as a Second Language (ESL) program fell every year, while those of the bilingually-schooled children continued to rise and topped national norms in the sixth grade.[3] The problem with the results of evaluations (apart from the fact that many programs being evaluated are not actually bilingual) may be that they, and the programs evaluated, cover too short a period. Had the Rock Point program stopped at the end of the third grade, one would have reasonably concluded that it was not as effective as the ESL program. The real benefits did not begin to appear until the fourth year, and reached a peak in the sixth year. To be significantly effective, bilingual programs may need to be continued for at least five years. Ironically, some politicians are trying to insist that children should not be allowed more than one year in a federally funded bilingual program, further underscoring the compensatory conception that other languages have no educational value in themselves, and should be begrudged only as a temporary bridge to English.

Such a myopic view holds serious dangers for the future of this country. Today we bask in the hubris of the dominant international position of English, an accidental legacy of British imperialism and the role of the United States in World War II and the period of recovery. However, the Spenglerian zeitgeist, having followed the course of empire westward from Europe in the nineteenth century to the United States in this, has already winged it way to Japan and in time will move on to China, home to one-fifth of the world's population. It has been said that "language follows the dollar," but the dollar, having been devalued once by Nixon and again by Reagan, no longer commands the position it formerly did. The decline in the international position of the United States, coupled with the rising status of other parts of the world, inevitably will lead to a decline in the international importance of English, just as French declined before it, and Latin before that. I predict (and I am joined in this prediction by Isaac Asimov) that by the year 2025 — within the lifetimes of many reading this — English will cease to be the dominant international language, and will be replaced for a period by regionally dominant languages: German in a united Europe, Spanish in Latin America, Arabic in the Middle East and North Africa, Russian in the Soviet Union, English in the English-speaking countries, and Chinese in much of Asia. By the middle of the next century, Chinese should emerge as the single most important international language, and efforts may even develop to write English in Chinese characters.

For the foreseeable future it will be in the economic and political best interests of the United States to cultivate the development among its population of advanced skills in as many languages as possible. The time has already passed when we can confidently expect to sell to the rest of the world in English. The Japanese are well aware of the need to use other languages, and train people, for example, in French to sell products in French West Africa. We have been so focused on the goal of eliminating other languages in our midst, however, using bilingual education as a humane form of linguicide, that we have failed to recognize the languages children bring to school as a national resource that could be built upon and developed in the national interest. Although, as I have noted, the foreign-language teaching profession in this country was actively involved in supporting the initiation of bilingual education, once the latter began to develop as a field of its own, contact between the two areas virtually ceased. Ironically, in spite of the fact that both groups are involved in teaching many of the same languages, there has been little interaction between them. One of the few people to recognize the inherent connection was former Secretary of Education Terrell Bell, who, had he remained in office a few months longer, intended to merge the bilingual education and foreign language education divisions in the Department of Education. I was one of three persons asked to draw up a policy statement to be used by the secretary in making this change. (Unfortunately, as we know, he decided to resign, and was replaced by William Bennett, who began his tenure by making a major and badly misinformed policy speech attacking bilingual education.) Secretary Bell, in looking back at the millions of dollars the government had spent following Sputnik to support the teaching of foreign languages in high schools and colleges, recognized that many of these same languages are being spoken by children in bilingual programs, and that it would make good logical and economic sense to broaden the purview of the foreign-language teaching profession, and apply its expertise to help develop the resources that we already had at hand.

There is in this country a kind of paranoia that bilingual education programs might encourage separatism and threaten the fabric of the American union. One thing that is extraordinary about such statements is the confidence with which they are asserted, yet anyone at all familiar with bilingual programs, which are, as I have tried to indicate, for the most part almost pathetically assimilation-oriented, would find the assertions laughably uninformed. Such often-inflammatory statements only reflect the ignorance of their makers, and should be recognized as such. In twenty years of involvement with bilingual education programs (always for the purpose of trying to improve their quality), I have never heard one word spoken in support of linguistic or political separatism. Nor is it conceivable that bilingualism — which might at most be the ideal goal of a truly dual-language program — could tear the nation asunder. Indeed the opposite is true: the experience of nations throughout history is that it is only political and economic suppression that leads to linguistic separatism and revolution. The isolation of Jews in ghettos in Europe, for example, led to the development and survival of Yiddish for many centuries; conversely, in New York City, which has the largest Jewish population in the world, Yiddish has begun to disappear, since the society is open and Yiddish is no longer necessary for survival. The best way to create political instability is to deny equal educational and economic opportunity to minorities. If compensatory bilingual education realized its principal goal of equal educational opportunity, it would in fact enhance political stability by helping to co-opt minorities into the system. Dual-language education would do the same, and in addition would strengthen the nation's linguistic resources.

The irrational fear of linguistic separatism expressed by many opponents of bilingual education again betrays an ignorance of the facts of language shift taking place in this country. The large and growing numbers of Spanish speakers in Los Angeles and south Florida create a spurious impression that Spanish speakers are not "giving up" their language as readily as have other immigrant groups in the past. (In any event, this view of the past is a convenient myth: James Alatis reports that his father lived most of his adult life in a Greek neighborhood in Cleveland, and never needed to learn English.) López (1982) has shown that in Los Angeles, the usual pattern of shift is taking place, with the first generation using Spanish in the home 90 percent of the time, the second generation 50 percent of the time, and the third generation only 10 percent of the time. It is only the continuing influx of immigrants, which for the time being is replenishing the linguistic pool, that has obscured the actual loss of Spanish that is going on. Veltman (1983, 66, 101) shows a generally similar picture at the national level, with a decline from 83 percent for the second generation to 35 percent for the third generation for Hispanics. In New Mexico, where rural isolation preserved Spanish through more than a century of American control, paved roads, television, and access to education are rapidly eroding the language.

Even in Miami, birthplace of U.S. English, the same pattern is found. One of my students, while doing research there for his dissertation, was confronted by a Puerto Rican street gang, and after some nervous moments persuaded the gang to let him interview them. The gang members assured him that they spoke Spanish to their parents to be polite, but used only English with one another. Thus, even hard-core dropouts who reject most of the appurtenances of middle-class school culture are switching to English. (Perhaps this will be comforting to know for some of those who may be mugged by them.) The clear picture that emerges is that minority languages in the United States, including even Spanish, are an endangered species, and even without any special legislation or coercion to hasten their demise, are doomed to extinction. The social and economic forces working against their preservation are so pervasive, and so inexorable, that it is unlikely that even the most massive school-based programs could do more than delay the process by one or two generations.

To turn to a different topic, I should like to commend the research reported in Christine Rossell's paper on the bilingual and ESL programs in the Berkeley schools, as one of the most exemplary quantitative treatments I have seen. Her findings are compelling, and should clearly cause advocates of transitional bilingual education as well as of ESL to rethink some of their long-standing assumptions. It is notable, for example, that she did not find any cumulative effect from time in program. Her paper, regrettably, did not entirely escape Mannheim's Paradox, as seen in its somewhat subliminal adversarial tone; the argumentation would have been more persuasive if it were presented in a more disinterested way. However, I should like to concur heartily with her concluding recommendation, given in her oral presentation of the paper, that she would like to see a bilingual program from grades K–12 made available in the Berkeley schools for those parents and students who want it, and that others who need special programs should be allowed to opt for the intensive language program. Such a choice might even conceivably produce a healthy competition between the two, to the benefit of all concerned.[4]

In 1978 I said

While the AIR study [the national evaluation of Title VII programs by the American Institutes for Research] can and should be faulted for its inadequacies . . . not all of the negative findings can be easily dismissed, and bilingual educators should take this report seriously as a challenge to improve the quality of programs. To ignore it because of its weaknesses and pretend that all is well would be disastrous for bilingual education, as well as for the students it is intended to serve. (P. 16)

So far as I am aware, this caveat went largely unheeded by those in the field of bilingual education. The findings reported in Rossell's paper, and her own recommendation, should certainly cause supporters of bilingual education to reconsider whether, and under what circumstances, bilingual programs should be mandated, and should encourage more open experimentation, with better documentation of procedures. As I have mentioned earlier, many such programs are at best pseudobilingual, and are perpetrating a fraud on mandating and sponsoring agencies.

The root of the problem lies in the venality of human nature (for which I regrettably have no solution), which is sometimes laid bare by the attraction of money. Thus the Delano, California, school district, the home of César Chávez, reported to the state department of education that it had no limited-English-proficient (LEP) students in its boundaries, when it thought reporting them might obligate it to provide services. When Title VI desegregation funds became available, however, suddenly seven thousand LEP students were found to be on the rolls. At the same time, a year following the *Lau* decision, the San Francisco school district reported that the number of LEP students had declined from about three thousand to two thousand, suggesting that the district was well on the way to solving the problem that had prompted the decision. When the district realized that it was eligible for Title VI funding, the number of LEP students was discovered to have mushroomed in a year to around twenty-one thousand, and the district collected over one million dollars in aid. It would be nice if people did things because they recognized that it was right and needed doing; the evidence, however, is sadly the other way. The lure of money can sometimes entice a school system to do what a court case could not force it to do. At other times, the availability of money can merely be corrupting (at least spiritually, not necessarily criminally).

It has been my belief from the very first year of federal funding for bilingual education through Title VII of the Elementary and Secondary Education Act in 1968, when it was a mere $7.5 million, that too much money was made available too soon for it to be well used. It would have been far better, in the original spirit of a demonstration program, for the funding to have started out much smaller, and to have grown much more slowly. A model in this regard, at least in its early years when it was closely monitored, was the funding for bilingual vocational training, which had a strongly catalytic effect far beyond the rather-meager amounts spent. Many superintendents saw Title VII funds merely as a way to pad their budgets, but gave no administrative support to the programs, and not infrequently marginalized them, even physically. Many programs were of poor quality, because in a subtle form of discrimination, no one in the central administration cared, and minority program directors were encouraged to create their own mini power bases.

Required evaluations in Title VII programs were generally meaningless, since evaluators depended on the good will of program directors for continued contracts, and evaluations were ignored anyway. Mediocre programs continued to be funded by Washington, even over the objections of state directors, because not expending the funds would lead Congress to lower funding in subsequent years. Program officers in the Office of Bilingual Education (the office's title was later expanded to include: and Minority Language Affairs) often knew little about bilingual education and rarely visited programs because of budget cuts for travel. And as we have seen, funds supposedly targeted for bilingual instruction actually supported many ESL programs, contrary to the assumptions of those who merely read the letter of the law. This dolorous list could easily be extended, and could probably be replicated for almost any other large, federally funded program. My own axiom concerning educational research (which might as well be called Troike's Law), that is, that "the quality and significance of research is often in inverse relation to the amount of money expended on it," appears to apply to program funding as well.

I do not raise these points to criticize the many good and worthwhile efforts that have been made thanks to Title VII funding. I have seen small amounts of funds used with a multiplier effect that would make a banker envious; and I have seen millions of dollars wasted in ways that could at best be called fraudulent (though any such amounts inevitably pale into insignificance in comparison with problems with defense or public housing projects). Perhaps the most lasting positive benefit of the Bilingual Education Act (Title VII) will be in the way that it led to a dropping of legal barriers against the use of other languages in schools. In the aftermath of the outpouring of xenophobia generated by World War I in this country, many states passed laws prohibiting the use of languages other than English for purposes of instruction.[5] When the Bilingual Education Act was signed into law in 1968, many schools found themselves unable to apply for funding because of these restrictive state laws. Although temporary waivers were often obtained for experimental purposes, pressure from school districts anxious to secure the dollars eventually led most legislatures to rescind these laws (at last count, two states still have them). Having grown up in a period when Spanish-speaking students were often kept after school (*Spanish detention* was the standard term) or otherwise punished for speaking their native language to one another anywhere on the school grounds, I hope we never again find ourselves returning to such a regressive state of affairs.

The unhappy history of the effect of rigid mandates in education is vividly illustrated by the graphic stories of bureaucracies run amok in imposing a single model of bilingual education.[6] Equally vivid converse examples could be given, however, of schools evading mandates by reporting false figures to the state on amounts of native-language use; in a particularly blatant example of evasion in Chicago, a superintendent ordered staff to prepare an impressive printed and illustrated brochure purporting to show what was being done for minority-language children, while no changes were actually made in the grossly inadequate existing programs. I also recall, on my first visit to a bilingual classroom in San Francisco, being told by a teacher, in response to a question probing why students' Spanish seemed so inadequate, that she used Spanish about 50 percent of the time, and hearing a student sitting nearby loudly whisper, "You lie!" I also recall a major school system in Texas using Title I monies to purchase new equipment, which was placed in schools on the affluent side of town, while used equipment was then placed in the schools for which the funding was intended.

Atrocities abound in all bureaucracies, and always deserve to be exposed and challenged. I find Peterson's report distressing, and believe that it gives further evidence for the need for greater overt flexibility in seeking the most effective treatment for particular children in particular settings (as I have indicated earlier, there is already a great deal of surreptitious flexibility being practiced). It would appear from the description of the Spanish as a Second Language class in Peterson's paper that some unconscionably bad teaching is being allowed to occur, which suggests that a serious problem with instructional leadership in the school exists that perhaps extends beyond the bilingual program.

Although mandates are sometimes necessary to get people to do what they should be doing in the first place, they may have a downside in merely stimulating more inventive solutions to nullify their effects. Thus for example, when the Houston, Texas, school district was ordered to desegregate some years ago, they conveniently counted Hispanics as Anglos for desegregation purposes (as they traditionally had done under legal segregation), and "integrated" schools by combining black and Hispanic students only. It took a separate court action to redress this inequity. We would like to think that all educators are primarily concerned about the academic best interests of their students, and the vast majority certainly are, but ideology or prejudice may take precedence with some, and Mannheim's Paradox hovers over even some of those with the best intentions.

While there are unquestionably many bad bilingual programs, bad ESL programs, and bad regular school programs, there are equally unquestionably many bad schools in which the attitude of administration and staff overweigh whatever good even the best-designed program might do, and good schools in which almost any program might succeed. On a visit to a number of Bureau of Indian Affairs (BIA) schools some years ago, I was told resignedly by principal after principal, all career BIA employees, that in spite of their best efforts, their school had about an average 40 percent absenteeism rate, because Indian parents were not interested in their children's education, and kept them home on the slightest pretext, such as herding sheep or caring for a sick relative. When I reached one school and learned that the principal was a newly retired Air Force colonel, I feared for the worst. Accordingly I was astonished to be told that the school had an absenteeism rate of only 5 percent and in disbelief had to ask for the figure to be repeated to make sure I had heard right. When asked how he had accomplished such a miracle, he expressed surprise that it should be surprising, and proceeded to explain how he had arranged for bus drivers to return to the homes of children who did not appear for the bus, and if the child was not ill, to try to persuade the parents to let the child come to school. If this did not work, he referred the matter to the educational representative on the tribal council, who then also visited the parents. In addition, he had established a parent-a-week program, bringing a parent or grand-parent in on the bus and letting them observe classes or participate in teaching traditional arts and skills. These simple administrative actions had almost eliminated absenteeism from the school, and children were actively and cheerfully involved in learning activities. We have seen more recently on television "The George McKenna Story," which dramatizes how one principal in a ghetto school in Los Angeles was able to build community support and change staff attitudes to move the school from being one of the worst in the Los Angeles area to one of the best.

I cite these examples in order to pose the issue of whether educational problems are better approached by solutions imposed from above, or whether they are better left, as is often urged, to those who supposedly "know the local situation best." One might have expected the veteran BIA educators to understand the needs of their students best, and they would probably have agreed, but it took a former Air Force colonel with no negative presuppositions about Indian behavior to institute a change that revolutionized attendance — and without massive funding to do it. The problematic nature of this issue with regard to the education of minority-language students is shown by a study conducted by David Adcock (1986) in Colorado, to determine what had happened after the legislature there had de-mandated bilingual education and mandated ESL, leaving bilingual education as a local option. He conducted interviews in four sites, two of which had continued with bilingual education and two of which had switched to ESL. In the former, he found staff and community expressions of close and mutually supportive cooperation and positive attitudes, and plans to extend their programs from the third to the sixth grades, at local expense and with parental involvement — hardly the dire picture of children trapped in a dead-end program depicted at Peterson's Glenwood School. In the sites that had taken the opportunity to switch to ESL, interviews reflected a sharp alienation between school and community: parents were said not to be interested in the education of their children, and higher administrative personnel expressed strong views that bilingual education was not successful or appropriate. More research is clearly needed to learn what factors led to such strikingly different outcomes, but it should be abundantly evident that local wisdom may be influenced by various factors in very different ways, and cannot always be expected to arrive at the best solutions for children who have historically been inadequately served. (Note where faith in local wisdom and the rejection of governmental supervision has gotten us in the Savings and Loan debacle.) A further moral is that mere quantitative data are not a reliable guide to policy making, unless carefully validated through qualitative research.

To sum up, I feel that the conference from which these papers derive, more so than the individual papers themselves as they will be encountered in isolation by readers, provided a unique and valuable forum for the exchange of views on how to deal with the complex and perplexing problem of providing the best possible education for linguistic minorities in American society. If, as I feel, the conference participants were drawn closer to a consensus on this as a goal, rather than remaining polarized in ideological adherence to an English-only or native-language-only advocacy, then the conference was a success, and there is hope for more collaborative searches for solutions in the future in the place of continuing nonproductive antagonistic standoffs.

One common core of concern on which we can unite is that of the best interests of the individual children affected. As they comprise a growing percentage of the population, their best interests are ultimately in the nation's best interest. Further, with the prospect of the international decline of English in the coming century, the preservation and cultivation of the languages that many of these children speak may become not merely a matter of personal preference, but a necessity for our national survival.

We should, therefore, begin to recognize the languages that children bring to school not as handicaps to learning, or ciphers to be replaced with English as quickly as possible, but rather as valid cognitive systems that wherever and however possible should be harnessed in the cause of learning, and as nonrenewable national resources, which, like the ozone layer, we deplete at our peril. If we can recognize that we are all still ignorant of many things, then the awareness of our ignorance can be the beginning of wisdom. Accepting that no one is the possessor of ultimate truth in these matters, we can begin in an atmosphere of cooperation and mutual respect to work toward better solutions to the urgent problems facing our schools in providing effective and equitable educational programs for the still-growing number of children and adults from other language backgrounds whom they must serve.

I should first of all like to thank Gary Imhoff for organizing the conference where these papers were presented, and for inviting me to serve as a commentator. I believe that he has performed a valuable service in bringing people of different persuasions together to discuss issues concerning bilingual education in a relatively unemotional atmosphere. I hope that the first steps to some sort of rapprochement may have come out of the conference.

By way of background for interested readers, I should mention that I was involved in the early years of the organization of Teachers of English to Speakers of Other Languages (TESOL), including serving on the executive committee, and my wife, Muriel Saville-Troike, served as president in 1974–75. I have taught English abroad in Turkey and Taiwan, and, as director of the Center for Applied Linguistics (1972–77), worked closely with the British Council and the English-Speaking Union. In 1970 I was elected director of the Commission on the English Language of the National Council of Teachers of English. I have been a member of the English departments at the University of Texas and currently at the University of Arizona, and coincidentally have twice served on committees with former Senator S. I. Hayakawa.

Notes

1. This is particularly true in considering my own involvement and that of other linguists in founding the ESL (English as a Second Language) movement in this country, and urging it upon the schools. In the 1950s and 1960s, many of us had been actively involved in teaching English abroad or to foreign students in universities here, using the behavioristic "audio-lingual" method, which had been found during World War II to be effective for training (usually highly motivated) adults in intensive programs. The method, which emphasized pronunciation and grammatical patterns within a limited vocabulary, involved a great deal of repetition of sentences after a teacher model, on the theory that language was a kind of habit, and mechanical repetition would condition learners to automatic responses. The method reflected the state of linguistics of the period, which emphasized the phonology and grammar of a language, and language as purely spoken, and downplayed the importance of vocabulary or writing.

Few of us had had any experience inside an elementary school class-room, but we had such strong faith in the scientific correctness of the method that we thought it would solve all of the problems of non-English-speaking children in the schools. At the same time, we con-vinced teachers that they did not need to learn the language of their students, since the application of the method alone would work. As a result, we produced a generation of ESL specialists in the schools who knew nothing about the school curriculum, and felt that language could be taught by itself apart from any connection with what children needed for conceptual learning. Happily, newer approaches are em-phasizing the teaching and learning of language as incidental to the learning of content, which research is showing to be the most effective way for younger children.

2. Similarly, I was recently asked by the Canada Council to review a proposal for a sociolinguistic study of Eskimo. Although I have never studied French, by combining my schema knowledge of the subject, my knowledge of English and Spanish, and the occasional use of a dictionary, I was able to read the proposal and write a critique (in English!). A colleague who knows French checked my comments to make sure I had not misunderstood, and expressed amazement that I could have read the document. Such a top-down approach has been taken in teaching Russian at the University of Colorado, and has been tried successfully in a graduate German reading course at the Universi-ty of Illinois.

3. Professor Edwards, in his paper in this volume, raises some questions about the Rock Point program, which I can answer in part, since I have some familiarity with the history of the program. Historical acci-dent being what it is, one can never with perfect confidence compare two cohorts taken at different points in time, but in this case it seems reasonable to do so. The ESL and subsequent bilingual programs were developed and administered by essentially the same group of people, so that change of personnel can be ruled out as a major factor. Agnes Holm once told me that it was her impression that children who lived nearer the school site and knew more English on school entry did less well in school than those who began without any knowledge of En-glish. The school is currently extending the dual-language curriculum through the twelfth grade.

4. Quantitative data, as I averred earlier, cry out for qualitative informa-tion to explain them. Would Professor Rossell conclude from her fig-ures showing the superior achievement of Asians in mathematics that a genetic explanation was warranted? Or can cultural or teacher expec-tancy factors be implicated? I would very much like to see descriptive information on actual classroom practices in the two programs to try to understand what made the differences in results. The information that the Berkeley schools had been required by the state department of education to increase the amount of native language in the bilingual

program the year before suggests that it had not been very bilingual in the past, and perhaps had not been conducted with much enthusiasm by teachers. How was the program administered, and what materials were used? Were any of the ESL instructors bilingual, and was the child's language ever used in the ESL pullout sessions? How was instruction negotiated in regular classrooms when children did not understand what was being said?

I pose these types of questions not to raise doubts about the findings reported in Rossell's paper, but rather to illustrate some of the kinds of intervening processual variables that may affect program outcomes, and that need to be understood if we are to improve the quality of any program. ESL, structured immersion, and bilingual education are not mechanical formulas that can be automatically replicated everywhere; they need detailed explication in each case. Esther Eisenhower, director of the well-known ESL program in Fairfax County, Virginia, for example, credits the success of her program (she having no professional training!) to her insistence that all of the teachers in the program must be certified in reading (rather than ESL), and points to another program in Virginia that attempted to replicate her model but without this requirement, and failed to achieve comparable success (personal communication). Before we can really use statistical data from any program in any conclusive way (my own examples cited above included), we need careful descriptive information about the program, including detailed observations of classroom interaction, curriculum content, teacher attitudes, school climate, and community relations.

5. Muriel Saville-Troike has on several occasions noted that she ran afoul of this law on her first job in California, where she was teaching Spanish-speaking children of migrant laborers and was almost fired by the school board because she used a few words of Spanish in class to help the children understand. (She saved her job only by suggesting to the board members, many of whom were from a German background, that German lessons might also be offered in the school.)

6. For example, see Sally Peterson's article in this volume.

References

Adcock, David. 1986. "Equality, Workability, and Excellence: A Search for Compatibility in State Educational Policy Regarding Limited English Proficient Students." Ph.D. dissertation, University of Illinois at Urbana-Champaign.

Chesarek, Steve. 1981. "Cognitive Consequences of Home or School Education in a Limited Second Language: A Case Study in the Crow Indian Bilingual Community." Paper presented at the Language Proficiency Assessment Symposium, Airlie House, Va.

Clay, Marie M. 1970. "Language Skills: A Comparison of Maori, Samoan, and Pakeha Children Aged Five to Seven Years."*New Zealand Journal of Education Studies* 5(2):153–62. Reprinted in *Observing Young Readers*, M. M. Clay, Exeter, N.H.: Heinemann.

Edelsky, Carol, and Sarah Hudelson. 1979. "Resistance to the Acquisition of Spanish by Native English Speakers in a Bilingual Setting." *Journal of the Linguistic Association of the Southwest* 3(2):102–11.

González, L. Antonio. 1986. "The Effects of First Language Education on the Second Language and Academic Achievement of Mexican Immigrant Elementary School Children in the United States." Ph.D. Dissertation, University of Illinois at Urbana-Champaign.

Leyba, Charles F. 1978. *Longitudinal Study, Title VII Bilingual Program, Santa Fe Public Schools, Santa Fe, N.M.*. Los Angeles: National Dissemination and Assessment Center, California State University.

López, David E. 1982. *Language Maintenance and Shift in the United States Today: The Basic Patterns and their Social Implications*. Vol. 3, *Hispanics and Portuguese*. Los Alamitos, Calif.: National Center for Bilingual Research.

O'Malley, J. Michael. 1981. "Instructional Time and Other Components of All-English and Bilingual Programs." *Cutting Edge* (Aspira of America, N.Y.) 2(1):2–3.

Ogbu, John. 1978. *Minority Education and Caste*. New York: Academic Press.

Serna, Irene A. 1988. "A Description of Navajo Spatial Concepts and Language in Young Children." Ph.D. dissertation, University of New Mexico.

Troike, Rudolph C. 1978. "Research Evidence for the Effectiveness of Bilingual Education." *NABE Journal* 3(1):13–24.

_____. 1984. "SCALP: Social and Cultural Aspects of Language Proficiency." In *Language Proficiency and Academic Achievement*, edited by Charlene Rivera. Clevedon, England: Multilingual Matters, Ltd.

U.S. General Accounting Office 1976. "Bilingual Education: An Unmet Need. Report to the Congress by the Comptroller General of the United States." Washington, D.C.: U.S. Government Printing Office.

Veltman, Calvin. 1983. *Language Shift in the United States*. Berlin: Mouton Publishers.

Vorih, L., and Paul Rosier. 1978. "Rock Point Community School: An Example of a Navajo-English Bilingual Elementary School Program." *TESOL Quarterly* 12:263–71.

13

Comments on Some Points of Agreement and Disagreement

Glynn Custred

I think that we may see on the horizon a more explicit understanding of language policy for the United States. This has not been the case before in American history. In the past, any kind of legislative enactment or court ruling on language use has been specific and somewhat limited. These laws and rulings have been made in reaction to specific sets of circumstances: for example, the attempts by some groups—the French-speaking population in Louisiana and Germans in Pennsylvania in the nineteenth century—to attain official status for their languages. But these laws have never evolved into a comprehensive national language policy, largely because there has not been a pressing need for one. However, everything today seems to call for definitive public-policy statements on language from the federal government and from the state governments. If we're going to have a language policy, we first have to clarify what we're talking about, clarify what the fears are on both sides, and clarify the ideological underpinnings of the debate.

One of the reasons why this conference is being held is that there is a tremendous emotional debate over language policy in general, with bilingual education being only part of that debate. Professor Edwards mentioned the movements for Official English, the English Language Amendment to the Constitution, and the counter-movement for a constitutional amendment on cultural rights. These movements have been built upon two completely different ideologies and views of the American nation. We have had a dichotomy between assimilation and pluralism throughout American history. Obviously, there was a period during which assimilation was very definitely the aim. There was a Bureau of Americanization in the federal government in the early part of the twentieth century, when our last large influx of immigrants occurred. The idea of this bureau was to aid the rapid assimilation of immigrant students. In the 1970s, in response to our current large influx of immigrants, there was, instead, an interest in pluralism, and of course the bilingual education program was an outgrowth of that.

So far during this historic cycle, this issue has been argued emotionally, too emotionally, and one of the purposes of this meeting has been to raise the level of debate. The papers, as I have read them, have brought up some very good points that we can consider more dispassionately and in more detail in the future.

Both Professor Banks and Professor Edwards spoke about what I would call the dependent variable aspect of language, which means that language itself is not the primary causal factor. Linguistic pluralism flourishes under certain sociocultural conditions, which have not prevailed in the United States. Linguistic assimilation, language shift, has always been the case in the United States, despite what so many language-minority groups have tried to do to forestall it. Compare assimilation rates in the United States with those almost anywhere else. Assimilation has been extremely rapid here. The main reason, of course, has been that in the United States the butter is on the assimilation, the language shift, side of the bread and not on the other.

The same phenomenon that occurs with language shift happens with dialects, or variations of English. Professor Banks mentioned an interesting study, *The Truly Disadvantaged*, by William Julius Wilson (1987). Here, Wilson sets up some interesting parameters with regard to the contextual surroundings of language shift among blacks in the United States. We have what appears to be a divergence in English. Black English in certain areas and in the underclass (certainly not in the black middle class, where an assimilation process is going on) is shifting away from standard English. Here again, however, language is the dependent variable. The context for this change is that the black middle class began moving away from the central city at the same time that there was a shift in demand for urban labor. These and other contextual changes allowed for speedy language shift among lower-class blacks away from standard English.

Cultural change frequently follows contextual social changes. One definition of culture is that it is what you have to know and believe in order to behave in an appropriate manner within a given system, a given social group. Culture, in a sense, is adaptable; it adapts to external conditions. What Professor Ogbu has pointed out in terms of the attitudes of so many inner-city blacks toward achievement would in a sense be an aspect of a subculture (Ogbu 1978). This subculture isn't something inherent or generally determined in blacks; it is a part of this very complicated contextual shift. The question is more properly what our public policy should be towards that, rather than toward "Black English." I would agree with Professor Edwards that there shouldn't be a public policy towards language per se. Rather, we should have a public policy aimed at the contextual things that determine language use.

I am a strong supporter of teaching more foreign language in the public schools in the United States. The question, again, would be how we go about doing it effectively. What's going to work? I'm not a specialist in education or bilingualism. I'm an anthropologist interested in language and language diversity. So I don't know the nuts and bolts kinds of things that some of our other presenters do. Professor Edwards has thrown a little cold water on foreign-language education with his Canadian example. I tend to think that we're going to have a lot of difficulty. My fieldwork has been in South America, one of the many places in the world where monolingualism is very, very strong. English is the second language taught in Peru, where I've done most of my fieldwork, but very few people actually learn it. Brazil seems to be gloriously monolingual. And, of course, the United States and Great Britain have never supported the widespread use of languages other than English. I have not worked on this statistically, the way Professor Fishman has, but it seems to me that if you have a speech community in which the language is accepted over a wide geographic area or an economically self-sufficient area, it is going to be much more difficult to develop the linguistic skills we have said we would like to see. In small countries like Sweden or Holland or even Germany, where there is more of an obvious need to know other languages, second-language instruction is going to be more successful.

Still, it does seem reasonable to try to develop the very rich linguistic resources of our population; we have people who are speaking Spanish at home, we have people who are speaking Chinese and Japanese at home. But it isn't consistent with our society's values to stipulate that a certain group of people, because of their national origin or ethnic affiliation, should be in a bilingual program of a maintenance or transitional nature. I would prefer to see the emphasis placed on the individual interests of students and their families. If a Spanish-speaking family says, "We want our kids to know Spanish," and the children in fact are interested, we should help to develop those individual resources. But we should not mandate it if the parents or the children aren't interested.

Professor Banks and Professor Trueba made the very good point that the teacher should be engaged with the student and should understand the student, partially by understanding the cultural background from which the student comes. I think that's part of being a good teacher. I think that all good teachers would agree that they have to have an empathy with their kids, or else they're not going to get very far. One way to develop that empathy is to understand their students' backgrounds. There are a lot of different backgrounds, as Professor Trueba pointed out; in fact, there is a great deal more diversity in American schools than we imagine, unless we're out there on the front line, as Sally Peterson is. In this respect, I definitely agree with Professor Trueba and Professor Banks that a great deal of cultural awareness is necessary in order to make teaching more workable. However, I think that something else also has come out of this conference: that there should be a great deal more flexibility in methodologies or in teaching strategies.

There are also, we should remember, a lot of monolingual families that would like very much to get their children into an effective language program. I'm very interested in linguistic competence myself. I've heard several personal stories today; Professor Drake said that he put his child on a waiting list to get into a language class, and Professor Walberg's child studied Japanese and went to Japan. Maybe it wouldn't be out of the way to tell my story. My wife is from Transylvania—there really is such a place; it's real, believe me. Transylvania is a traditionally multiethnic, multilingual region, populated by Rumanians, Hungarians, and Germans. The Germans of Transylvania, known as Saxons, are diglossic. This is a very interesting case of education, by the way, a study that someone should do. I've done a little bit of it myself, but not nearly as much as it deserves. Practically every peasant in the Saxon community knows standard German. In fact, the Saxons were among the first in Europe to develop public schools. The Saxon peasants, however, spoke a dialect that wasn't comprehensible in Germany — the closest thing that it is comparable to is a dialect in Luxembourg, clear across the German linguistic territory. So in the Saxon schools the children learned standard German. They learned to read it; they learned to write it. You can read travelers' accounts of Transylvania written in the last century that express amazement at how well the Saxons spoke standard German. At the same time, the Saxons continued speaking their own dialect. This is the diglossic situation that Professor Fishman referred to in passing in his paper. My wife comes from a background that stressed this very effective diglossic education, and when we moved to California she insisted that our children would learn German language and culture, as her people had in Transylvania for the past eight hundred years. We have two children, both born in this country, and they both speak German. They wouldn't dream of speaking anything else at home. Of course, their language is all mixed up and there's constant code switching, as there is in all these situations. But I think my family situation demonstrates that I too am interested in the preservation of language and cultural identity on the personal level. I'm doing everything that I can to preserve it in my backyard. I think, really, that this is another point of commonality here, that we are interested in other languages, and we are trying in our own personal lives to expand it in our own families.

This brings me to another point. Everyone today has agreed, I believe, that we should have an overarching set of values and a common language. But how can we facilitate that? Professor Edwards, as well as other people, has said that the schools are not really the cutting edge. Schools can do certain kinds of jobs, but they can't do it all. The schools, I believe we agree, have a relatively limited role to play. Their role is important, but limited when compared with the external conditions of family life and of socioeconomic background. In other words, the schools can't do it all. The school is merely a part of society, one institution in society. Within schools, good solid teaching is the key to almost any achievement. In fact, as has been said, but not necessarily agreed upon here, good teaching is even more important than the language used in teaching.

One thing that a school can do is to give priority to the standard language, and to literacy in the standard language, as well as to the kinds of background knowledge necessary to be truly literate. Professor Banks stressed the relationship between language and culture. There is, in fact, a standard language, and there is in fact a certain set of standard cultural categories and information that we can't ignore if we want to be able to use the standard language in its full range of expressibility, that is, in the spoken and written media. If the school gives priority to the standard language, to English, is it really also capable of creating and maintaining societal diversity? When we think about this language policy that I believe is looming on the horizon, we should keep this question in mind, remembering that the school, and the language, as well as the culture, the subcultures, and the dialects, are all parts of much broader issues.

Unless I've misunderstood what's going on, one thing that I think all of us today have agreed upon is that non-English-speaking children should learn English, and that they should learn not only spoken English but also written English. What we don't agree upon, however, is on how this should be accomplished. While linguistic and cultural retention on a personal level should be encouraged, I don't think that a national language policy or a mandated program can focus on the maintenance of the languages of subcultures of ethnic groups. As much as possible, we should preserve and develop languages. But this is only a secondary priority. If we have limited resources — and we do — and if the school has limited time — and it does — and if the school is only one institution in society — and it is — the question is, What should our priority be? The first priority should be teaching English, both the spoken and the written language. This opinion is the conclusion of a very long train of thought on the nature of education, the nature of the nation-state, the nature of community. But time is marching on, and I'm not going to present that train of thought today. Maybe some other time.

References

Ogbu, John U. 1978. *Minority Education and Caste: The American System in Cross-Cultural Perspective*. N.Y.: Academic Press.
Wilson, William Julius. 1987. *The Truly Disadvantaged: The Inner City, the Underclass, and Public Policy*. Chicago: University of Chicago Press.

Contributors

JAMES A. BANKS is professor of education at the University of Washington, Seattle. He is a former chairman of curriculum and instruction and a past president of the National Council for the Social Studies. Professor Banks is a specialist in social studies education and multicultural education and has written over ninety articles in these fields. He has contributed to journals such as *Phi Delta Kappan, School Review, Educational Leadership*, and the *Elementary School Journal.* His books include *Teaching Strategies for Ethnic Studies, Multiethnic Education: Theory and Practice, Teaching Strategies for the Social Studies*, and (with Cherry A. McGee Banks), *Multicultural Education: Issues and Perspectives.* Professor Banks was named Distinguished Scholar/Researcher on Minority Education by the American Educational Research Association in 1986.

GLENDON F. DRAKE is currently a senior fellow with the American Association of State Colleges; and Universities as well as a professor at the University of Colorado. In universities, he has held the positions of chancellor, vice president, dean of arts and sciences, and linguistics department chair. He holds a doctorate in American culture with an emphasis in linguistics from the University of Michigan and a B.A. in classical humanities from Miami University of Ohio. His writings are in the areas of language and ethnicity, language policy, linguistic attitudes, history of linguistics, and American intellectual history.

JOHN EDWARDS is professor of psychology at St. Francis Xavier University in Nova Scotia. His general interests are sociolinguistic, including bilingual education, minority-language issues, and the language-group identity relationship. He is the author of *The Irish Language* (1983), *Linguistic Minorities, Policies and Pluralism* (1984), and *Language, Society and Identity* (1985), as well as of many articles and chapters on language and educational matters. Professor Edwards is the review editor of the *Journal of Language and Social Psychology*.

JOSHUA A. FISHMAN is distinguished university research professor in Social Sciences, Emeritus, at Yeshiva University. He has been a fellow at the Center for Advanced Study in the Behavioral Sciences at Palo Alto, the Institute for Advanced Projects of the East-West Center, the Institute for Advanced Study at Princeton, the Netherlands Institute for Advanced Study at Wassenaar, and the Israel Institute for Advanced Study at Jerusalem. He has written and co-written more than three hundred professional articles, reviews, and books. Among them are: *Language Loyalty in the United States* (1966), *Bilingualism in the Barrio* (1971), *Language and Nationalism* (1972), *Language in Socio-Cultural Change* (1972), *The Spread of English* (1977), *Bilingual Education: An International Sociological Perspective* (1976), *Never Say Die! A Thousand Years of Yiddish in Jewish Life and Letter* (1981), *Readings in the Sociology of Jewish Languages* (1985), *The Rise and Fall of the Ethnic Revival* (1985), *Ideology, Society and Language* (1987), and *Language and Ethnicity* (1989). He is the general editor of the *International Journal of the Sociology of Language* and the book series *Contributions to the Sociology of Language* and *Contributions to the Sociology of Jewish Languages*.

HARRY GLYNN CUSTRED, JR., is a professor in the Department of Anthropology at California State University, Hayward. He has specialized in linguistic, folklore, and anthropological studies in the high Andes of Peru. He edited *Land and Power in Latin America: New Approaches to Agrarian Economies and Social Processes in the Andes* with Benjamin Orlove, and is now working on a book on language among the Saxons of Transylvania.

GARY IMHOFF is a Washington writer who specializes in public policy issues. He co-wrote *The Immigration Time Bomb: The Fragmenting of America* with Governor Richard D. Lamm, and is now working on a book on successful antidrug programs in American cities.

SALLY PETERSON has been an elementary classroom teacher in California and Wisconsin for twenty-six years, specializing in the third grade and kindergarten. She is a master teacher and demonstration teacher. She is also president and founder of the Learning English Advocates Drive, LEAD, a national organization of teachers and friends dedicated to the reform of bilingual education to bring more focus on English development.

ROSALIE PEDALINO PORTER, a recent fellow of the Bunting Institute of Radcliffe College and a former visiting scholar at the University of London, is director of ESL/Bilingual Programs for the Newton, Massachusetts, Public Schools. She served from 1985 to 1988 as a member of the National Advisory Council on Bilingual Education, which advises the U.S. Congress on legislation in the field, and she has lectured on language policy on behalf of the United States Information Service in Finland, Italy, Japan, Turkey, and Bulgaria.

CHRISTINE H. ROSSELL is professor of political science at Boston University. Her research interests include school desegregation, bilingual education, and educational policy. She has recently written a book on school desegregation, *The Carrot or the Stick for School Desegregation Policy*, articles on school desegregation for *Urban Affairs Quarterly* and *Educational Evaluation and Policy Analysis*, and on bilingual education in the *Journal of Law and Education* and *Educational Policy*. She has testified for parties in twenty school desegregation cases and one bilingual education case.

RUDOLPH TROIKE is professor of English and linguistics at the University of Arizona. He has written over one hundred articles, books, and reviews in archaeology, American Indian linguistics, English dialectology and linguistics, linguistic theory, and applied linguistics. He edited *Language and Cultural Diversity in American Education* with Roger Abrahams and the *Proceedings of the First Inter-American Conference on Bilingual Education* with Nancy Modiano, and he compiled Volume I of *A Bibliography of Bibliographies of the Languages of the World*.

HENRY TRUEBA is the associate dean of the College of Letters and Science and director of the Division of Education at the University of California, Davis, and was formerly professor of educational psychology and crosscultural studies at the University of California, Santa Barbara. In 1987, he received the American Educational Research Association Distinguished Scholarship Award for Research on Linguistic Minorities. His most recent books include *Raising Silent Voices: Educating Linguistic Minorities to the 21st Century, School and Society: Learning Content through Culture* (edited with C. Delgado-Gaitan), and *Becoming Literate in English as a Second Language* (edited with S. Goldman).

HERBERT J. WALBERG is research professor of education at the University of Illinois at Chicago. Formerly assistant professor at Harvard University, he has served as an adviser on educational research and improvement to governmental and private agencies in the U.S. and a dozen other countries. He has written or edited thirty-five books and contributed more than three hundred articles to educational, psychological, and practitioner journals on such topics as achievement and language development, giftedness and talent, educational productivity, international comparisons, effective instruction, and parent education. He currently chairs the scientific committee for educational indicators of the Paris-based Organization for Economic and Cooperative Development, and chairs the editorial board of the *International Journal of Educational Research*.

BRIAN WEINSTEIN is a professor of political science at Howard University, where he has taught since 1966. During 1987–1988, he served as Fulbright lecturer at the Hebrew University in Jerusalem, Israel. He is the author of *The Civic Tongue: Political Consequences of Language Choices* (Longman, 1983) and the editor of *Language Policy and Political Development* (Ablex, 1990).

CAROL WHITTEN was the director of the Office of Bilingual Education and Minority Languages Affairs of the Department of Education from 1985 through 1987, and has held several other federal offices. She is currently a member of the National Advisory Council on Educational Research. She is the principal author of the chapter on "Federal Grant and Contract Management" in the Heritage Foundation's *Mandate for Leadership*, 1989.

Index

Language (*continued*)
reality, 204; and society, 163–165;
studies, 149–151; study, 265; and
successful learning, 80; in United
States, 10. *See also* Bilingualism;
Linguistics; Studies; U.S. English
Language, Society, and Identity
(Edwards), 198–199
Language minorities. *See* Linguistic
minorities
Language policies: in Africa, 167,
181–185; in Belguim, 171–172; and
economic policies, 168; and the
elites, 165–166; in France, 169–
171; in Haiti, 167–168, 178–179;
in India, 166–167, 176–178; in Israel, 179–180; in Japan, 174; and political goals, 171; in Quebec, 174–
175; restrictive, 166; and society,
169; in Soviet Union, 185–186; in
Spain, 172; and status quo, 165–
166; in Turkey, 179–181; in United
States, 173–174, 285–286
Language-skills-transference, theory
of, xvii–xviii
Lau Remedies: and Office for Civil
Rights, 234–235. *See also Lau v.
Nichols*
LAUSD. *See* Los Angeles Unified
School Discrict (LAUSD)
Lau v. Nichols, 173, 231, 241, 267;
compliance agreements, 234–235;
and limited-English students, 19.
See also Limited-English students
Laws: California state, bilingual,
232
LEAD. *See* Learning English Advo-
cates Drive (LEAD)
Learning: factors, 144, 159; and psy-
chology, 147
Learning English Advocates Drive
(LEAD), 252–256
Limited-English-proficient (LEP),
xviii–xix, 71, 73, 85–93, 107–108,
129, 140, 229; education programs
for, 71–72; and *Lau v. Nichols*, 19;
and socioeconomic backgrounds,
150–153, 159
Limited-English students, 20–21; demographics of, 21–22; native-lan-

guage instruction for, 21; and the
Supreme Court, 19
Linguistic; assimilation, 286; homogeneity, 217; pluralism, 286
Linguistic heterogeneity: charges
against, 209–210; and civil strife,
210–211, 213–215, 218, 220; and
factor analysis, 218–219; impact
on society of, xx; and inter-polity
hypothesis, 209–210; and inter-polity variation, 216; and negative
policies towards, 222; and per capita gross national product, 210–211,
218, 220; and positive consequences of, 220–221; and productivity, 209
Linguistic minorities, 126–127, 221–
222; bilingual education for, xii;
and cultural knowledge, 130; defined, xii; demographics of, 22; education for, 128–129, 261; and
learning in mother tongue, 132–
133; learning of English, 227; and
literacy problems, 130; and student
failures, 47–48; teachers of, 31,
123, 130–132. *See also* Immigrants;
Minorities
Linguistic: relativity notion and
women's liberation movement, 196;
study, 203
Linguistics. *See* Applied linguistics;
Linguists
Linguistics, applied. *See* Applied linguistics; Linguists
Linguists, 190; and bilingualism, 197;
· and social factors, 190
Literacy: and culture, 139–140; and
demographics, 139–140, 141–142;
English language, 142–143; and
family conditions, 141; international comparisons of, 140–141;
and minorities, 130–140; and poor
children, 152–154. *See also*
Illiteracy
López, David E., 272
Los Angeles Board of Education, 249
Los Angeles Unified School District (LAUSD), 241–242, 245,
254; Bilingual Master Plan,
249–250, 251